SAM'S

OYSTER SALOON,

101 St. Charles Street,

NEW ORLEANS.

This justly celebrated Saloon is fitted up on a scale of magnificence equal to any establishment in the Union. The Larder is always supplied with the CHOICEST FISH AND GAME; and the Oysters served are obtained exclusively for this establishment.

☞ The Bar is supplied with the choicest liquors; and servants well known for their excellent qualities, have been employed, including the best Cooks; in short, every thing has been done to render this Saloon worthy the patronage of a liberal community.

New Orleans, Dec. 1854.

D. H. HOLMES,

DIRECT IMPORTER OF, AND DEALER IN

FRENCH, ENGLISH, GERMAN AND DOMESTIC

DRY GOODS,

No. 148 TOURO AVENUE,

LATE CANAL STREET, AND

17 RUE THEVENOT,

PARIS.

New Orleans, Dec. 1854.

G. A. BREAUX,

Attorney at Law,

No. 68 CAMP STREET,

NEW ORLEANS.

Advocate Book-Bindery.

The Proprietors of the Daily and Weekly Advocate having purchased a new and splendid assortment of BOOK BINDING MATERIALS, are prepared to execute orders in their line in a manner unsurpassed in the State, and on terms that must be satisfactory.

Magazines, Pamphlets, Newspapers, Public Documents, Music, Blank Books, etc., can be turned out in a substantial and beautiful manner.

The Proprietors respectfully solicit a share of public patronage.

Baton Rouge, Dec. 1, 1854.

EXCELSIOR!

This cut is a fac simile of the medal for the best Boys' Clothing at the World's Fair, New York.

ALFRED MUNROE & Co.,

34 MAGAZINE STREET,

Corner of Gravier,

NEW ORLEANS.

HAVE NOW ON HAND THE

LARGEST STOCK OF CLOTHING

In the City of New Orleans, for MEN, BOYS, AND CHILDREN, and are constantly receiving from their Manufactory, 441 Broadway, New York. The principle of business adopted by them many years since is still adhered to—ONE PRICE, AND IN NO INSTANCE DEVIATED FROM.

They have polite, gentlemanly Clerks, speaking the French Language, as well as English, who show all their goods with pleasure, if parties should only call from curiosity. The stock embraces every style of Coats now in vogue; also every kind of Vesting and Pantaloons. They would ask particular attention to the WRAPPER OVERCOATS, TALMAS, and MONTEHCRISTO CLOAKS, all got up in magnificent style. BOYS' CLOTHING of every variety, among which are TALMAS and splendid DRESS JACKETS for Children and Boys. Annexed is a partial list.

They are the only agents in New Orleans for the

Union India Rubber Company,

Large Stock always on hand and sold AT MANUFACTURERS' PRICES.

Frock and Dress Coats.

Black, Blue, Brown, Olive and Golden Brown

Single-Breasted Frocks.

Black, Blue, Brown, Olive, Claret and Mulberry.

Single-Breasted Business Coats.

Devonshire Kersey, Oxford Mixed, Cloth, Plaid, Cassimere, Drab, Doeskin, Silver Gray, Cassimere and Mottled, Blue, Fancy and Gray Tweed.

Overcoats.

Blue and Brown Sultana Cloth Frock;
Black, Blue, Brown and Olive Devonshire Kersey.
Blue, Black, Gray, Whitney and Drab;
" " Pilot Cloth—some extra long;
Black, Blue and Brown Cloth—superior;
Drab Emb'd Cloth Sacs and Walking Coats.

Blanket Coats.

Blue, Drab and Mottled Sacs and Frocks.

Cloaks.

Black and Blue Cloth—some extra fine—violet facings;
Real English Pilot Cloth;
Black and Blue Cloth Talmas and Monte-Christos.

Vestings.

Plain black Satin, Figured Silk and Satin;
" " Silk and Fancy " "
Black Cloth and Fancy Cassimere;
Black and Fancy Velvet;
Fancy Velvet and Silk Ball Vests;
In all the above goods D. B. and half D. B. and R. Collars.

Stocks and Ties

of all descriptions—impossible to enumerate.

Pantaloons.

Black and Fancy Colored Doeskin;
" " Cassimeres;
" and Buckskin "
Devonshire Kersey and Oxford Mixed do
Black, Blue and Fancy Colored Satinet;
French and American Cottonade.

Furnishing Goods.

Silk, Merino, all wool, red, gray and white Flannel and Cotton Flannel Undershirts and Drawers;
All Linen and Cotton Shirts;
☞ The Shirts sold by us are made expressly for our own retail sales. A fit guaranteed in all instances.

Half-Hose.

Orkney and Shetland Wool, Merino, white and gray Lambs' Wool, English and German. Cotton, white and colored.

Gloves.

Black, white and colored Kid Gloves;
Thread Silk and Neapolitan Plush do
Drab Buck Gloves and Gauntlets.

Cravats.

Black fancy Satin and Silk Cravats.

BOYS' & CHILDREN'S CLOTHING

Black and colored Cloth Frocks;
Black and colored Cloth Sacs;
Cassimere and Tweed Frocks and Sacs;
Black and colored Cloth Overcoats;
Mottled, gray and brown Whitney Frocks and Sacs;
Black, blue and brown Cloth Jackets;
Olive, green and Cadet " "

Vests.

Black Cloth, black and fancy Silk Vests;
Tweed and colored Cassimere "

Pantaloons.

Black and fancy colored Cassimere and Doeskin;
Satinet, Tweed and Cottonade;
Children's black and colored Cloth Suits;
" " " " Jackets;
" " " " Cutaways

Furnishing Goods.

Merino Shirts, Cotton and Cotton Flannel Drawers;
Muslin Shirts, Linen Bosoms, Collars and Wristbands;
Cotton and Wool Half-Hose, Cash. Gloves;
Suspenders, Hdkfs, Ties and Elastic Belts.
TRUNKS, CARPET BAGS and VALISES;
Silk, Cotton and Gingham UMBRELLAS.

Agency of the Union India Rubber Company.

INDIA RUBBER GOODS.

Coats and Ponchos, all kinds;
Overalls, Pantaloons, Mechanics' Aprons, Wading and Baptismal Pants, Riding and Walking Leggins, Caps, Traveling, Navy, Saddle, Gas and Coal Bags; also bags for hot and cold water, Life Preservers, Cushions, Blankets, Crumb Cloths, Table Covers, Bathing Mats, Air Beds and Pillows, Tarpaulins, Wagon Aprons, Horse Covers, Carriage and Hospital Cloth, Hoof, Knee and Ankle Boots for Horses, Stationer's Gum, Fire Buckets, Gun Covers, Canteens, &c.

ALFRED MUNROE & Co.,
34 Magazine Street,
Corner of Gravier.

☞ This Store is open every night in the week until eight and Saturday night until nine o'clock, and not open on Sunday.

J. C. MORGAN,

Bookseller and Stationer,

EXCHANGE PLACE,

Adjoining the Post Office,

NEW ORLEANS,

Always keeps on hand a large and varied stock of

Standard and Miscellaneous Books:

also receives the latest works as soon as issued from the Press—together with all the

REVIEWS, MAGAZINES, &c., &c.

☞Orders solicited.

New Orleans, Dec. 1, 1854.

Southwestern Book Store.

H. D. McGINNIS,

(SUCCESSOR TO JOHN BALL,)

BOOKSELLER & STATIONER,

No. 36 CAMP STREET,

NEW ORLEANS.

Always on hand a large assortment of—

LAW, MEDICAL, THEOLOGICAL, STANDARD

and Miscellaneous Books, Cheap Periodicals, &c.

School Books and Stationery at wholesale and retail.

Blank Books of every description.

Printing and Book-Binding executed with neatness and dispatch.

New Orleans, Dec. 1, 1854.

C. M. SIMPSON,

DEALER IN DRY GOODS,

NO. 116 CANAL STREET,

TOURO'S ROW, NEW ORLEANS.

In referring you to my card above, I would respectfully invite your attention to my large and well selected stock of

STAPLE, DOMESTIC, SILK AND FANCY DRY GOODS;

ALSO,

GENTLEMEN'S FURNISHING GOODS,

all of which have been selected with good care and with a view to the wants of the Southern trade, which enables me to place before my customers a *larger* and *better* assorted stock than can be found elsewhere in this city.

Particular attention has been paid in the selection of

PLANTATION AND HOUSEKEEPING GOODS,

an assortment of which will be found complete, thereby saving the necessity of making purchases in several houses to fill orders for Dry Goods. An early call is respectfully solicited.

C. M. SIMPSON,
No. 116 CANAL STREET, Touro's Row,
NEW ORLEANS,

☞ *Particular attention paid to Orders.*

THE STATE REGISTER:

COMPRISING AN HISTORICAL AND

Statistical Account of Louisiana,

FROM ITS EARLIEST SETTLEMENT AS A TERRITORY
DOWN TO ITS PRESENT PERIOD AS A STATE;

TOGETHER WITH AN

ACCURATE LIST OF ALL

STATE AND PARISH OFFICERS.

COMPILED BY A. W. BELL.

BATON ROUGE:
T. B. R. HATCH & CO., PUBLISHERS.
Printed at the "Daily Advocate" Book and Job Office,
1855.

ENTERED

In conformity to An Act of Congress, entitled "an Act to amend the several acts relating to copy rights," approved 3d February, A. D., 1831,

BY AMOS W. BELL,

In the Clerk's Office of the United States District Court for the Eastern District of Louisiana

INTRODUCTION.

In compiling the "State Register," the undersigned desires it to be fully understood that he sets forth no claim to originality.

The task was undertaken with the sole view of condensing from promiscuous sources, such historical facts and matters of interest relative to the State, which would be found to meet the wants of every citizen.

If he has succeeded in performing this labor, in a manner making it worthy the approbation of the reader, his highest ambition is accomplished. The many errors and omissions which may be found, must be attributed to the many changes which are taking place in various portions of the State, which are at times months in being made known at the Seat of Government.

After the next State election shall have taken place the Work will be revised and published anew, with all the changes necessary to make it a correct Register of the State.

A. W. BELL.

Baton Rouge, December, 1854.

THE STATE REGISTER.

CONSTITUTION OF THE UNITED STATES.

WE, the people of the United States, in order to form a more perfect union, establish justice, insure domestic tranquility, provide for the common defence, promote the general welfare, and secure the blessings of liberty to ourselves and our posterity, *do ordain and establish this Constitution for the United States of America.*

ARTICLE I.

Section I.—All legislative power herein granted shall be vested in a Congress of the United States, which shall consist of a Senate and House of Representatives.

Section II.—1. The House of Representatives shall be composed of members chosen every second year, by the people of the several States; and the electors in each State shall have the qualifications requisite for electors, of the most numerous branch of the State Legislature.

2. No person shall be a representative who shall not have attained the age of twenty-five years, and been seven years a citizen of the United States, and who shall not, when elected, be an inhabitant of the State in which he shall be chosen.

3. Representatives and direct taxes shall be apportioned among the several States which may be included within this Union according to their respective numbers, which shall be determined by adding to the whole number of free persons, including those bound to service for a term of years, and excluding Indians not taxed, three-fifths of all other persons. The actual enumeration shall be made within three years after the first meeting of the Congress of the United States, and within every subsequent term of ten years, in such manner as they shall by law direct. The number of representatives shall not exceed one for every thirty thousand, but each State shall have at least one representative; and until such enumeration shall be made,

the State of New Hampshire shall be entitled to choose three; Massachusetts, eight; Rhode Island and Providence Plantations, one; Connecticut, five; New York, six; New Jersey, four; Pennsylvania, eight; Delaware, one; Maryland, six; Virginia, ten; North Carolina, five; South Carolina, five; and Georgia, three.

4. When vacancies happen in the representation from any State, the executive authority thereof shall issue writs of election to fill such vacancies.

5. The House of Representatives shall choose their Speaker and other officers, and shall have the sole power of impeachment.

Section III.—1. The Senate of the United States shall be composed of two senators from each State, chosen by the Legislature thereof, for six years; and each senator shall have one vote.

2. Immediately after they shall be assembled in consequence of the first election, they shall be divided, as equal as may be, into three classes. The seats of the senators of the first class shall be vacated at the expiration of the second year; of the second class, at the expiration of the fourth year; and of the third class, at the expiration of the sixth year; so that one-third may be chosen every second year; and if vacancies happen by resignation or otherwise during the recess of the Legislature of any State, the executive thereof may make temporary appointments until the next meeting of the Legislature, which shall then fill such vacancies.

3. No person shall be a senator who shall not have attained to the age of thirty years, and been nine years a citizen of the United States, and who shall not, when elected, be an inhabitant of that State for which he shall be chosen.

4. The Vice-President of the United States shall be President of the Senate, but shall have no vote unless they be equally divided.

5. The Senate shall choose their other officers, and also a President *pro tempore*, in the absence of the Vice-President, or when he shall exercise the office of President of the United States.

6. The Senate shall have the sole power to try all impeachments. When sitting for that purpose they shall be on oath or affirmation. When the President of the United States is tried, the chief justice shall preside; and no person shall be convicted without the concurrence of two-thirds of the members present.

7. Judgment in cases of impeachment shall not extend further than to removal from office, and disqualification to hold and enjoy any office of honor, trust or profit under the United States; but the party convicted shall, nevertheless, be liable and subject to indictment, trial, judgment and punishment according to law.

Section IV.—1. The times, places and manner of holding elections for senators and representatives, shall be prescribed in each State by the Legislature thereof; but the Congress may, at any time, by law, make or alter such regulations, except as to the places of choosing senators.

2. The Congress shall assemble at least once in every year, and such meeting shall be on the first Monday in December, unless they shall by law appoint a different day.

Section V.—1. Each house shall be the judge of the elections, returns and qualifications of its own members, and a majority of each shall constitute a *quorum* to do business; but a smaller number may adjourn from day to day, and may be authorized to compel the attendance of absent members in such manner and under such penalties as each house may provide.

2. Each house may determine the rules of its proceedings, punish its members for disorderly behavior, and, with the concurrence of two-thirds, expel a member.

3. Each house shall keep a journal of its proceedings, and from time to time publish the same, except such parts as may, in their judgment, require secrecy; and the yeas and nays of the members of either house, on any question, shall, at the desire of one-fifth of those present, be entered on the journal.

4. Neither house, during the session of Congress, shall, without the consent of the other, adjourn for more than three days, nor to any other place than that in which the two houses shall be sitting.

Section VI.—1. The senators and representatives shall receive a compensation for their services, to be ascertained by law, and paid out of the treasury of the United States. They shall, in all cases, except treason, felony, and breach of the peace, be privileged from arrest during their attendance at the session of their respective houses, and in going to and returning from the same; and for any speech or debate in either house, they shall not be questioned in any other place.

2. No senator or representative shall, during the time for which he was elected, be appointed to any civil office under the authority of the United States, which shall have been created, or the emoluments whereof shall have been increased during such time; and no person holding any office under the United States, shall be a member of either house during his continuance in office.

Section VII.—1. All bills for raising revenue shall originate in the House of Representatives; but the Senate may propose or concur with amendments, as on other bills.

2. Every bill which shall have passed the House of Representatives and the Senate, shall, before it becomes a law, be presented to the President of the United States; if he approve, he shall sign it; but if not, he shall return it, with his objections, to that house in which it shall have originated, who shall enter the objections at large, on their journal, and proceed to reconsider it. If after such re-consideration, two-thirds of that house shall agree to pass the bill, it shall be sent, together with the objections, to the other house, by which it shall likewise be reconsidered, and if approved by two-thirds of that house it shall become a law. But in all such cases the votes of both houses shall be determined by yeas and nays; and the names of the persons voting for and against the bill, shall be entered on the journal of each house respectively. If any bill shall not be returned by the President within ten days (Sundays excepted) after it shall have been presented to him, the same shall be a law, in the like manner as if he had signed it, unless the Congress, by adjournment, prevent its return, in which case it shall not be a law.

3. Every order, resolution or vote to which the concurrence of the Senate and House of Representatives may be necessary, (except on a question of adjournment,) shall be presented to the President of the United States, and before the same shall take effect, shall be approved by him, or being disapproved by him, shall be re-passed by two-thirds of the Senate and House of Representatives, according to the rules and limitation prescribed in the case of a bill.

Section VIII.—1. The Congress shall have power to lay and collect taxes, duties, imposts and excises, to pay the debts and provide for the common defence and general welfare of the United States; but all duties, imposts and excises, shall be uniform throughout the United States:

2. To borrow money on the credit of the United States:

3. To regulate commerce with foreign nations, and among the several States, and with the Indian tribes:

4. To establish an uniform rule of naturalization, and uniform laws on the subject of bankruptcies throughout the United States:

5. To coin money, regulate the value thereof, and of foreign coin, and fix the standard of weights and measures:

6. To provide for the punishment of counterfeiting the securities and current coin of the United States:

7. To establish post offices and post roads:

8. To promote the progress of science and useful arts, by securing for limited times, to authors and inventors the exclusive right to their respective writings and discoveries:

9. To constitute tribunals inferior to the Supreme Court: to define and punish piracies and felonies committed on the high seas, and offences against the law of nations:

10. To declare war, grant letters of marque and reprisal, and make rules concerning captures on land and water:

11. To raise and support armies; but no appropriation of money to that use shall be for a longer term than two years:

12. To provide and maintain a navy:

13. To make rules for the government and regulation of the land and naval forces:

14. To provide for calling forth the militia to execute the laws of the Union, suppress insurrections and repel invasions:

15. To provide for organizing, arming and disciplining the militia, and for governing such part of them as may be employed in the service of the United States, reserving to the States respectively, the appointment of the officers, and the authority of training the militia, according to the discipline prescribed by Congress:

16. To exercise exclusive legislation in all cases whatsoever, over such district (not exceeding ten miles square) as may by cession of particular States, and the acceptance of Congress, become the seat of the government of the United States, and to exercise like authority over all places purchased by the consent of the Legislature of the State in which the same shall be, for the erection of forts, magazines, arsenals, dock yards, and other needful buildings: and

17. To make all laws which shall be necessary and proper for

carrying into execution the foregoing powers, and all other powers vested by this Constitution in the government of the United States, or in any department or officer thereof.

Section IX.—1. The migration or importation of such persons as any of the States now existing shall think proper to admit, shall not be prohibited by the Congress prior to the year one thousand eight hundred and eight; but a tax or duty may be imposed on such importation, not exceeding ten dollars for each person.

2. The privilege of the writ of *habeas corpus* shall not be suspended, unless when in cases of rebellion or invasion the public safety may require it.

3. No bill of attainder or *ex post facto* law shall be passed.

4. No capitation or other direct tax shall be laid, unless in proportion to the *census* or enumeration herein before directed to be taken.

5. No tax or duty shall be laid on articles exported from the State. No preference shall be given by any regulation of commerce or revenue to the ports of one State over those of another; nor shall vessels bound to or from one State be obliged to enter, clear or pay duties in another.

6. No money shall be drawn from the treasury, but in consequence of appropriations made by law; and a regular statement and account of the receipts and expenditures of all public money shall be published from time to time.

7. No title of nobility shall be granted by the United States; and no person holding any office of profit or trust under them shall, without the consent of the Congress, accept of any present, emolument, office, or title of any kind whatever, from any King, Prince, or foreign State.

Section X.—1. No State shall enter into any treaty, alliance or confederation; grant letters of marque and reprisal; coin money; emit bills of credit; make anything but gold and silver coin a tender in payment of debts; pass any bill of attainder, *ex post facto* law, or law impairing the obligation of contracts, or grant any title of nobility.

2. No State shall, without the consent of the Congress, lay any imposts or duties on imports or exports, except what may be absolutely necessary for executing its inspection laws; and the nett produce of all duties and imposts, laid by any State on imports or exports, shall be for the use of the treasury of the United States, and all such laws shall be subject to the revision and control of the Congress. No State shall without the consent of Congress, lay any duty on tonnage, keep troops or ships of war in time of peace, enter into any agreement or compact with another State, or with a foreign power, or engage in war, unless actually invaded, or in such imminent danger as will not admit of delay.

ARTICLE II.

Section I.—1. The *executive power* shall be vested in a President of the United States of America. He shall hold his office during the term of four years, and together with the Vice-President, chosen for the same term, be elected as follows:

2. Each State shall appoint, in such manner as the legislature thereof may direct, a number of electors, equal to the whole number of senators and representatives to which the State may be entitled in Congress; but no senators or representatives or persons holding an office of trust or profit under the United States shall be appointed an elector.

3. The electors shall meet in their respective States, and vote by ballot for two persons, of whom one at least shall not be an inhabitant of the same State with themselves. And they shall make a list of all the persons voted for, and of the number of votes for each; which list they shall sign and certify, and transmit, sealed, to the seat of government of the United States, directed to the President of the Senate. The President of the Senate shall, in the presence of the Senate and House of Representatives, open all the certificates, and the votes shall then be counted. The person having the greatest number of votes shall be the President, if such number be a majority of the whole number of electors appointed; and if there be more than one who have such majority, and have an equal number of votes, then the House of Representatives shall immediately choose, by ballot, one of them for President; and if no person have a majority, then from the five highest on the list the said house shall in like manner choose the President. But in choosing the President, the votes shall be taken by States, the representation from each State having one vote; a quorum for this purpose shall consist of a member or members from two-thirds of the States, and a majority of all the States shall be necessary to a choice. In every case, after the choice of the President, the person having the greatest number of votes of the electors shall be Vice-President. But if there should remain two or more who have equal votes, the Senate shall choose from them, by ballot, the Vice-President. [*Annulled, see amendments, Article,* 12.]

4. The Congress may determine the time of choosing the electors, and the day on which they shall give their votes; which day shall be the same throughout the United States.

5. No person except a natural born citizen, or a citizen of the United States at the time of the adoption of this Constitution, shall be eligible to the office of President; neither shall any person be eligible to that office who shall not have attained to the age of thirty-five years, and been fourteen years a resident within the United States.

6. In case of the removal of the President from office, or of his death, resignation, or inability to discharge the powers and duties of the said office, the same shall devolve on the Vice-President; and the Congress may by law provide for the case of removal, death, resignation, or inability, both of the President and Vice-President,

declaring what officer shall then act as President; and such officer shall act accordingly, until the disability be removed, or a President shall be elected.

7. The President shall, at stated times, receive for his services, a compensation which shall neither be increased nor diminished during the period for which he shall have been elected; and he shall not receive within that period any other emolument from the United States, or any of them.

8. Before he enter on the execution of his office, he shall take the following oath or affirmation :

"I do solemnly swear (or affirm) that I will faithfully execute the office of President of the United States; and will to the best of my ability, preserve, protect and defend the Constitution of the United States."

Section II.—1. The President shall be Commander-in-Chief of the army and navy of the United States, and of the militia of the several States, when called into the actual service of the United States; he may require the opinion, in writing, of the principal officer of each of the executive departments, upon any subject relating to the duties of their respective offices; and he shall have power to grant reprieves and pardons for offences against the United States, except in cases of impeachment.

2. He shall have power, by and with the advice and consent of the Senate, to make treaties, provided two-thirds of the senators present concur; and he shall nominate, and by and with the advice and consent of the Senate, shall appoint ambassadors, other public ministers and consuls, judges of the Supreme Court, and all other officers of the United States, whose appointments are not herein otherwise provided for, and which shall be established by law; but the Congress may, by law, vest the appointment of such inferior officers as they think proper, in the President alone, in the courts of law, or in the heads of departments.

3. The President shall have power to fill up all vacancies that may happen during the recess of the Senate, by granting commissions which shall expire at the end of the next session.

Section III.—1. He shall, from time to time, give to the Congress information of the state of the Union, and recommend to their consideration such measures as he shall judge necessary and expedient; he may on extraordinary occasions, convene both houses, or either of them, and in case of disagreement between them, with respect to the time of adjournment, he may adjourn them to such time as he shall think proper; he shall receive ambassadors and other public ministers; he shall take care that the laws be faithfully executed, and shall commission all the officers of the United States.

Section IV.—The President, Vice-President, and all civil officers of the United States, shall be removed from office on impeachment for, and conviction of treason, bribery, or other high crimes and misdemeanors.

ARTICLE III.

Section I.—The *judicial* power of the United States shall be vested in one Supreme Court, and in such inferior Courts as the Congress may, from time to time, ordain and establish. The judges, both of the Supreme and inferior courts, shall hold their offices during good behavior; and shall, at stated times, receive for their services a compensation, which shall not be diminished during their continuance in office.

Section II.—1. The judicial power shall extend to all cases in law and equity, arising under this Constitution, the laws of the United States, and treaties made, or which shall be made under their authority; to all cases affecting ambassadors, other public ministers and consuls; to all cases of admiralty and maritime jurisdiction; to controversies to which the United States shall be a party; to controversies between two or more States, between a State and citizen of another State, between citizens of different States, between citizens of the same State claiming lands under grants of different States, and between a State, or the citizens thereof, and foreign States, citizens or subjects. [*See a restriction of this provision, amendments, Article* 11.]

2. In all cases affecting ambassadors, other public ministers and consuls, and those in which a State shall be a party, the Supreme Court shall have original jurisdiction. In all other cases before mentioned, the Supreme Court shall have appellate jurisdiction, both as to law and fact, with such exceptions and under such regulations as the Congress shall make.

3. The trial of all crimes, except in cases of impeachment, shall be by jury; and such trial shall be held in the State where the said crimes shall have been committed; but when not committed within any State, the trial shall be at such place or places as the Congress may by law have directed.

Section III.—1. Treason against the United States shall consist only in levying war against them, or in adhering to their enemies, giving them aid and comfort. No person shall be convicted of treason, unless on the testimony of two witnesses to the same overt act, or on confession in open court.

2. The Congress shall have power to declare the punishment of treason, but no attainder of treason shall work corruption of blood, or forfeiture, except during the life of the person attainted.

ARTICLE IV.

Section I.—Full faith and credit shall be given in each State to the public acts, records and judicial proceedings of every other State. And the Congress may, by general laws, prescribe the manner in which such acts, records and proceedings shall be proved, and the effect thereof.

Section II.—1. The citizens of each State shall be entitled to all the privileges and immunities of citizens in the several States.

2. A person charged, in any State, with treason, felony, or other crime, who shall flee from justice and be found in another State, shall, on demand of the executive authority of the State from which he fled, be delivered up, to be removed to the State having jurisdiction of the crime.

3. No person held to service or labor in one State, under the laws thereof, escaping into another, shall, in consequence of any law or regulation therein, be discharged from such service or labor, but shall be delivered up on claim of the party to whom such service or labor may be due.

Section III.—1. New States may be admitted by the Congress of this Union; but no new State shall be formed or erected within the jurisdiction of another State, nor any State be formed by the junction of two or more States, or parts of States, without the consent of the Legislatures of the States concerned, as well as of the Congress.

2. The Congress shall have power to dispose of, and make all needful rules and regulations respecting the Territory or other property belonging to the United States; and nothing in this Constitution shall be so construed as to prejudice any claims of the United States or of any particular State.

Section IV.—The United States guarantee to every State in this Union, a republican form of government, and shall protect each of them against invasion; and on application of the Legislature, or of the executive, (when the Legislature cannot be convened,) against domestic violence.

ARTICLE V.

The Congress, whenever two-thirds of both houses shall deem it necessary, shall propose amendments to this Constitution, or, on the application of the Legislatures of two-thirds of the several States, shall call a convention for proposing amendments, which, in either case shall be valid, to all intents and purposes, as part of this Constitution, when ratified by the Legislatures of three-fourths of the several States, or by conventions of three-fourths thereof, as the one or the other mode of ratification may be proposed by the Congress: *Provided*, That no amendment which may be made prior to the year one thousand eight hundred and eight, shall in any manner affect the first and fourth clauses in the ninth section of the first article; and that no State, without its consent, shall be deprived of its equal suffrage in the Senate.

ARTICLE VI.

1. All debts contracted and engagements entered into before the adoption of this Constitution, shall be as valid against the United States under this Constitution as under the Confederation.

2. This Constitution, and the laws of the United States which

shall be made in pursuance thereof, and all treaties made, or which shall be made under the authority of the United States, shall be the supreme law of the land; and the judges in every State shall be bound thereby; any thing in the Constitution or laws of any State to the contrary notwithstanding.

3. The senators and representatives before mentioned, and the members of the several State Legislatures, and all executive and judicial officers, both of the United States and of the several States, shall be bound by oath or affirmation, to support this Constitution; but no religious test shall ever be required as a qualification to any office or public trust under the United States.

ARTICLE VII.

The ratification of the Conventions of nine States shall be sufficient for the establishment of this Constitution between the States so ratifying the same.

Done in convention, by the unanimous consent of the States present, the seventeenth day of September, in the year of our Lord, one thousand seven hundred and eighty-seven, and of the Independence of the United States of America the twelfth. In witness whereof we have hereunto subscribed our names.

GEORGE WASHINGTON,
President, and Deputy from Virginia.

New Hampshire.
JOHN LANGDON,
NICHOLAS GILMAN.

Massachusetts.
NATHANIEL GORMAN,
RUFUS KING.

Connecticut.
WILLIAM SAMUEL JOHNSON,
ROGER SHERMAN.

New York.
ALEXANDER HAMILTON.

New Jersey.
WILLIAM LIVINGSTON,
DAVID BREARLY.
WILLIAM PATTERSON,
JONATHAN DAYTON.

Pennsylvania.
BENJAMIN FRANKLIN,
THOMAS MIFFIN,
ROBERT MORRIS,
GEORGE CYLMER,
THOMAS FITZSIMMONS,
JARED INGERSOL,
JAMES WILSON,
GOUVENEUR MORRIS.

Delaware.
GEORGE READ,
GUNNING BEDFORD, JR.,
JOHN DICKINSON,
RICHARD BASSETT,
JACOB BROOM.

Maryland.
JAMES M'HENRY,
DAN. OF ST. THOMAS JENIFER,
DANIEL CARROL.

Virginia.
JOHN BLAIR,
JAMES MADISON, JR.,

North Carolina.
WILLIAM BLOUNT,
RICHARD DOBBS SPAIGHT,
HU. WILLIAMSON.

South Carolina.
J. RUTLEDGE,
CHAS. COTESWORTH PINCKNEY,
CHARLES PINCKNEY,
PIERCE BUTLER.

Georgia.
WILLIAM FEW,
ABR. BALDWIN.

Attest, WILLIAM JACKSON, *Secretary.*

AMENDMENTS TO THE

CONSTITUTION OF THE UNITED STATES.

ARTICLE I. Congress shall make no law respecting an establishment of religion, or prohibiting the free exercise thereof; or abridging the freedom of speech, or of the press; or of the right of the people peaceably to assemble, and to petition the government for a redress of grievances.

ARTICLE II. A well regulated militia being necessary to the security of a free state, the right of the people to keep and bear arms shall not be infringed.

ARTICLE III. No soldier shall in time of peace be quartered in any house, without the consent of the owner; nor in time of war, but in a manner to be prescribed by law.

ARTICLE IV. The right of the people to be secure in their persons, houses, papers and effects, against unreasonable searches and seizures, shall not be violated, and no warrants shall issue, but on probable cause, supported by oath or affirmation, and particularly describing the place to be searched, and the persons or things to be seized.

ARTICLE V. No person shall be held to answer for a capital or otherwise infamous crime, unless on a presentment or indictment of a grand jury, except in cases arising in the land or naval forces, or in the militia when in actual service in time of war or public danger; nor shall any person be subject for the same offence to be twice put in jeopardy of life or limb; nor he, shall be compelled, in any criminal case, to be witness against himself, nor be deprived of life, liberty, or property, without due process of law; nor shall private property be taken for public use without just compensation.

ARTICLE VI. In criminal prosecutions the accused shall enjoy, the right to a speedy and public trial, by an impartial jury of the State and district wherein the crime shall have been committed, which district shall have been previously ascertained by law, and to be informed of the nature and cause of the accusation, to be confronted with the witnesses against him; to have compulsory process for obtaining witnesses in his favor, and to have the assistance of counsel for his defence.

ARTICLE VII. In suits at common law, where the value in controversy shall exceed twenty dollars, the right of trial by jury shall be preserved, and no fact, tried by a jury, shall be otherwise re-examined in any court of the United States, than according to the rules of the common law.

ARTICLE VIII. Excessive bail shall not be required, nor excessive fines imposed, nor cruel and unusual punishment inflicted.

ARTICLE IX. The enumeration in the Constitution, of certain

rights, shall not be construed to deny or disparage others retained by the people.

ARTICLE X. The powers not delegated to the United States by the Constitution, nor prohibited by it to the States, are reserved to the States respectively, or to the people

ARTICLE XI. The judicial power of the United States shall not be construed to extend to any suit in law or equity, commenced or prosecuted against one of the United States by citizens of another State, or by citizens or subjects of any foreign State.

ARTICLE XII. 1. The electors shall meet in their respective states, and vote by ballot for President and Vice-President, one of whom, at least, shall not be an inhabitant of the same State with themselves; they shall name in their ballot the person voted for as President, and in distinct ballots the person voted for as Vice-President, and they shall make distinct lists of all persons voted for as President, and of all persons voted for as Vice-President, and of the number of votes for each, which lists they shall sign and certify, and transmit sealed to the seat of government of the United States, directed to the President of the Senate; the President of the Senate shall, in the presence of the Senate and House of Representatives, open all the certificates and the votes shall then be counted. The person having the greatest number of votes for President shall be President, if such number be a majority of the whole number of electors appointed; and if no person have such majority, then from the persons having the highest numbers not exceeding three on the list of those voted for as President, the House of Representatives shall choose immediately, by ballot, the President. But in choosing the President, the votes shall be taken by States, the representation from each State having one vote; a quorum for this purpose shall consist of a member or members from two thirds of the States, and a majority of all the States shall be necessary to a choice. And if the House of Representatives shall not choose a President whenever the right of choice shall devolve upon them, before the fourth day of March next following, then the Vice-President shall act as President, as in the case of the death or other Constitutional disability of the President.

2. The person having the greatest number of votes as Vice-President, shall be the Vice-President, if such number be a majority of the whole number of electors appointed and if no person have a majority, then from the two highest numbers on the list, the Senate shall choose the Vice-President; a quorum for this purpose shall consist of two thirds of the whole number of Senators, and a majority of the whole number shall be necessary to a choice.

3. But no person constitutionally ineligible to the office of President shall be eligible to that of Vice-President of the United States.

ARTICLE XIII. If any citizen of the United States shall accept, claim, receive or retain any title of nobility or honor, or shall without the consent of Congress, accept and retain any present, pension, office or emolument of any kind whatever, from any emperor, king, prince or foreign power, such person shall cease to be a citizen of the United States, and shall be incapable of holding any office of trust or profit under them, or either of them.

[*The other articles proposed as amendments to the Constitution of the United States, not having been ratified by the constitutional number of the Legislatures of the several States, have not become law.*]

TREATY BETWEEN THE UNITED STATES OF AMERICA AND THE FRENCH REPUBLIC.

The President of the United States of America and the first consul of the French Republic, in the name of the French people, desiring to remove all sources of misunderstanding relative to objects of discussion mentioned in the second and fifth articles of the convention of the eighth Vendemaire An. 9, (thirtieth September, one thousand eight hundred) relative to the rights claimed by the United States, in virtue of the treaty concluded at Madrid, the twenty-seventh October, one thousand seven hundred and ninety five, between his catholic majesty and the said United States, and willing to strengthen the union and friendship which at the time of the said convention was happily re-established between the two nations, have respectively named their plenipotentiaries, to wit: the President of the United States of America, by and with the advice and consent of the Senate of the said States, Robert R. Livingston, minister plenipotentiary of the United States, and James Monroe, minister plenipotentiary and envoy extraordinary of the said States, near the government of the French Republic: and the first consul, in the name of the French people, citizen Francis Barbé Marbois, minister of the public treasury, who, after having respectively exchanged their full powers, have agreed to the following articles:

ARTICLE I. WHEREAS, by the article the third of the treaty concluded at St. Ildelfonso, the 9th Vendemaire, An 9. (1st October, 1800) between the First Consul of the French Republic and his Catholic majesty, it was agreed as follows: "His Catholic majesty promises and engages on his part, to cede to the French Republic, six months after the full and entire execution of the conditions and stipulations herein relative to his royal highness the Duke of Parma, the colony or province of Louisiana, with the same extent that it now has in the hands of Spain and that it had when France possessed it; and such as it should be after the treaties subsequently entered into between Spain and other States." *And whereas*, in pursuance of the treaty, and particularly of the third article, the French Republic has an incontestible title to the domain and to the possession of the said territory; the First Consul of the French Republic desiring to give to the United States a strong proof of his friendship, doth hereby cede to the United States, in the name of the French Republic, forever and in full sovereignty, the said territory with all its rights and appurtenances, as fully and in the same manner as they have been acquired by the French Republic in virtue of the above mentioned treaty concluded with his Catholic majesty.

ARTICLE II. In the cession made by the preceeding article are included the adjacent islands belonging to Louisiana, all public lots and squares, vacant lands, and all public buildings, fortifications, barracks, and other edifices which are not private property. The archives, papers and documents, relative to the domain and sovereignty of Louisiana and its dependencies, will be left in the possession of the commissaries of the United States, and copies will be afterwards given in due form to the magistrates and municipal officers of such of the said papers and documents as may be necessary to them.

ARTICLE III. The inhabitants of the ceded territory shall be incorporated into the Union of the United States, and admitted as soon as possible, according to the principles of the Federal Constitution, to the enjoyment of all the rights, advantages and immunities of citizens of the United States: and in the mean time they shall be maintained and protected in the free enjoyment of their liberty, property, and the religion which they profess.

ARTICLE IV. There shall be sent by the Government of France a commissary to Louisiana, to the end that he do every act necessary, as well to receive from the officers of his Catholic Majesty the said country and its dependencies, in the name of the French Republic, if it has not been already done, as to transmit it in the name of the French Republic to the commissary or agent of the United States.

ARTICLE V. Immediately after the ratification of the present treaty by the President of the United States, and in case that of the First Consul shall have been previously obtained, the commissary of the French Republic shall remit all the military posts of New Orleans, and other parts of the ceded territory, to the commissary or commissaries named by the President to take possession; the troops, whether of France or Spain, who may be there shall cease to occupy any military post from the time of taking possession, and shall be embarked as soon as possible, in the course of three months after the ratification of this treaty.

ARTICLE VI. The United States promise to execute such treaties and articles as may have been agreed between Spain and the tribes and nations of Indians, until by mutual consent of the United States and the said tribes or nations, other suitable articles shall have been agreed upon.

ARTICLE VII. As it is reciprocally advantageous to the commerce of France and the United States to encourage the communication of both nations, for a limited time, in the country ceded by the present treaty, until general arrangements relative to the commerce of both nations may be agreed on; it has been agreed between the contracting parties, that the French ships coming directly from France or any of her colonies, loaded only with the produce or manufactures of France or her said colonies, and the ships of Spain, coming directly from Spain or any of her colonies, loaded only with the produce or manufactures of Spain or her colonies, shall be admitted during the space of twelve years in the port of New Orleans, and in all other legal ports of entry within the ceded territory, in the same manner as the ships of the United States coming directly from France or Spain or any of their colonies, without being subject to any other or greater duty on merchandise, or other or greater tonnage than those paid by the citizens of the United States.

During the space of time above mentioned, no other nation shall have a right to the same privileges in the ports of the ceded Territory; the twelve years shall commence three months after the exchange of ratifications, if it shall take place in France, or three months months after it shall have been notified at Paris to the French Government, if it shall take place in the United States; it is, however, well understood that the object of the above article is to favor the manufactures, commerce, freight and navigation of France and of Spain, so far as relates to the importations that the French and Spanish shall make into the said ports of the United States, without in any sort affecting the regulations that the United States may make concerning the exportation of the produce and merchandise of the United States, or any right they may have to make such regulations.

ARTICLE VIII. In future, and forever after the expiration of the twelve years, the ships of France shall be treated upon the footing of the most favored nations in the ports above mentioned.

ARTICLE IX. The particular convention signed this day by the respective ministers, having for its object to provide for the payment of debts due to the citizens of the United States by the French Republic, prior to the thirtieth of September, one thousand eight hundred, (eighth Vendemaire, An. 9,) is approved, and to have its execution in the same manner as if it had been inserted in the present treaty, and it shall be ratified in the same form and in the same time, so that the one shall not be ratified distinct from the other.

Another particular convention, signed at the same date as the present treaty, relative to a definitive rule between the contracting parties, is in the like manner approved and will be ratified in the same form and in the same time, and jointly.

ARTICLE X. The present treaty shall be ratified in good and due form, and the ratification shall be exchanged in the space of six months after the date of the signatures by the ministers plenipotentiaries, or sooner, if possible.

IN FAITH WHEREOF, The respective plenipotentiaries have signed these artices in the French and English languages; declaring, nevertheless, that the present treaty was originally agreed to in the French language; and have thereunto put their seals.

Done at Paris the tenth day of Floreal, in the eleventh year of the French Republic, and the thirtieth April, one thousand eight hundred and three.

ROBERT R. LIVINGSTON, [L. S.]
JAMES MONROE, [L. S.]
F. BARBE-MALBOIS. [L. S.]

ACTS OF CONGRESS.

1. *AN ACT to enable the people of the Territory of Orleans to form a Constitution and State Government, and for the admission of such State into the Union, on an equal footing with the original States, and for other purposes,* approved, February 16, 1811.

Section 1.—*Be it enacted by the Senate and House of Representatives of the United States of America in Congress assembled,* That the inhabitants of all that part of the Territory or country ceded under the name of Louisiana, by the treaty made at Paris, on the thirtieth day of April, one thousand eight hundred and three, between the United States and France, contained within the following limits, that is to say: beginning at the mouth of the river Sabine, thence by a line to be drawn along the middle of said river, including all its lands to the thirty-second degree of latitude; thence due North, to the Northermost part of the thirty-third degree of North latitude; thence along the said parallel of latitude to the river Mississippi; thence down the said river to the river Iberville; and from thence along the middle of the said river and lakes Maurepas and Ponchartrain, to the gulf of Mexico; thence bounded by the said gulf to the place of beginning, including all islands within three leagues of the coast, be, and they are hereby, authorized to form for themselves a Constitution and State government, and to assume such name as they may deem proper, under the provisions and upon the conditions hereinafter mentioned.

Section 2.—All free white male citizens of the United States, who shall have arrived at the age of twenty-one years, and resided within the said Territory at least one year previous to the day of election, and shall have paid a Teritorial, county, district, or parish tax; and all persons having, in other respects, the legal qualifications to vote for Representatives in the General Assembly of the Territory thereof, shall be and they are hereby authorized to choose Representatives to form a Convention, who shall be apportioned amongst the several counties, districts and parishes within the said Territory of New Orleans, in such manner as the Legislature of the said Territory shall by law direct. The number of the Representatives shall not exceed sixty; and the election for Representatives, aforesaid, shall take place on the third Monday in September next, and shall be conducted in the same manner as is now provided by the laws of said Territory for electing members for the House of Representatives.

Section 3.—The members of the Convention, when duly elected, shall be, and they are hereby, authorized to meet at the city of New Orleans, on the first Monday of November next, which Convention, when met, shall first determine, by the majority of the whole number elected, whether it be expedient or not, at that time, to form a Constitution or State Government, for the people within the said Territory, and if it be determined to be expedient, then the Convention shall, in like manner, declare in behalf of the people of the said Territory, that it adopts the Constitution of the United States; whereupon the said Convention shall be, and hereby is, authorized to form a Constitution and State Government, for the people of the said Territory: *Provided*, The Constitution to be formed, in virtue of the authority herein given, shall be republican, and consistent with the Constitution of the United States; that it shall contain the fundamental principles of civil and religious liberty; that it shall secure to the citizens the trial by jury in all criminal cases, and the privilege of the writ of *habeas corpus*, conformably to the provisions of the Constitution of the United States, and that after the admission of the said Territory of Orleans as a State in the Union, the laws which such State may pass shall be promulgated, and its records, of every description shall be preserved, and its judicial and legislative written proceedings conducted in the language in which the laws and the judicial and legislative written proceedings of the United States are now published and conducted: *And provided also*, That the said Convention shall provide by an ordinance, irrevocable, without the consent of the United States, that the people inhabiting the said Territory do agree and declare, that they do forever disclaim all right or title to the waste or unappropriated lands lying within the said Territory; and that the same shall be and remain at the sole and entire disposition of the United States; and, moreover, that each and every tract of land sold by Congress shall be and remain exempt from any tax laid by the order or under the authority of the State, county, township, parish, or any other purpose whatever, for the term of five years from and after the respective days of the sales thereof, and that the lands belonging to the citizens of the United States, residing without the said State, shall never be taxed higher than the lands belonging to persons residing therein; and that no taxes shall be imposed on lands, the property of the United States.

Section 4. In case the Convention shall declare its assent in behalf of the people of the said Territory, to the adoption of the Constitution of the United States, and shall form a Constitution and State Government for the people of the said Territory of Orleans, the said Convention, as soon thereafter as may be, is hereby required to cause to be transmitted to Congress, the instrument by which its assent to the Constitution of the United States is thus given and declared, and also a true and attested copy of such Constitution or frame of State Government, as shall be formed and provided by said Convention, and if the same shall not be disapproved by Congress, at their next session after the receipt thereof, the said State shall be admitted into the Union, upon the same footing with the original States.

Section 5. Five per centum of the nett proceeds of the sales of the public lands of the United States, and after the first day of January, shall be applied in laying out and constructing public roads and levees in the said State, as the Legislature thereof may direct.

2. *AN ACT for the admission of the State of Louisiana into the Union and to extend the laws of the United States to the said State,* approved, April, 8, 1812.

WHEREAS, The Representatives of the people of all that part of the Territory or country ceded, under the name of "Louisiana," by the treaty made at Paris, on the 30th day of April, one thousand eight hundred and three, between the United States and France, contained within the following limits, that is to say: beginning at the mouth of the river Sabine; thence, by a line to be drawn along the middle of said river, including all islands to the thirty-second degree of latitude; thence, due North, to the Northermost part of the thirty-third degree of North latitude; thence, along the said parallel of latitude, to the river Mississippi; thence, down the said river to the river Iberville; and from thence, along the middle of the said river, and lakes Maurepas and Ponchartrain, to the Gulf of Mexico; thence, bounded by the said Gulf, to the place of beginning, including all islands within three leagues of the coast, did, on the twenty-second day of January, one thousand eight hundred and twelve, form for themselves a Constitution and State Government, and give to the said State the name of Louisiana, in pursuance of an act of Congress, entitled, "an Act to enable the people of the Territory of Orleans to form a Constitution and State Government, and for the admission of the said State into the Union, on an equal footing with the original States, and for other purposes;" and the said Constitution having been transmitted to Congress, and by them being hereby approved: therefore,

Section 1. *Be it enacted by the Senate and House of Representatives of the United States of America, in Congress assembled,* That the said State shall be one, and is hereby declared to be one of the United States of America, and admitted into the Union on an equal footing with the original States, in all respects whatever, by the name and title of the State of Louisiana: *Provided,* That it shall be taken as a condition upon which the said State is incorporated into the Union, that the river Mississippi, and the navigable rivers and waters leading into the same, and into the gulf of Mexico, shall be common highways, and forever free, as well to the inhabitants of the said State as to the inhabitants of other States and the Territories of the United States, without any tax, duty, impost or toll therefor, imposed by the said State, and that the above condition, and also all other the conditions and terms contained in the third section of the act, the title whereof is herein before recited, shall be considered, deemed and taken, fundamental conditions and terms, upon which the said State is incorporated in the Union.

Section 2. Until the next general census and apportionment of Representatives, the said State shall be entitled to one Representative in the House of Representatives of the United States; and all the laws of the United States, not locally inapplicable, shall be extended to the said State, and shall have the same force and effect within the same as elsewhere within the United States.

Section 3. The said State, together with the residue of that portion of country which was comprehended within the Territory of Orleans, as constituted by the act, entitled, "an Act erecting Louisiana into two Territories, and providing for the temporary government thereof," shall be one district, and be called the Louisiana district; and there shall be established in the said district, a District Court, to consist of one Judge, who shall reside therein and be called the District Judge; and there shall be, annually, four stated sessions of the said court held at the city of Orleans; the first to commence on the third Monday of July next, and the three other sessions progressively, on the third Monday of every calender month thereafter. The said Judge shall, in all things, have and exercise the same jurisdiction and powers, which, by the act, the title whereof is in this section recited, were given to the District Judge of the Territory of Orleans; and he shall be allowed an annual compensation of three thousand dollars, to be paid quarter yearly at the Treasury of the United States. The said Judge shall appoint a clerk of the said Court, who shall reside and keep the records of the Court, in the city of Orleans, and shall receive for the services performed by him, the same fees heretofore allowed to the clerk of the Orleans Territory.

Section 4. There shall be appointed in the said district, a person, learned in the law, to act as Attorney for the United States, who shall, in addition to his stated fees, be paid six hundred dollars, annually, as a full compensation for all extra services. There shall also be appointed a Marshal for the said district, who shall perform the same duties, be subject to the same regulations and penalties, and be entitled to the same fees to which Marshals in other districts are entitled for similar services; and shall, moreover, be paid two hundred dollars, annually, as a compensation for all extra services.

Section 5. Nothing in this act shall be construed to repeal the fourth section of an act, entitled, "act Act for laying and collecting the duties on imports and tonnage within the Territories ceded to the United States, by the treaty of the thirtieth of April, one thousand eight hundred and three, between the United States and the French Republic; and for other purposes;" and the Collection District shall be and remain as thereby established.

Section 6. This act shall commence and be in force from and after the thirtieth day of April, 1812.

3. *AN ACT to enlarge the limits of the State Louisiana*, approved, April 14, 1812.

Section 1. *Be it enacted by the Senate and House of Representatives of the United States of America in Congress assembled*, That in case the Legislature of the State of Louisiana shall consent thereto, all that tract of country comprehended within the following bounds, to wit: beginning at the junction of the Iberville, with the river Mississippi; thence along the middle of the Iberville, the river Amite, and of the lakes Maurepas and Ponchartrain to the eastern mouth of the

Pearl river; thence up the Eastern branch of Pearl river to the thirty-first degree of North latitude; thence along the said degree of latitude to the river Mississippi; thence down the said river to the place of beginning, shall become and form a part of the said State of Louisiana, and be subject to the Constitution and laws thereof, in the same manner, and for all intents and purposes as if it had been included within the original boundaries of the said State.

Section 2. It shall be incumbent on the Legislature of the State of Louisiana, in case they consent to the incorporation of the territory aforesaid, within their limits, at their first session, to make provision by law for the representation of the said territory in the Legislature of the State, upon the principles of the Constitution, and for the securing to the people of the said territory, equal rights, privileges, benefits and advantages, with those enjoyed by the people of the other parts of the State; which law shall be liable to revision, modification and amendment by Congress, and also in the manner provided for the amendment of the State Constitution, but shall not be liable to change or amendment by the Legislature of the State.

[*See the resolution passed by the Legislature on the 4th of August,* 1812, 2. *Digest,* 415, *by which the aforesaid enlargement of limits, was assented to.*]

4 *AN ACT granting to the Governor of the State of Louisiana, for the time being, and his successors in office, a lot of ground and the buildings thereon, in the city of New Orleans,* approved, April 29, 1812.

Be it enacted by the Senate and House of Representatives of the United States of America, in Congress assembled, That all the right and claim of the United States to the use, possession and occupancy of a space of three hundred and thirty-six by two hundred and twenty feet of a lot of ground in the city of New-Orleans, bounded by Chartres and Levee streets, and by Toulouse street and the lot of widow Castillon, together with the house on the above described lot, known by the name of the Government House, and the other buildings thereon, be, and the same are hereby vested in, and conveyed to the Governor of the State of Louisiana for the time being, and his successors in the same office, for the sole use and benefit of the said State of Louisiana forever: *Provided however,* that this act shall not effect the claim or claims of any individual or individuals, if any such there be.

5. *AN ACT supplementary to an act entitled "an act for the admission of the State of Louisiana into the Union, and to extend the laws of the United States to the said State,* approved, May 22, 1812.

Section 1. *Be it enacted by the Senate and House of Representatives of the United States of America in Congress assembled,* That all causes, actions, indictments, libels, pleas, processes and proceedings whatsoever, returnable, commenced, depending or in any manner existing in the District Court established in the Territory of Orleans, in and by the act entitled "an act erecting Louisiana into two

Territories and providing for the temporary government thereof," be and the same are hereby transferred to the District Court established by the act to which this is a supplement, and may be proceeded in, shall exist and have like incidents and effects as if they had been originated and been proceeded in, in the Court established by the act to which this is a supplement,

Section 2. The dockets, books, records, papers and seal, belonging to the said District Court of the Orleans Territory, shall be transferred to, and become the dockets, books, records and papers of the District Court of the Louisiana District.

Section 3. The eighth section of the act aforesaid, entitled, "an Act erecting Louisiana into two Territories, and providing for the temporary government thereof," and also, all acts within the purview of this act, and the one to which this is a supplement, shall be, and the same are hereby repealed.

CONSTITUTION OR FORM OF GOVERNMENT OF THE STATE OF LOUISIANA.

WE, the representatives of the people of all that part of the Territory or country ceded under the name of Louisiana, by the treaty made at Paris, on the thirtieth day of April, one thousand eight hundred and three, between the United States and France, contained in the following limits, to wit: beginning at the mouth of the river Sabine, thence by a line to be drawn along the middle of said river, including all its islands, to the thirty-second degree of latitude; thence, due North to the Northermost part of the thirty-third degree of North latitude; thence, along the said parallel of latitude to the river Mississippi; thence, down the said river to the river Iberville; and from thence, along the middle of the said river and lakes Maurepas and Ponchartrain to the gulf of Mexico; thence, bounded by the said gulf, to the place of beginning, including all islands within three leagues of the coast, in Convention assembled, by virtue of an act of Congress, entitled, "an Act to enable the people of the Territory of Orleans to form a Constitution and State Government, and for the admission of said State into the Union, on an equal footing with the original States, and for other purposes;" in order to secure to all the citizens thereof, the enjoyment of the right of life, liberty and property, do ordain and establish the following Constitution or form of government, and do mutually agree with each other to form ourselves into a free and independent State, by the name of the State of Louisiana.

ARTICLE I.

Concerning the Distribution of the Powers of Government.

Section 1. The powers of the Government of the State of Louisiana shall be divided into three distinct departments, and each of them be confided to a separate body of magistracy, viz: those which are legislative, to one; those which are executive, to another; and those which are judiciary, to another.

Section 2. No person or collection of persons, being one of those departments, shall exercise any power properly belonging to either of the others; except in the instances hereinafter expressly directed or permitted.

ARTICLE II.

Concerning the Legislative Department.

Section 1. The legislative power of this State shall be vested in two distinct branches, the one to be styled the House of Representatives; the other, the Senate; and both together, the General Assembly of the State of Louisiana.

Section 2. The members of the House of Representatives shall continue in service for the term of two years from the day of the commencement of the general election.

Section 3. Representatives shall be chosen on the first Monday in July, every two years; and the General Assembly shall convene on the first Monday in January in every year, unless a different day be appointed by law, and their sessions shall be held at the seat of government.

Section 4. No person shall be a Representative who, at the time of his election, is not a free white male citizen of the United States, and hath not attained to the age of twenty-one years, and resided in the State two years next preceding his election, and the last year thereof, in the county for which he may be chosen, or in the district for which he is elected, in case the said counties may be divided into separate districts of election, and has not held, for one year, in the said county or district, landed property to the value of five hundred dollars, agreeably to the last list.

Section 5. Elections for Representatives for the several counties entitled to representation, shall be held at the places of holding their respective Courts, or in the several election precincts into which the Legislature may think proper, from time to time, to divide any or all of those counties.

Seetion 6. Representation shall be equal and uniform in this State, and shall be forever regulated and ascertained by the number of qualified electors therein. In the year one thousand eight hundred and thirteen, and every fourth year thereafter, an enumeration of all the electors shall be made in such manner as shall be directed by law. The number of Representatives shall, in the several years of making these enumerations, be so fixed as not to be less than twenty-five nor more than fifty.

Section 7. The House of Representatives shall choose its Speaker and other officers.

Section 8. In all elections for Representatives every free white male citizen of the United States, who, at the time being hath attained to the age of twenty-one years and resided in the county in which he offers to vote one year next preceding the election, and who in the last six months prior to the said election, shall have paid a State tax, shall enjoy the right of an elector: Provided however, That every free white male citizen of the United States who shall have purchased land from the United States, shall have the right of voting whenever he shall have the other qualifications of age and residence above prescribed. Electors shall, in all cases, except treason, felony, breach of surety of peace, be privileged from arrest during their attendance at, going to, or returning from elections.

Section 9. The members of the Senate shall be chosen for the term of four years; and when assembled, have the power to choose its officers annually.

Section 10. The State shall be divided into fourteen Senatorial Districts, which shall forever remain indivisible, as follows: the parish of St. Bernard and Plaquemine including the country above as far as the land (Des Pécheurs,) on the East of the Mississippi, and on the West as far as Bernoudy's canal, shall form one district. The city of New Orleans, beginning at the Nun's Plantation above and extending below as far as the above mentioned canal (Des Pécheurs,) including the inhabitants of the bayou St. John, shall form the second district, the remainder of the county of Orleans shall form the third district. The counties of German Coast, Acadia, Lafourche, Iberville, Point Coupée, Concordia, Attakapas, Opelousas, Rapides, Natchitoches and Ouachita, shall each form one district, and each district shall elect a Senator.

Section 11. At the session of the General Assembly after this Constitution takes effect, the Senators shall be divided by lot, as equally as may be, into two classes; the seats of the Senators of the first class shall be vacated at the expiration of the second year; of the second class, at the expiration of the fourth year; so that one half shall be chosen every two years, and a rotation thereby kept up perpetually.

Section 12. No person shall be a Senator who, at the time of his election, is not a citizen of the United States, and who hath not attained to the age of twenty-seven years, resided in this State four years next preceding his election, and one year in the district in which he may be chosen; and unless he holds within the same a landed property to the value of one thousand dollars agreeably to the tax list.

Section 13. The first election for Senators shall be general throughout the State, and at the same time that the general election for Representatives is held; and thereafter there shall be a biennial election of Senators to fill the place of those whose term of service may have expired.

Section 14. Not less than a majority of the members of each House of the General Assembly, shall form a quorum to do business; but a smaller number may adjourn from day to day, and shall be authorized by law to compel the attendance of absent members, in such manner and under such penalties as may be prescribed thereby.

Section 15. Each House of the General Assembly shall judge of the qualifications, elections and returns of its members, but a contested election shall be determined in such manner as shall be directed by law.

Section 16. Each House of the General Assembly may determine the rules of its proceedings, punish a member for disorderly behavior, and with the concurrence of two-thirds, expel a member, but not a second time for the same offence.

Section 17. Each House of the General Assembly shall keep and publish weekly, a journal of its proceedings, and the yeas and nays of the members on any question, shall, at the desire of any two of them, be entered on their journal.

Section 18. Neither House, during the session of the General Assembly, shall, without the consent of the other, adjourn for more than three days, nor to any other place than that in which they may be sitting.

Section 19. The members of the General Assembly shall, severally, receive from the public treasury, a compensation for their services, which shall be four dollars per day, during their attendance on, going to and returning from the sessions of their respective houses: Provided, That the same may be increased or diminished by law; but no alteration shall take effect during the period of service of the members of the House of Representative, by whom such alterations shall have been made.

Section 20. The members of the General Assembly shall, in all cases except treason, felony, breach of surety of the peace, be privileged from arrest, during their attendance at the sessions of their respective houses, and in going to or returning from the same, and for any speech or debate in either house they shall not be questioned in any other place.

Section 21. No Senator or Representative shall, during the term for which he was elected, nor for one year thereafter, be appointed or elected to any civil office of profit under this State, which shall have been created, or the emoluments of which shall have been increased during the time such Senator or Representative was in office, except to such offices or appointments as may be filled by the elections of the people.

Section 22. No person, while he continues to exercise the functions of a clergyman, priest or teacher of any religious persuasion, society or sect, shall be eligible to the General Assembly, or to any office of profit or trust under this State.

Section 23. No person who, at any time, may have been a collector of taxes for the State, or the assistant or deputy of such collector, shall be eligible to the General Assembly, until he shall have obtained a *quietus* for the amount of such collection, and for all public moneys for which he may be responsible.

Section 24. No bill shall have the force of a law until, on three several days, it be read over in each House of the General Assembly, and free discussion allowed thereon; unless in case of urgency, four-fifths of the House where the bill shall be depending, may deem it expedient to dispense with this rule.

Section 25. All bills for raising revenue shall originate in the House of Representatives, but the Senate may propose amendments, as in other bills: Provided, That they shall not introduce any new matter, under the color of an amendment, which does not relate to raising a revenue.

Section 26. The General Assembly shall regulate, by law, by whom and in what manner writs of election shall be issued to fill vacancies which may happen in either branch thereof.

ARTICLE III.

Concerning the Executive Department.

Section 1. The supreme executive power of the State shall be vested in a chief magistrate, who shall be styled the Governor of the State of Louisiana.

Section 2. The Governor shall be elected for the term of four years, in the following manner: the citizens entitled to vote for Representatives shall vote for a Governor at the time and place of voting for Representatives and Senators. Their votes shall be returned by the persons presiding over the elections to the seat of government, addressed to the President of the Senate; and on the second day of the General Assembly, the members of the two houses shall meet in the House of Representatives, and immediately after, the two candidates who shall have obtained the greatest number of votes shall be balloted for, and the one having a majority of votes shall be Governor: Provided, however, That if more than two candidates have obtained the highest number of votes, it shall be the duty of the General Assembly to ballot for them in the manner above prescribed, and in case several candidates should obtain an equal number of votes, next to the candidate who has obtained the highest number, it shall be the duty of the General Assembly to select in the same manner, the candidate who is to be balloted for with him who has obtained the highest number of votes.

Section 3. The Governor shall be ineligible for the succeeding four years after the expiration of the time for which he shall have been elected.

Section 4. He shall be at least thirty-five years of age, and a citizen of the United States, and have been an inhabitant of this State at least six years preceding his election, and shall hold in his own right a landed estate of five thousand dollars value, agreeably to the tax list.

Section 5. He shall commence the execution of his office on the fourth Monday succeeding the day of his election, and shall continue in the execution thereof, until the end of four weeks next succeeding the election of his successor, and until his successor shall have taken the oaths or affirmations prescribed by this Constitution.

Section 6. No member of Congress, or person holding any office under the United States, or minister of any religious society, shall be eligible to the office of Governor.

Section 7. The Governor shall, at stated times, receive for his services a compensation which shall neither be increased nor diminished during the term for which he shall have been elected.

Section 8. He shall be Commander-in-Chief of the army and navy of this State, and of the militia thereof, except when they shall be called into the service of the United States, but he shall not command personally in the field, unless he shall be advised so to do by a resolution of the General Assembly.

Section 9. He shall nominate and appoint, with the advice and consent of the Senate, Judges, Sheriffs, and all other officers whose offices are established by this Constitution, and whose appointments are not herein otherwise provided for: Provided, however, That the Legislature shall have a right to prescribe the mode of appointment of all other offices to be established by law.

Section 10. The Governor shall have power to fill up vacancies that may happen during the recess of the Legislature, by granting commissions which shall expire at the end of the next session.

Section 11. He shall have power to remit fines and forfeitures, and, except in cases of impeachment, to grant reprieves and pardons, with the approbation of the Senate. In cases of treason he shall have power to grant reprieves until the end of the next session of the General Assembly in which the power of pardoning shall be vested.

Section 12. He may require information, in writing, from the officers in the executive department, upon any subject relating to the duties of their respective offices.

Section 13. He shall, from time to time, give to the General Assembly information respecting the situation of the State, and recommend to their consideration such measures as he may deem expedient.

Section 14. He may, on extraordinary occasions, convene the General Assembly at the seat of government, or at a different place if that should have become dangerous from an enemy or from contagious disorders; and in case of disagreement between two houses with respect to the time of adjournment, he may adjourn them to such time as he may think proper, not exceeding four months.

Section 15. He shall take care that the laws be faithfully executed.

Section 16. It shall be his duty to visit the different counties at least once in every two years, to inform himself of the state of the militia and the general condition of the country.

Section 17. In case of the impeachment of the Governor, his removal from office, death, refusal to qualify, resignation, or absence from the State, the President of the Senate shall exercise all the power and authority appertaining to the office of Governor, until another be duly qualified, or the Governor absent or impeached shall return or be acquitted.

Section 18. The President of the Senate, during the time he administers the government, shall receive the same compensation which the Governor would have received had he been employed in the duties of his office.

Section 19. A Secretary of State shall be appointed and commissioned during that time for which the Governor shall have been elected, if he shall so long behave himself well; he shall keep a fair register, and attest all official acts and proceedings of the Governor, and shall, when required, lay the same, and all papers, minutes and vouchers relative thereto, before either House of the General Assembly, and shall perform such other duties as may be enjoined him by law.

Section 20. Every bill which shall have passed both houses shall be presented to the Governor, if he approve, he shall sign it, if not, he shall return it, with his objections, to the house in which it shall have originated, who shall enter the objections at large upon their journal, and proceed to reconsider it; if, after such reconsideration, two-thirds of all the members elected to that house shall agree to pass the bill, it shall be sent, with the objections, to the other house, by which it shall likewise be reconsidered, and if approved by two-thirds of all the members elected to that house, it shall be a law; but in such cases, the votes of both houses shall be determined by yeas and nays, and the names of the members voting for and against the bill shall be entered on the journal of each house, respectively. If any bill shall not be returned by the Governor within ten days, (Sundays excepted,) after it shall have been presented to him, it shall be a law in like manner as if he had sighed it, unless the General Assembly, by adjournment, prevent its return, in which case it shall be a law, unless sent back within three days after their next meeting.

Section 21. Every order, resolution, or vote, to which the concurrence of both houses may be necessary, except on a question of adjournment, shall be presented to the Governor, and, before it shall take effect, be approved by him; or being disappoved shall be repassed by two-thirds of both houses.

Section 22. The free white men of this State shall be armed and disciplined for its defense; but those who belong to religious societies whose tenets forbid them to carry arms, shall not be compelled so to do, but shall pay an equivolent for personal services.

Section 23. The militia of this State shall be organized in such manner as may be hereafter deemed most expedient by the Legislature.

ARTICLE IV.

Concerning the Judiciary Department.

Section 1. The judiciary power shall be vested in a Supreme Court and inferior Courts.

Section 2. The Supreme Court shall have appellate jurisdiction only, which jurisdiction shall extend to all civil cases when the matter in dispute shall exceed the sum of three hundred dollars.

Section 3. The Supreme Court shall consist of not less than three judges, nor more than five; the majority of whom shall form a *quorum;* each of said judges shall receive a salary of five thousand dollars, annually. The Supreme Court shall hold its sessions at the places hereinafter mentioned; and for that purpose the State is hereby divided into two districts of appellate jurisdiction, in each of which the Supreme Court shall administer justice in the manner hereinafter prescribed. The Eastern District to consist of the counties of New Orleans, German Coast, Acadia, Lafourche, Iberville and Point Coupée; the Western District to consist of the counties of Attakapas, Opelousas, Rapides, Concordia, Natchitoches and Ouachita. The Supreme Court shall hold its sessions in each year; for the Eastern District, in New Orleans, during the months of November, December, January, February, March, April, May, June and July; and for the Western District, at the Opelousas, during the months of August, September and October, for five years: Provided however, That every five years the Legislature may change the place of holding said Court in the Western District. The said Court shall appoint its own clerks.

Section 4. The Legislature is authorized to establish such inferior Courts as may be convenient to the administration of justice.

Section 5. The judges, both of the Supreme and inferior Courts, shall hold their offices during good behavior; but for any reasonable cause which shall not be sufficient ground for impeachment, the Governor shall remove any of them, on the address of three-fourths of each House of the General Assembly: Provided, however, That the cause or causes for which such removal may be required, shall be stated at length in the address, and inserted on the journal of each house.

Section 6. The judges, by virtue of their offices, shall be conservators of the peace throughout the State; the style of all process shall be "the State of Louisiana." All prosecutions shall be carried on in the name and by the authority of the State of Louisiana, and conclude "against the peace and dignity of the same."

Section 7. There shall be an Attorney General for the State, and as many other prosecuting attorneys for the State as may be hereafter found necessary. The said attorneys shall be appointed by the Governor, with the advice and approbation of the Senate. Their duties shall be determined by law.

Section 8. All commissions shall be in the name and by the authority of the State of Louisiana, and sealed with the State seal, and signed by the Governor.

Section 9. The State Treasurer, and Printer or Printers of the State shall be appointed annually, by the joint vote of both houses of the General Assembly: Provided, That during the recess of the same, the Governor shall have power to fill vacancies which may happen in either of the said offices.

Section 10. The clerks of the several Courts shall be removable for beach of good behavior, by the Court of Appeals only, who shall be judge of the fact as well as of the law.

Section 11. The existing laws in this Territory, when this Constitution goes into effect, shall continue to be in force until altered or abolished by the Legislature: Provided, however, That the Legislature shall never adopt any system or code of laws, by a general reference to the said system or code; but in all cases, shall specify the several provisions of the laws it may enact.

Section 12. The judges of all the Courts within this State shall, as often as it may be possible so to do, in every definite judgment, refer to the particular law, in virtue of which such judgment may have been rendered; and in all cases, adduce the reasons on which their judgment is founded.

ARTICLE V.

Concerning Impeachment.

Section 1. The power of impeachment shall be vested in the House of Representatives alone.

Section 2. All impeachments shall be tried by the Senate. When sitting for that purpose the Senators shall be upon oath or affirmation, and no person shall be convicted without the concurrence of two-thirds of the members present.

Section 3. The Governor and all civil officers shall be liable to impeachment for any misdemeanor in office, but judgment, in such cases, shall not extend further than to the removal from office and disqualification to hold any office of honor, trust or profit under this State; but the parties convicted shall, nevertheless, be liable and subject to indictment, trial and punishment, according to law.

ARTICLE VI.

General Provisions.

Section 1. Members of the General Assembly and all officers, executive and judicial, before they enter upon the execution of their respective offices, shall take the following oath or affirmation: "I, (A. B.,) do solemnly swear (or affirm) that I will faithfully and impartially discharge and perform all the duties incumbent upon me as———, according to the best of my abilities and understanding, agreeably to the rules and regulations of the Constitution, and the laws of the State, so help me God."

Section 2. Treason against the State shall consist only in levying war against it, or in adhering to its enemies, giving them aid and comfort. No person shall be convicted of treason, unless on the testimony of two witnesses to the same overt act, or his own confession in open Court.

Section 3. Every person shall be disqualified from serving as Governor, Senator, or Representative, for the term for which he shall have been elected, who shall have been convicted of having given or offered any bribe to procure his election.

Section 4. Laws shall be made to exclude from office and from suffrage those who shall thereafter be convicted of bribery, perjury, forgery, or other high crimes or misdemeanors. The privilege of free suffrage shall be supported by laws regulating elections, and prohibiting, under adequate penalties, all undue influence thereon, from power, bribery, tumult, or other improper practices.

Section 5. No money shall be drawn from the treasury but in pursuance of appropriations made by law; nor shall any appropriation of money for the support of an army be made for a longer term than one year; and a regular statement and account of the receipts and expenditures of all public money shall be published annually.

Section 6. It shall be the duty of the General Assembly to pass such laws as may be necessary and proper to decide differences by arbitrators, to be appointed by the parties, who may choose that summary mode of adjustment.

Section 7. All civil officers for the State at large shall reside within the State; and all district or county officers within their respective districts or counties, and shall keep their respective offices at such places therein as may be required by law.

Section 8. The Legislature shall determine the time of duration of the several public offices when such time shall not have been fixed by this Constitution; and all civil officers except the Governor and judges of the superior and inferior Courts shall be removable by an address of two-thirds of the members of both houses, except those, the removal of whom has been otherwise provided for by this Constitution.

Section 9. Absence on the business of this State or of the United States shall not forfeit a residence once obtained, so as to deprive one of the right of suffrage, or of being elected or appointed to any office under this State, under the exceptions contained in this Constitution.

Section 10. It shall be the duty of the General Assembly to regulate by law, in what cases, and what deduction from the salaries of public officers shall be made for neglect of duty in their official capacity.

Section 11. Returns of all elections for the members of the General Assembly shall be made to the Secretary of State for the time being.

Section 12. The Legislature shall point out the manner in which a man coming into the country shall declare his residence.

Section 13. In all elections by the people, and also by the Senate and House of Representatives, jointly or separately, the vote shall be given by ballot.

Section 14. No member of Congress, nor person holding or exercising any office of trust or profit under the United States, or either of them, or under any foreign powers, shall be eligible as a member of the General Assembly of this State, or hold or exercise any office of trust or profit under the same.

Section 15. All the laws that may be passed by the Legislature, and the public records of this State, and the judicial and legislative written proceeding of the same, shall be promulgated, preserved and conducted in the language in which the Constitution of the United States is written.

Section 16. The General Assembly shall direct, by law, how persons who are now, or may hereafter become securities for public offices, may be relieved or discharged on account of such securityship.

Section 17. No power of suspending the laws of this State shall be exercised, unless by the Legislature or its authority.

Section 18. In all criminal prosecutions the accused have the right of being heard by himself or counsel, of demanding the nature and cause of the accusation against him, of meeting the witnesses face to face, of having compulsory process for obtaining witnesses in his favor, and prosecutions by indictment or information, a speedy public trial by an impartial jury of the vicinage, nor shall he be compelled to give evidence against himself.

Section 19. All prisoners shall be bailable by sufficient securities, unless for capital offences, where the proof is evident or the presumption great; and the privileges of the writ of *habeas corpus* shall not be suspended unless when in cases of rebellion or invasion the public safety may require it.

Section 20. No *ex post facto* law nor any law impairing the obligation of contracts shall be passed.

Section 21. Printing presses shall be free to every person who undertakes to examine the proceedings of the Legislature, or any other branch of the Government, and no law shall ever be made to restrain the right thereof. The free communications of thoughts and opinions is one of the invaluable rights of man, and every citizen may freely speak, write and print on any subject, being responsible for the abuse of that liberty.

Section 22. Emigration from the State shall not be prohibited.

Section 23. The citizens of the town of New Orleans shall have the right of appointing the several public officers necessary for the administration and the police of the said city, pursuant to the mode of election which shall be prescribed by the Legislature: Provided, That the Mayor and Recorder be ineligible to a seat in the General Assembly.

Section 24. The seat of government shall continue at New Orleans until removed by law.

Section 25. All laws contrary to this Constitution shall be null and void.

ARTICLE VII.

Mode of Revising the Constitution.

Section 1. When experience shall point out the necessity of amending this Constitution, and a majority of all the members elected to each House of the General Assembly shall, within the first twenty days of their stated annual session, concur in passing a law, specifying the alterations intended to be made, for taking the sense of the good people of this State, as to the necessity and expediency of calling a Convention, it shall be the duty of the several returning officers, at the next general election which shall be held for Representatives after the passage of such a law, to open a poll for, and make return to the Secretary for the time being, of the names of all those entitled to vote for Representatives, who have voted for calling a Convention; and if thereupon, it shall appear that a majority of all the citizens of this State entitled to vote for Representatives, have voted for a Convention, the General Assembly shall direct that a similar poll shall be opened, and taken for the next year; and if thereupon, it shall appear that a majority of all the citizens of this State entitled to vote for Representatives, have voted for a Convention, the General Assembly shall, at their next session, call a Convention, to consist of as many members as there shall be in the General Assembly, and no more, to be chosen in the same manner and proportion, at the same places and at the same time that Representatives are, by citizens entitled to vote for Representatives; and to meet within three months after the said election, for the purpose of readopting, amending, or changing this Constitution. But if it shall appear by the vote of either year, as aforesaid, that a majority of all the citizens entitled to vote for Representatives, did not vote for a Convention, a Convention shall not be called.

SCHEDULE.

Section 1. That no inconveniences may arise from the change of a Territorial to a permanent State Government, it is declared by the Convention that all rights, suits, actions, prosecutions, claims and contracts, both as it respects individuals and bodies corporate, shall continue as if no change had taken place in this Government in virtue of the laws now in force.

Section 2. All fines, penalties and forfeitures, due and owing to the Territory of Orleans shall inure to the use of the State. All bonds executed to the Governor or any other officer, in his official capacity, in the Territory, shall pass over to the Governor or to the officers of the State and their successors in office, for the use of the State, by him or by them to be respectively assigned over to the use of those concerned, as the case may be.

Section 3. The Governor, Secretary and Judges, and all other officers under the Territorial Government, shall continue in the exercise of the duties of their respective departments until the said officers are superceded under the authority of this Constitution.

Section 4. All laws now in force in this Territory, not inconsistent with this Constitution, shall continue and remain in full effect until repealed by the Legislature.

Section 5. The Governor of this State shall make use of his private seal until a State seal be procured.

Section 6. The oaths of office herein directed to be taken, may be administered by any justice of the peace, until the Legislature shall otherwise direct.

Section 7. At the expiration of the time after which this Constitution is to go into operation, or immediately after official information shall have been received that Congress have approved of the same, the President of the Convention shall issue writs of election to the proper officers in the different counties, enjoining them to cause an election to be held for Governor and members of the General Assembly, in each of their respective districts. The election shall commence on the fourth Monday following the day of the date of the President's proclamation, and shall take place on the same day throughout the State. The mode and duration of the said election shall be determined by the laws now in force: Provided, however, that in case of absence or disability of the President of the Convention to cause the said election to be carried into effect, the Secretary of the Convention shall discharge the duties hereby imposed on the President; and that in case of absence of the Secretary, a committee of Messrs. Blanque, Brown and Urquhart, or a majority of them, shall discharge the duties herein imposed on the Secretary of the Convention; and the members of the General Assembly thus elected, shall assemble on the fourth Monday thereafter at the seat of government. The Governor and members of the General Assembly, for this time only, shall enter upon the duties of their respective offices immediately after their election, and shall continue in office in the manner and during the same period they would have done had they been elected on the first Monday of July, one thousand eight hundred and twelve.

Section 8. Until the first enumeration shall be made, as directed in the sixth section of the second article of this Constitution, the county of Orleans shall be entitled to six Representatives, to be elected as follows: one by the First Senatorial District within the said county, four by the Second District, and one by the Third District. The county of German Coast, to two Representatives; the county of Acadia, to two Representatives; the county of Iberville, to two Representatives; the county of Lafourche, to two Representatives, to be elected as follows: one by the parish of Assumption, and the other by the parish of the interior; the county of Rapides, to two Representatives; the county of Natchitoches, to one Representative; the county of Concordia, to one Representative; the county of Ouachita, to one Representative; the county of Opelousas, to two Representatives; the county of Attakapas to three Representatives, to be elected as follows; two by the parish of St. Martin, and the third by the parish of St. Mary; and the respective Senatorial Districts created by this Constitution, to one Senator each.

Done in Convention, at New Orleans, the twenty-second day of the month of January, in the year of our Lord, one thousand eight hundred and twelve, and in the Independence of the United States of America, the thirty-sixth.

J. POYDRAS,
President of the Convention.

J. D. Degoutin Bellechasse,
J. Blanque,
F. J. Le Breton D'Orgenoy,
Mgre. Guichard,
S. Henderson,
Denis Delaronde,
F. Livaudais,
B. Marigny,
Thomas Urquhart,

Jaques Villere,
John Watkins,
Samuel Winter,
of the county of Orleans,
James Brown,
Jean-Noel Destrehan,
Alex. La Branche,
of the county of German Coast,

MICHEL CANTRELLE,
J. M. REYNAUD,
GENEZI ROUSSIN,
of the county of Acadia,
AMAND HEBERT,
WILLIAM WIKOFF, Jr.,
of the county of Iberville,
P. BOSSIER,
J. PRUD'HOMME,
of the county of Natchitoches,
WILLIAM GOFORTH,
BELA HUBBARD, Jr.,
ST. MARTIN,
H. S. THIBODEAUX,
of the county of Lafourche,
S. HIRIART,
of the county of Point Coupée,
R. HALL,
THOS. F. OLIVER,
LEVI WELLS,
of the county of Rapides,
JAMES DUNLAP,
DAVID B. MORGAN,
of the county of Concordia,
HENRY BRY,
of the county of Ouachita,
ALLAN B. MAGRUDER,
D. J. SUTTON,
JOHN THOMPSON,
of the county of Opelousas,
LOUIS DE BLANC,
HENRY JOHNSON,
W. C. MAQUILLE,
CHAS. OLIVER,
ALEXANDER PORTER,
of the county of Attakapas,

ELIGIUS FROMETIN,
Secretary of the Convention.

CONSTITUTION OF 1845.

PREAMBLE.

We, the People of the State of Lonisiana, do ordain and establish this Constitution.

TITLE I.—DISTRIBUTION OF POWERS.

ART. 1. The powers of the Government of the State of Louisiana shall be divided into three distinct departments, and each of them be confined to a separate body of magistracy, to wit: those which are legislative to one; those which are executive to another; and those which are judicial to another.

ART. 2. No one of these departments, nor any person holding office in one of them, shall exercise power properly belonging to either of the others, except in the instances hereinafter expressly directed or permitted.

TITLE II.—LEGISLATIVE DEPARTMENT.

ART. 3. The Legislative powers of the State shall be vested in two distinct branches, the one to be styled the "House of Representatives," the other "The Senate," and both, the "General Assembly of the State of Louisiana."

ART. 4. The members of the House of Representatives shall continue in service for the term of two years from the day of the closing of the general elections.

ART. 5. Representatives shall be chosen on the first Monday in November, every two years; and the election shall be completed in one day. The General Assembly shall meet every second year, on the third Monday in January next ensuing the election, unless a different day be appointed by law, and their session shall be held at the seat of government.

ART. 6. No person shall be a Representative who at the time of his election is not a free white male, and has not been for three years a citizen of the United States, and has not attained the age of twenty-one years, and resided in the State for the three years next preceding the election, and the last year thereof in the perish for which he may be chosen.

ART. 7. Elections for Representatives for the several parishes or representative districts shall be held at the several election precincts established by law. The Legislature may delegate the power of establishing election precincts to the parochial or municipal authorities.

ART. 8. Representation in the House of Representatives shall be equal and uniform, and shall be regulated and ascertained by the number of qualified electors. Each parish shall have at least one representative; no new parish shall be created with a territory less than six hundred and twenty-five square miles, nor with a number of electors less than the full number entitling it to a representative, nor when the creation of such new parish would leave any other parish without the said extent of territory and number of electors.

The first enumeration to be made by the State authorities under this Constitution, shall be made in the year 1847; the second, in the year 1855; and the subsequent enumerations shall be made every tenth year thereafter, in such manner as shall be prescribed by law for the purpose of ascertaining the total population and the number of qualified electors in each parish and election district.

At the first regular session of the Legislature after the making of each enumeration, the Legislature shall apportion the representation amongst the several parishes and election districts on the basis of qualified electors as aforesaid. A representative number shall be fixed, and each parish and election district shall have as many representatives as the aggregate number of its electors will entitle it to, and an additional representative for any fraction exceeding one-half the representative number. The number of representatives shall not be more than one hundred, nor less than seventy.

That part of the parish of Orleans situated on the left bank of the Mississippi shall be divided into nine representative districts, as follows, viz:

1st. First district to extend from the line of the parish of Jefferson to the middle of Benjamin, Estelle and Thalia streets.

2d. Second district to extend from the last mentioned limits to the middle of Julia street, until it strikes the New Orleans Canal, thence down said Canal to the Lake.

3d. Third district to comprise the residue of the Second Municipality.

4th. Fourth district to extend from the middle of Canal street to the middle of St. Louis street, until it reaches the Metairie road, thence along said road to the New Orleans Canal.

5th. Fifth district to extend from the last mentioned limits to the middle of St. Philip street, thence down said street until its intersection with the Bayou St. John, thence along the middle of said bayou until it intersects the Metairie road, thence along said road until it reaches St. Louis street.

6th. Sixth district to compose the residue of the First Municipality.

7th. Seventh district, from the middle of Esplanade street to the middle of Champs Elysees street.

8th. Eighth district, from the middle of Champs Elysees street to the middle of Enghein street and Lafayette avenue.

9th. Ninth district, from the middle of Enghein street and Lafayette avenue to the lower limits of the parish.

ART. 9. The House of Representatives shall choose its Speaker and other officers.

ART. 10 In all elections by the people, every free white male, who has been two years a citizen of the United States, who has attained the age of twenty-one years, and resided in the State two consecutive years next preceding the election, and the last year thereof, in the parish in which he offers to vote, shall have the right of voting: *Provided*, That no person shall be deprived of the right of voting, who, at the time of the adoption of this Constitution, was entitled to that right under the Constitution of 1812. Electors shall, in all cases except treason, felony, breach of surety of the peace, be privileged from arrest during their attendance at, going to, or returning from elections.

ART. 11. Absence from the State for more than ninety consecutive days, shall interrupt the acquisition of the residence required in the preceding section, unless the person absenting himself shall be a housekeeper, or shall occupy a tenement for carrying on business, and his dwelling-house or tenements for carrying on business shall be actually occupied during his absence by his family or servants, or some portion thereof, or by some one employed by him.

ART. 12. No soldier, seaman, or marine in the Army or Navy of the United States, no pauper, no person under interdiction, nor under conviction of any crime punishable with hard labor, shall be entitled to a vote at any election in this State.

ART. 13. No person shall be entitled to vote at any election held in this State, except in the parish of his residence, and in cities and towns divided into election precincts, in the election precinct in which he resides.

ART. 14. The members of the Senate shall be chosen for the term of four years. The Senate, when assembled, shall have the power to choose its officers every two years.

ART. 15. The Legislature, in every year in which they shall apportion representation in the House of Representatives, shall divide the State into Senatorial districts. No parish shall be divided in the formation of a Senatorial district, the parish of Orleans excepted. And whenever a new parish shall be created, it shall be attached to the Senatorial district from which most of its territory was taken, or to another contiguous district, at the discretion of the Legislature; but shall not be attached to more than one district. The number of Senators shall be thirty-two, and they shall be apportioned among the Senatorial districts according to the total population contained in the several districts: *Provided*, That no parish shall be entitled to more than one-eighth of the whole number of Senators.

ART. 16. In all apportionments of the Senate, the population of the city of New Orleans shall be deducted from the population of the whole State, and the remainder of the population divided by the number twenty-eight, and the result produced by this division shall be the Senatorial ratio entitling a Senatorial district to a Senator. Single or contiguous parishes shall be formed into districts having a population the nearest possible to the number entitling a district to a Senator; and if, in the apportionment to be made, a parish or district fall short of or exceed the ratio one-fifth, then a district may be formed having not more than two Senators, but not otherwise. No new apportionment shall have the effect of abridging the term of service of any Senator already elected at the time of making the apportionment. After an enumeration has been made as directed in the (eighth) article, the Legislature shall not pass any law until an apportionment of representation in both houses of the General Assembly be made.

ART. 17. At the first session of the General Assembly after this Constitution takes effect, the Senators shall be equally divided by lot into two classes; the seats of the Senators of the first class shall be vacated at the expiration of the second year; of the second class, at the expiration of the fourth year; so that one-half shall be chosen every two years, and a rotation thereby kept up perpetually. In case any district shall have elected two or more Senators, said Senators shall vacate their seats respectively at the end of two and four years, and lots shall be drawn between them.

ART. 18. No person shall be a Senator, who, at the time of his election, has not been a citizen of the United States ten years, and who has not attained the age of twenty-seven years, and resided in the State four years next preceding his election, and the last year thereof in the district in which he may have been chosen.

ART. 19. The first election for Senators shall be general throughout the State, and at the same time that the general election for Representatives is held; and thereafter there shall be biennial elections to fill the places of those whose time of service may have expired.

ART. 20. Not less than a majority of the members of each House of the General Assembly shall form a quorum to do business; but a smaller number may adjourn from day to day, and shall be authorized by law to compel the attendance of absent members.

ART. 21. Each House of the General Assembly shall judge of the qualification, election, and returns of its members; but a contested election shall be determined in such manner as shall be directed by law.

ART. 22. Each House of the General Assembly may determine the rules of its proceedings, punish a member for disorderly behaviour, and with the concurrence of two-thirds, expel a member, but not a second time for the same offence.

ART. 23. Each House of the General Assembly shall keep and publish a weekly journal of its proceedings; and the yeas and nays of the members on any question, shall, at the desire of any two of them, be entered on the journal.

ART. 24. Each House may punish by imprisonment, any person not a member, for disrespectful and disorderly behaviour in its presence, or for obstructing any of its proceedings. Such imprisonment shall not exceed ten days for any one offence,

ART. 25. Neither House, during the session of the General Assembly, shall, without the consent of the other, adjourn for more than three days, nor to any other place than that in which they may be sitting.

ART. 26. The members of the General Assembly shall receive from the public treasury a compensation for their services, which shall be four dollars per day during their attendance, going to and returning from the session of their respective Houses. The compensation may be increased or diminished by law; but no alteration shall take effect during the period of service of the members of the House of Representatives by whom such alteration shall have been made. No session shall extend to a period beyond sixty days, to date from its commencement, and any legislative action had after the expiration of the said sixty days, shall be null and void. This provision shall not apply to the first Legislsture which is to convene after the adoption of this Constitution.

ART. 27. The members of the General Assembly shall, in all cases except treason, felony, breach of surety of the peace, be privileged from arrest during their attendance at the sessions of their respective Houses, and going to or returning from the same; and for any speech or debate in either House, they shall not be questioned in any other place.

ART. 28. No Senator or Representative shall, during the term for which he was elected, nor for one year thereafter, be appointed or elected to any civil office of profit under this State, which shall have been created, or the emoluments of which shall have been increased during the time such Senator or Representative was in office, except to such offices or appointments as may be filled by the elections of the people.

ART. 29. No person, while he continues to exercise the functions of a clergyman, priest, or teacher of any religious persuasion, society or sect, shall be eligible to the General Assembly.

ART. 30. No person who at any time may have been a collector of taxes, or who may have been otherwise entrusted with public money, shall be eligible to the General Assembly or to any office of profit or trust under the State government until he shall have obtained a discharge for the amount of such collections, and for all public moneys with which he may have been entrusted.

ART. 31. No bill shall have the force of a law until on three several days it be read over in each House of the General Assembly, and free discussion allowed thereon; unless in case of urgency, four-fifths of the House where the bill shall be pending, may deem it expedient to dispense with this rule.

ART. 32. All bills for raising revenue shall originate in the House of Representatives, but the Senate may propose amendments, as in other bills: *Provided*, they shall not introduce any new matter under color of an amendment, which does not relate to raising revenue.

Art. 33. Tbe General Assembly shall regulate by law, by whom and in what manner writs of election shall be issued to fill vacancies which may happen in either branch thereof.

Art. 34. A majority of the members elected to the Senate shall be required for the confirmation or rejection of officers to be appointed by the Governor, with the advice and consent of the Senate; and the Senate in deciding thereon, shall vote by yeas and nays, and the names of the Senators voting for and against the appointments respectively, shall be entered on a journal to be kept for that purpose, and made public at the end of each session, or before.

Art. 35. Returns of all elections for members of the General Assembly shall be made to the Secretary of State.

Art. 36. A Treasurer of the State shall be elected biennially by joint ballot of the two Houses of the General Assembly. The Governor shall have power to fill any vacancy that may happen in that office during the recess of the Legislature.

Art. 37. In the year in which a regular election for a Senator of the United States is to take place, the members of the General Assembly shall meet in the Hall of the House of Representatives on the Monday following the meeting of the Legislature, and proceed to the said election.

TITLE III—EXECUTIVE DEPARTMENT.

Art. 38. The Supreme Executive power of the State shall be vested in a Chief Magistrate, who shall be styled the Governor of the State of Louisiana. He shall hold his office during the term of four years; and, together with the Lieutenant Governor, chosen for the same term, be elected as follows: The qualified electors for Representatives shall vote for a Governor and Lieutenant Governor, at the time and place of voting for representatives; the returns of every election shall be sealed up and transmitted by the proper returning officer to the Secretary of State, who shall deliver them to the Speaker of the House of Representatives on the second day of the session of the General Assembly then next to be holden. The members of the General Assembly shall meet in the House of Representatives to examine and count the votes. The person having the greatest number of votes for Governor shall be declared duly elected; but if two or more persons shall be equal, and the highest in the number of votes polled for Governor, one of them shall immediately be chosen Governor, by joint vote of the members of the General Assembly. The person having the greatest number of votes for Lieutenant Governor, shall be Lieutenant Governor; but if two or more persons shall be equal, and highest in the number of votes polled for Lieutenant Governor, one of them shall be immediately chosen Lieutenant Governor by joint vote of the members of the General Assembly.

Art. 39. No person shall be eligible to the office of Governor or Lieutenant Governor, who shall not have attained the age of thirty-five years, been fifteen years a citizen of the United States, and a resident within the State for the same space of time next preceeding his election.

ART. 40. The Governor shall enter on the discharge of his duties on the fourth Monday of January next ensuing his election, and shall continue in office until the Monday next succeeding the day that his successor shall be declared duly elected, and shall have taken the oath or affirmation prescribed by the Constitution.

ART. 41. The Governor shall be ineligible for the succeeding four years after the expiration of the time for which he shall have been elected.

ART. 42. No member of Congress or person holding any office under the United States, or minister of any religious society, shall be eligible to the office of Governor or Lieutenant Governor.

ART. 43. In case of the impeachment of the Governor, his removal from office, death, refusal or inability to qualify, resignation or absence from the State, the powers and duties of the office shall devolve upon the Lieutenant Governor for the residue of the term, or until the Governor, absent or impeached, shall return or be acquitted. The Legislature may provide by law for the case of removal, impeachment, death, resignation, disability or refusal to qualify, of both the Governor and Lieutenant Governor, declaring what officer shall act as Governor; and such officer shall act accordingly, until the disability be removed, or for the residue of the term.

ART. 44. The Lieutenant Governor or other officer discharging the duties of Governor, shall, during his administration, receive the same compensation to which the Governor would have been entitled had he continued in office.

ART. 45. The Lieutenant Governor shall, by virtue of his office, be President of the Senate, but shall have only a casting vote therein. Whenever he shall administer the Government, or shall be unable to attend as President of the Senate, the Senators shall elect one of their own members as President of the Senate for the time being.

ART. 46. While he acts as President of the Senate, the Lieutenant Governor shall receive for his services the same compensation which shall for the same period be allowed to the Speaker of the House of Representatives, and no more.

ART. 47. The Governor shall have power to grant reprieves for all offences against the State, and except in cases of impeachment, shall, with the consent of the Senate, have power to grant pardons and remit fines and forfeitures after conviction. In cases of treason, he may grant reprieves until the end of the next session of the General Assembly, in which the power of pardoning shall be vested.

ART. 48. The Governor shall, at stated times, receive for his services a compensation, which shall neither be increased nor diminished during the term for which he shall have been elected.

ART. 49. He shall be Commander-in-Chief of the Army and Navy of this State and of the Militia thereof, except when they shall be called into the service of the United States.

ART. 50. He shall nominate, and by and with the advice and consent of the Senate, appoint all officers whose offices are established by this Constitution, and whose appointment is not therein otherwise provided for: *Provided*, however, that the Legislature shall have a right to prescribe the mode of appointment to all other offices established by law.

ART. 51. The Governor shall have power to fill vacancies that may happen during the recess of the Senate, by granting commissions which shall expire at the end of the next session, unless otherwise provided for in this Constitution; but no person who has been been nominated for office and rejected by the Senate, shall be appointed to the same office during the recess of the Senate.

ART. 52. He may require information in writing from the officers in the Executive Department, upon any subject relating to the duties of their respective offices.

ART. 53. He shall, from time to time, give to the General Assembly information respecting the situation of the State, and recommend to their consideration such measures as he may deem expedient.

ART. 54. He may, on extraordinary occasions, convene the General Assembly at the Seat of Government, or at a different place, if that should have become dangerous from an enemy or from epidemic; and in case of disagreement between the two houses as to the time of adjournment, he may adjourn them to such time as he may think proper, not exceeding four months.

ART. 55. He shall take care that the laws be faithfully executed.

ART. 56. Every bill which shall have passed both houses, shall be presented to the Governor; if he approve, he shall sign it, if not, he shall return it, with his objections, to the house in which it originated, which shall enter the objections at large upon its journal and proceed to reconsider it. If, after such reconsideration, two-thirds of all the members elected to that house shall agree to pass the bill, it shall be sent, with the objections, to the other house, by which it shall likewise be reconsidered, and if approved by two-thirds of all the members elected to that house, it shall be a law; but in such cases the vote of both houses shall be determined by yeas and nays, and the names of the members voting for and against the bill shall be entered on the journal of each house, respectively. If any bill shall not be returned by the Governor within ten days, (Sundays excepted,) after it shall have been presented to him, it shall be a law in like manner as if he had signed it, unless the General Assembly, by adjournment, prevent its return, in which case it shall be a law, unless sent back within three days after their next session.

ART. 57. Every order, resolution, or vote to which the concurrence of both houses may be necessary, except on a question of adjournment, shall be presented to the Governor, and, before it shall take effect, be approved by him; or, being disapproved, shall be repassed by two-thirds of the members elected to each House of the General Assembly.

ART. 58. There shall be a Secretary of State, who shall hold his office during the time for which the Governor shall have been elected. The records of the State shall be kept and preserved in the office of the Secretary; he shall keep a fair register of the official acts and proceedings of the Governor, and, when necessary, shall attest them. He shall, when required, lay the said register, and all papers, minutes and vouchers relative to his office, before either House of the General Assembly, and shall perform such other duties as may be enjoined on him by law.

ART. 59. All commissions shall be in the name and by the authority of the State of Louisiana, and shall be sealed with the State seal and signed by the Governer.

ART. 60. The free white men of the State shall be armed and disciplined for its defence; but those who belong to religious societies, whose tenets forbid them to carry arms, shall not be compelled so to do, but shall pay an equivalent for personal services.

ART. 61. The militia of the State shall be organized in such manner as may be hereafter deemed most expedient by the Legislature.

TITLE IV—JUDICIARY DEPARTMENT.

ART. 62. The judicial power shall be vested in a Supreme Court, in District Courts, and in Justices of the Peace.

ART. 63. The Supreme Court, except in cases hereinafter provided, shall have appellate jurisdiction only, which jurisdiction shall extend to all cases when the matter in dispute shall exceed three hundred dollars, and to all cases in which the constitutionality or legality of any tax, toll, or impost, of any kind or nature soever, shall be in contestation, whatever may be the amount thereof; and likewise to all fines, forfeitures and penalties imposed by municipal corporations; and in criminal cases, on questions of law alone; whenever the punishment of death or hard labor may be inflicted, or when a fine exceeding three hundred dollars is actually imposed.

ART. 64. The Supreme Court shall be composed of one Chief Justice and three Associate Justices, a majority of whom shall constitute a quorum. The Chief Justice shall receive a salary of six thousand dollars, and each of the Associate Justices a salary of five thousand dollars annually. The Court shall appoint its own Clerks. The Judges shall be appointed for the term of eight years.

ART. 65. When the first appointments are made under this Constitution, the Chief Justice shall be appointed for eight years, one of the Associate Judges for six years, one for four years, and one for two years; and in the event of the death, resignation or removal of any of said Judges, before the expiration of the period for which he was appointed, his successor shall be appointed only for the remainder of his term; so that the term of service of no two of said Judges shall expire at the same time.

ART. 66. The Supreme Court shall hold its sessions in New Orleans, from the first Monday of the month of November to the end of the month of June, inclusive. The Legislature shall have power to fix the sessions elsewhere during the rest of the year; until otherwise provided, the sessions shall be held as heretofore.

ART. 67. The Supreme Court, and each of the Judges thereof,

shall have power to issue writs of *habeas corpus* at the instance of all persons in actual custody, under process, in all cases in which they may have appellate jurisdiction.

ART. 68. In all cases in which the Judges shall be equally divided in opinion, the judgment appealed from shall stand affirmed; in which case each of the Judges shall give his separate opinions in writing.

ART. 69. All Judges, by virtue of their office, shall be conservators of the peace throughout the State. The style of all process shall be "The State of Louisiana." All prosecutions shall be carried on in the name and by the authority of the State of Louisiana, and conclude, against the peace and dignity of the same.

ART. 70. The Judges of all the Courts within this State shall, as often as may be possible so to do, in every definitive judgment, refer to the particular law in virtue of which such judgment may be rendered, and in all cases, adduce the reasons on which their judgment is founded.

ART. 71. No Court or Judge shall make any allowance by way of fee or compensation in any suit or proceedings, except for the payment of such fees to ministerial officers as may be established by law.

ART. 72. No duties or functions shall be attached by law to the Supreme or District Courts, or to the several judges thereof, but such as are judicial; and the said Judges are prohibited from receiving any fees of office, or other compensation than their salaries, for any civil duties performed by them.

ART. 73. The Judges of all Courts shall be liable to impeachment; but for any reasonable cause, which shall not be sufficient ground for impeachment, the Governor shall remove any of them on the address of three-fourths of the members present of each House of the General Assembly. In every such case, the cause or causes for which such removal may be required, shall be stated at length in the address and inserted in the journal of each house.

ART. 74. There shall be an Attorney General for the State, and as many District Attorneys as may hereafter be found nesessary. They shall hold their offices for two years; their duties shall be determined by law.

ART. 75. The first Legislature assembled under this Constitution shall divide the State into Judicial Districts, which shall remain unchanged for six years, and be subject to reorganization every sixth year thereafter.

The number of Districts shall not be less than twelve nor more than twenty.

For each District, one Judge, learned in the law, shall be appointed, except in the Districts in which the cities of New Orleans and Lafayette are situated, in which the Legislature may establish as many District Courts as the public interest may require.

ART. 76. Each of the said Judges shall receive a salary to be fixed by law, which shall not be increased or diminished during his term of office, and shall never be less than two thousand five hundred dollars annually. He must be a citizen of the United States, over the age of thirty years, and have resided in the State for six years next preceding his appointment, and have practised law therein for the space of five years.

ART. 77. The Judges of the District Courts shall hold their offices for the term of six years. The Judges first appointed shall be divided, by lot, into three classes, as nearly equal as may be, and the term of office of the Judges of the first class shall expire at the end of two years; of the second class, at the end of four years; and of the third class, at the end of six years.

ART. 78. The District Courts shall have original jurisdiction in all civil cases when the amount in dispute exceeds fifty dollars, exclusive of interest. In all criminal cases, and in all matters connected with successions, their jurisdiction shall be unlimited.

ART. 79. The Legislature shall have power to vest in Clerks of Courts, authority to grant such orders and do such acts as may be deemed necessary for the furtherance of the administration of justice, and in all cases, the powers thus granted shall, be specified and determined.

ART. 80. The Clerks of the several Courts shall be removable for breach of good behavior by the Judges thereof; subject, in all cases, to an appeal to the Supreme Court.

ART. 81. The Jurisdiction of Justices of the Peace shall never exceed, in civil cases, the sum of one hundred dollars, exclusive of interest, subject to appeal to the District Court in such cases as shall be provided for by law. They shall be elected by the qualified voters of each parish for the term of two years, and shall have such criminal jurisdiction as shall be provided for by law.

ART. 82. Clerks of the District Courts in this State shall be elected by the qualified electors in each parish, for the term of four years; and should a vacancy occur subsequent to an election, it shall be filled by the Judge of the Court in which such vacancy exists, and the person so appointed shall hold his office until the next general election.

ART. 83. A Sheriff and a Coroner shall be elected in each parish, by the qualified voters thereof, who shall hold their offices for the term of two years, unless sooner removed.

Should a vacancy occur in either of these offices subsequent to an election, it shall be filled by the Governor; and the person so appointed shall continue in office until his successor shall be elected and qualified.

TITLE V—IMPEACHMENT.

ART. 84. The power of impeachment shall be vested in the House of Representatives.

ART. 85. Impeachments of the Governor, Lieutenant Governor, Attorney General, Secretary of State, State Treasurer, and of the Judges of the District Courts, shall be tried by the Senate; the Chief Justice of the Supreme Court, or the senior Judge thereof, shall preside during the trial of such impeachment. Impeachments of the Judges of the Supreme Court shall be tried by the Senate. When sitting as a Court of Impeachment, the Senators shall be upon oath or affirmation, and no person shall be convicted without the concurrence of two-thirds of the Senators present.

ART. 86. Judgments in cases of impeachment shall extend only to removal from office and disqualification from holding any office of honor, trust or profit, under this State; but the convicted parties shall, nevertheless, be subject to indictment, trial and punishment, according to law.

ART. 87. All officers against whom articles of impeachment may be preferred, shall be suspended from the exercise of their functions during the pendency of such impeachment; the appointing power may make a provisional appointment to replace any suspended officer unlil the decision on the impeachment.

ART. 88. The Legislature shall provide by law for the trial, punishment and removal from office of all other officers of the State, by indictment or otherwise.

TITLE VI—GENERAL PROVISIONS.

ART. 89. Members of the General Assembly, and all officers, before they enter upon the duties of their offices, shall take the following oath or affirmation:

I, (A. B.,) do solemnly swear (or affirm) that I will faithfully and impartially discharge and perform all the duties incumbent on me as ———, according to the best of my abilities and understanding, agreeably to the Constitution and laws of the United States, and of this State; and I do further solemnly swear (or affirm) that since the adoption of the present Constitution, I, being a citizen of this State, have not fought a duel, with deadly weapons, within this State, nor out of it, with a citizen of this State, nor have I sent or accepted a challenge to fight a duel with deadly weapons with a citizen of this State, nor have I acted as second in carrying a challenge, or aided, advised, or assisted any person thus offending, so help me God."

ART, 90. Treason against the State shall consist only in levying war against it, or in adhering to its enemies, giving them aid and comfort. No person shall be convicted of treason, unless on the testimony of two witnesses to the same overt act, or his own confession in open court.

ART. 91. Every person shall be disqualified from holding any office of trust or profit in this State, who shall have been convicted of having given, or offered a bribe to procure his election or appointment.

ART. 92. Laws shall be made to exclude from office, and from the right of suffrage, those who shall hereafter be convicted of bribery, perjury, forgery, or other high crimes or misdemeanors. The privilege of free suffrage shall be supported by laws regulating elections, and prohibiting under adequate penalties, all undue influence thereon, from power, bribery, tumult or other improper practice.

ART. 93. No money shall be drawn from the Treasury but in pursuance of specific appropriation made by law, nor shall any appropriation of money be made for a longer term than two years. A regular statement and account of the receipts and expenditures of all public moneys shall be published annually, in such manner as shall be prescribed by law.

ART. 94. It shall be the duty of the General Assembly to pass such laws as may be proper and necessary to decide differences of arbitration.

ART. 95. All civil officers for the State at large, shall reside within the State, and all district or parish officers within their district or parishes, and shall keep their offices at such places therein as may be required by law. And no person shall be elected or appointed to any parish office, who shall not have resided in such parish long enough before such election or appointment to have acquired the right of voting in such parish; and no person shall be elected or appointed to any district office who shall not have resided in such district, or an adjoining district, long enough before such appointment or election to have acquired the right of voting for the same.

ART. 96. The duration of all offices not fixed by this Constitution shall never exceed four years.

ART. 97. All civil officers, except the Governor, and Judges of the Supreme and District Courts, shall be removable by an address of a majority of the members of both houses, except those the reremoval of whom has been otherwise provided for by this Constitution.

ART. 98. Absence on the business of this State or of the United States shall not forfeit a residence once obtained, so as to deprive any one of the right of suffrage, or of being elected or appointed to any office under the exceptions contained in this Constitution.

ART. 99. It shall be the duty of the Legislature to provide by law for deductions from the salaries of public officers who may be guilty of a neglect of duty.

ART. 100. The Legislature shall point out the manner in which a person coming into the State shall declare his residence.

ART. 101. In all elections by the people the vote shall be by ballot, and in all elections by the Senate and House of Representatives, jointly or separately, the vote shall be given *viva voce.*

ART. 102. No member of Congress, nor person holding or exercising any office of trust or profit under the United States, or either of them, or under any foreign power, shall be eligible as a member of the General Assembly, or hold or exercise any office of trust or profit under the State.

ART. 103. The laws, public records, and the judicial and legislative written proceedings of the State, shall be promulgated, preserved and conducted in the language in which the Constitution of the United States is written.

ART. 104. The Secretary of the Senate and Clerk of the House of Representatives, shall be conversant with the French and English languages, and members may address either House in the French or English language.

ART. 105. The General Assembly shall direct by law how persons who are now, or may hereafter become sureties for public officers, may be discharged from such suretyship.

ART. 106. No power of suspending the laws of this State shall be exercised, unless by the Legislature or by its authority.

ART. 107. Prosecutions shall be by indictment or information. The accused shall have a speedy public trial by an impartial jury of the vicinage: he shall not be compelled to give evidence against himself; he shall have the right of being heard by himself or counsel: he shall have the right, unless he shall have fled from justice, of meeting the witnesses face to face, and shall have compulsory process for obtaining witnesses in his favor.

ART. 108. All prisoners shall be bailable by sufficient sureties, unless for capital offences, where the proof is evident, or presumption great; and the privilege of the writ of *habeas corpus* shall not be suspended, unless when in case of rebellion or invasion the public safety may require it.

ART. 109. No *ex post facto* law, nor any law impairing the obligation of contracts, shall be passed, nor vested rights be divested, unless for purposes of public utility, and for adequate compensation previously made.

ART. 110. The press shall be free. Every citizen may freely speak, write and publish his sentiments on all subjects; being responsible for an abuse of this liberty.

ART. 111. Emigration from the State shall not be prohibited.

ART. 112. The General Assembly which shall meet after the first election of Representatives under this Constitution, shall, within the first month after the commencement of the session, designate and fix the seat of Government at some place not less than sixty miles from the city of New Orleans, by the nearest travelling route, and if on the Mississippi river, by the meanders of the same; and when so fixed, it shall not be removed without the consent of four-fifths of the members of both Houses of the General Assembly. The sessions shall be held in New Orleans until the end of the year 1848.

ART. 113. The Legislature shall not pledge the faith of the State for the payment of any bonds, bills or other contracts of obligations for the benefit or use of any person or persons, corporation or body politic whatever. But the State shall have the right to issue new bonds in payment of its outstanding obligations or liabilities, whether due or not; the said new bonds, however, are not to be used for a larger amount or at a higher rate of interest than the original obligations they are intended to replace.

ART. 114. The aggregate amount of debts hereafter contracted by the Legislature, shall never exceed the sum of one hundred thousand dollars, except in the case of war, to repel invasions or suppress insurrections, unless the same be authorized by some law, for some single object or work to be distinctly specified therein; which law shall provide ways and means, by taxation, for the payment of running interest during the whole time for which said debt shall be contracted, and for the full and punctual discharge at maturity of the capital borrowed; and said law shall be irrepealable until the principal and interest are fully paid and discharged, and shall not be put into execution until after its enactment by the first Legislature returned by a general election after its passage.

ART. 115. The Legislature shall provide by law for a change of venue in civil and criminal cases.

ART. 116. No Lottery shall be authorized by this State, and the buying and selling of lottery tickets within the State is prohibited.

ART. 117. No divorce shall be granted by the Legislature.

ART. 118. Every law enacted by the Legislature shall embrace but one object, and that shall be expressed in the title.

ART. 119. No law shall be revised or amended by reference to its title; but in such case, the act revised, or section amended, shall de re-enacted and published at length.

ART. 120. The Legislature shall never adopt any system or code of laws by general reference to such system or code of laws, but in all cases shall specify the several provisions of the laws it may enact.

ART. 121. The State shall not become subscriber to the stock of any corporation or joint stock company.

ART. 122. No corporate body shall be hereafter created, renewed or extended, with banking or discounting privileges.

ART. 128. Corporations shall not be created in this State by special laws, except for political or municipal purposes, but the Legislature shall provide, by general laws, for the organization of all other corporations, except corporations with banking or discounting privileges, the creation of which is prohibited.

ART. 124. From and after the month of January, 1890, the Legislature shall have the power to revoke the charters of all corporations whose charters shall not have expired previous to that time, and no corporation hereafter to be created, shall ever endure for a longer term than twenty-five years, except those which are political or municipal.

ART. 125. The General Assembly shall never grant any exclusive privilege or monopoly for a longer period than twenty years.

ART. 126. No person shall hold or exercise, at the same time more than one civil office of emolument, except that of Justice of the Peace.

ART. 127. Taxation shall be equal and uniform throughout the State. After the year 1848, all property on which the taxes may be levied in this State shall be taxed in proportion to its value, to be ascertained as directed by law. No one species of property shall be taxed higher than another species of property of equal value, on which taxes shall be levied; the Legislature shall have power to levy an income tax, and to tax all persons pursuing any occupation, trade or profession.

ART. 128. The citizens of the city of New Orleans shall have the right of appointing the several public officers necessary for the administration of the police of the said city, pursuant to the mode of elections which shall be prescribed by the Legislature; *Provided*, that the Mayor and Recorders shall be ineligible to a seat in the General Assembly; and the Mayor, Recorders and Aldermen shall be commissioned by the Governor as Justices of the Peace, and the Legislature may vest in them such criminal jurisdiction as may be necessary for the punishment of minor crimes and offences, and as the police and good order of said city may require.

ART. 129. The Legislature may provide by law in what cases officers shall continue to perform the duties of their offices until their successors shall have been inducted into office.

ART. 130. Any citizen of this State who shall, after the adoption of this Constitution, fight a duel with deadly weapons with a citizen of this State, or send or accept a challenge to fight a duel with deadly weapons, either within this State or out of it, with a citizen of this State, or who shall act as second, or knowingly aid and assist in any manner those thus offending, shall be deprived of holding any office of profit, and of enjoying the right of suffrage under this Constitution.

ART. 131. The Legislature shall have power to extend this Constitution and the jurisdiction of this State over any territory acquired by compact with any State, or with the United States, the same being done by the consent of the United States.

ART. 132. The Constitution and Laws of this State shall be promulgated in the English and French languages.

TITLE VII.—PUBLIC EDUCATION.

ART. 133. There shall be appointed a Superintendent of Public Education, who shall hold his office for two years. His duties shall be prescribed by law. He shall receive such compensation as the Legislature may direct.

ART. 134. The Legislature shall establish free Public Schools throughout the State, and shall provide means for their support by taxation on property or otherwise.

ART. 135. The proceeds of all lands heretofore granted by the United States to this State for the use or support of schools, and of all lands which may hereafter be granted or bequeathed to the State, and not expressly granted or bequeathed for any other purpose, which hereafter may be disposed of by the State, and the proceeds of the estates of deceased persons, to whieh the State may become entitled by law, shall be held by the State as a loan, and shall be and remain a perpetual fund, on which the State shall pay an annual interest of six per cent.; which interest, together with all the rents of the unsold lands, shall be appropriated to the support of such schools, and this appropriation shall remain inviolable.

ART. 136. All moneys arising from the sales which have been or may hereafter be made of any lands heretofore granted by the United States to this State, for the use of a seminary of learning, and from any kind of donation that may hereafter be made for that purpose, shall be and remain a perpetual fund, the interest of which, at six per cent. per annum, shall be appropriated to the support of a seminary of learning for the promotion of literature and the arts and sciences, and no law shall ever be made diverting said fund to any other use than to the establishment and improvement of said seminary of learning.

ART. 137. An University shall be established in the city of New Orleans. It shall be composed of four faculties, to wit: one of law, one of medicine, one of the natural sciences, and one of letters.

ART. 138. It shall be called the "University of Louisiana," and the Medical College of Louisiana, as at present organized, shall constitute the faculty of medicine.

ART. 139. The Legislature shall provide by law for its further organization and government, but shall be under no obligation to contribute to the establishment or support of said University by appropriations.

TITLE VIII.—MODE OF REVISING THE CONSTITUTION.

ART. 140. Any amendment or amendments to this Constitution may be proposed in the Senate or House of Representatives, and if the same shall be agreed to by three-fifths of the members elected to each house, and approved by the Governor, such proposed amendments shall be entered on their journals, with the yeas and nays taken thereon, and the Secretary of State shall cause the same to be published, three months before the next general election, in at least one newspaper in French and English, in every parish in the State in which a newspaper shall be published; and if in the Legislature next afterwards chosen, such proposed amendment or amendments shall be agreed to by a majority of the members elected to each house, the Secretary of State shall cause the same again to be published in the manner aforesaid, at least three months previous to the next general election for Representatives to the State Legislature, and such proposed amendment or amendments shall be submitted to the people at said election; and if a majority of the qualified electors shall approve and ratify such amendment or amendments, the same shall become a part of the Constitution. If more than one amendment be submitted at a time, they shall be submitted in such manner and form that the people may vote for or against each amendment separately.

TITLE IX.—SCHEDULE.

ART. 141. The Constitution adopted in eighteen hundred and twelve is declared to be superceded by this Constitution, and in order to carry the same into effect, it is hereby declared and ordained as follows:

ART. 142. All rights, actions, prosecutions, claims and contracts, as well of individuals as of bodies corporate, and all laws in force at the time of the adoption of this Constitution, and not inconsistent therewith, shall continue as if the same had not been adopted.

ART. 143. Until the first enumeration shall be made as directed in Article Eighth of this Constitution, the parish of Orleans shall have twenty representatives, to be elected as follows: Eight by the First Municipality, seven by the Second Municipality, and four by the Third Municipality, to be distributed among the nine representative districts as follows, by allotting to the

First District	Two	Sixth District	Two
Second "	Two	Seventh "	Two
Third "	Three	Eighth "	One
Fourth "	Three	Ninth "	One
Fifth "	Three		

And to that part of the parish on the right bank of the Mississippi....One

Parish of Plaquemines shall have	Three	Parish of W. Baton Bouge	One
" St. Bernard	One	" East Baton Rouge	Three
" Jefferson	Three	" West Feliciana	Two
" St. Charles	One	" East Feliciana	Three
" St. John the Baptist	One	" St. Helena	One
" St. James	Two	" Washington	One
" Ascension	Two	" Livings.on	One
" Assumption	Three	" St. Tammany	One
" Lafourche Interior	Three	" Pointe Coupée	One
" Terrebonne	Two	" Concordia	One
" Iberville	Two	" Tensas	One
" Carroll	One	" Madison	One
" Franklin	One	" Sabine	Two
" St. Mary	Two	" Caddo	One
" St. Martin	Three	" De Soto	One
" Vermillion	One	" Ouachita	One
" Lafayette	Two	" Morehouse	One
" St. Landry	Five	" Union	One
" Calcasieu	One	" Jackson	One
" Avoyelles	Two	" Caldwell	One
" Rapides	Three	" Catahoula	Two
" Natchitoches	Three	" Claiborne	Two
		" Bossier	One

Total.........Ninety-Eight.

And the State shall be divided into the following Senatorial Districts:

All that portion of the parish of Orleans lying on the east side of the Mississippi river, shall compose one Senatorial district, and shall elect four Senators.

The parishes of Plaquemines, St. Bernard, and that part of the parish of Orleans on the right bank of the river, shall compose one district, with one Senator.

The parish of Jefferson shall compose one district, with one Senator.

The parishes of St. Charles and St. John the Baptist shall compose one district, with one Senator.

The parish of St. James shall compose one district with one Sneator.

The parish of Ascension shall compose one district, with one Senator.

The parishes of Assumption, Lafourche Interior, and Terrebonne shall compose one district, with two Senators.

The parishes of Iberville and West Baton Rouge shall compose one district, with one Senator.

The parish of East Baton Rouge shall compose one district with one Senator.

The parish of Pointe Coupée shall compose one district, with one Senator.

The parish of Avoyelles shall compose one district, with one Senator.

The parish of St. Mary shall compose one district, with one Senator.

The parish of St. Martin shall compose one district, with one Senator.

The parishes of Lafayette and Vermillion shall compose one district, with one Senator

The parishes of St. Landry and Calcasieu shall compose one district, with two Senators.

The parish of West Feliciana shall compose one district, with one Senator.

The parish of East Feliciana shall compose one district, with one Senator.

The parishes of St. Helena and Livingston shall compose one district, with one Senator.

The parishes of Washington and St. Tammany shall compose one district, with one Senator.

The parishes of Concordia and Tensas shall compose one district, with one Senator.

The parishes of Carroll and Madison shall compose one district, with one Senator.

The parishes of Jackson, Union, Morehouse and Ouachita shall compose one district, with one Senator.

The parishes of Caldwell, Franklin, and Catahoula shall compose one district, with one Senator.

The parish of Rapides shall compose one district, with one Senator.

The parishes of Bossier and Claiborne shall compose one district, with one Senator.

The parish of Natchitoches shall compose one district, with one Senator.

The parishes of Sabine, De Soto and Caddo shall compose one district, with one Senator.

Art. 144. In order that no inconvenience may result to the public service from the taking effect of this Constitution, no office shall be superseded thereby : but the laws of the State relative to the duties of the several officers, Executive, Judicial and Military, shall remain in full force, though the same be contrary to this Constitution, and the several duties shall be performed by the respective officers of the State, according to the existing laws, until the organization of the Government under this Constitution, and the entering into office of the new officers to be appointed under said Government, and no longer.

Art. 145. Appointments to office by the Executive under this Constitution, shall be made by the Governor, to be elected under its authority.

Art. 146. The provisions of Article 28, concerning the inability of members of the Legislature to hold certain offices therein mentioned, shall not be held to apply to the members of the first Legislature elected under this Constitution.

Art. 147. The time of service of all officers chosen by the people, at the first election under this Constitution, shall terminate as though the election had been holden on the first Monday in November, 1845., and they had entered on the discharge of their duties at the time designated therein.

Art. 148. The Legislature shall provide for the removal of all causes now pending in the Supreme or other Courts of the State under the Constitution of 1812, to Courts created by this Constitution.

Art. 149. Appeals to the Supreme Court from the parishes of Jackson, Union, Morehouse, Catahoula, Caldwell, Ouachita, Franklin, Carroll, Madison, Tensas, and Concordia shall, until otherwise provided for, be returnable to New Orleans.

TITLE X.—ORDINANCE.

Art. 150. Immediately after the adjournment of the Convention, the Governor shall issue his proclamation, directing the several officers of this State authorized by law to hold elections for members of the General Assembly, to open and hold a poll in every parish of the State, at the places designated by law, upon the first Monday of November next, for the purpose of taking the sense of the good people of this State in regard to the adoption or rejection of this Constitution; and it shall be the duty of said officers to receive the votes of all persons entitled to vote under the old Constitution and this Constitution. Each voter shall express his opinion by depositing in the ballot box a ticket, whereon shall be written "the Constitution accepted," or "the Constitution rejected," or some such word as will distinctly convey the intention of the voter. At the conclusion of said election, which shall be conducted in every respect as the general State election is now conducted, the parish Judges and Commissioners designated to preside over the same, shall carefully examine and shall forthwith make due returns thereof to the Secretary of State, in conformity to the provisions of the existing law upon the subject of elections.

Art. 151. Upon the receipt of the said returns, or on the first Monday of December, if the returns be not sooner received, it shall be the duty of the Governor, the Secretary of State, the Attorney

General and the State Treasurer, in the presence of all such persons as may choose to attend, to compare the votes given at the said poll for the ratification and rejection of this Constitution, and if it shall appear from said returns that a majority of all the votes given are for ratifiying this Coestitution, then it shall be the duty of the Governor to make proclamation of that fact, and thenceforth this Constitution shall be ordained and established as the Constitution of the State of Louisiana. But whether this Constitution be accepted or rejected, it shall be the duty of the Governor to cause to be published in the State paper, the result of the polls, showing the number of votes cast in each parish for and against the said Constitution.

ART. 152. Should this Constitution be accepted by the people, it shall also be the duty of the Governor forthwith to issue his proclamation, declaring the present Legislature, elected under the old Constitution, to be dissolved, and directing the several officers of the State authorized by law to hold elections for members of the General Assembly, to hold an election, at the places designated by law, upon the third Monday in January next, (1846,) for Governor, Lieutenant Governor, members of the General Assembly, and all other officers whose election is provided for pursuant to the provisions of this Constitution. And the said election shall be conducted, and the returns thereof made, in conformity to the existing laws upon the subject of State elections.

ART. 153. The General Assembly elected under this Constitution shall convene at the State House, in the city of New Orleans, upon the second Monday of February next (1846) after the election; and the Governor and Lieutenant Governor elected at the same time, shall be duly installed in office during the first week of the session, and before it shall be competent for the said General Assembly to proceed with the transaction of business.

JOSEPH WALKER,
President of the Convention.

Attest:

HORATIO DAVIS,
Secretary of the Convention.

CONSTITUTION OF 1852.

PREAMBLE.

We, the People of the State of Louisiana, do ordain and establish this Constitution.

TITLE I.—DISTRIBUTION OF POWERS.

Art. 1. The powers of the Government of the State of Louisiana shall be divided into three distinct departments, and each of them be confined to a separate body of magistracy, to wit: those which are legislative to one; those which are executive to another; and those which are judicial to another.

Art. 2. No one of these departments, nor any person holding office in one of them, shall exercise power properly belonging to either of the others, except in the instances hereinafter expressly directed or permitted.

TITLE II.—LEGISLATIVE DEPARTMENT.

Art. 3. The Legislative power of the State shall be vested in two distinct branches, the one to be styled the "House of Representatives," the other "The Senate," and both, the "General Assembly of the State of Louisiana."

Art. 4. The members of the House of Representatives shall continue in service for the term of two years from the day of the closing of the general elections.

Art. 5. Representatives shall be chosen on the first Monday in November, every two years; and the election shall be completed in one day. The General Assembly shall meet annually, on the third Monday in January, unless a different day be appointed by law, and their sessions shall be held at the seat of government.

Art. 6. Every duly qualified elector under this Constitution shall be eligible to a seat in the General Assembly; provided that no person shall be a Representative or Senator, unless he be at the time of his election, a duly qualified voter of the Representative or Senatorial District from which he is elected.

ART. 7. Elections for members of the General Assembly shall be held at the several election precincts established by law. The Legislature may delegate the power of establishing election precincts to the parochial or municipal authorities.

ART. 8. Representation in the House of Representatives shall be equal and uniform, and shall be regulated and ascertained by the total population of each of the several parishes of the State. Each parish shall have at least one Representative; no new parish shall be created with a territory less than six hundred and twenty-five square miles, nor with a population less than the full number entitling it to a representative, nor when the creation of such new parish would leave any other parish without the said extent of territory and amount of population.

The first enumeration by the State authorities under this Constitution shall be made in the year 1853, the second in the year 1858, the third in the year 1865; after which time the General Assembly shall direct in what manner the census shall be taken, so that it be made at least once in every period of ten years, for the purpose of ascertaining the total population in each Parish and election district.

At the first regular session of the Legislature after the making of each enumeration, the Legislature shall apportion the representation amongst the several parishes and election districts on the basis of the total population as aforesaid. A representative number shall be fixed, and each parish and election district shall have as many representatives as the aggregate population shall entitle it to, and an additional representative for any fraction exceeding one-half the representative number. The number of representatives shall not be more than one hundred, nor less than seventy.

Until an apportionment shall be made, and elections held under the same, in accordance with the first enumeration to be made as directed in this article, the representation in the Senate and House of Representatives shall be and remain as at present established by law.

The limits of the parish of Orleans are hereby extended, so as to embrace the whole of the present city of New Orleans, including that part of the Parish of Jefferson, formerly known as the City of Lafayette.

All that part of the Parish of Orleans which is situated on the left bank of the Mississippi river, shall be divided by the Legislature into not more than ten Representative Districts, and until a new apportionment shall be made according to the first census to be taken under this Constitution, that part of the City of New Orleans which was comprised within the former limits of the City of Lafayette, shall vote for Senators from the Parish of Orleans, and form the Tenth Representative District, and shall elect two out of the three Reprensatives now apportioned by law to the Parish of Jefferson; the other Representative Districts shall remain as they are now established.

ART. 9. The House of Representatives shall choose its Speaker and other officers.

ART. 10. Every free white male who has attained the age of twenty-one years, and who has been a resident of the State twelve months next preceding the election, and the last six months thereof in the Parish in which he offers to vote, and who shall be a citizen of the United States, shall have the right of voting, but no voter, on removing from one Parish to another, within the State, shall lose the right of voting in the former, until he shall have acquired it in the latter. Electors shall, in all cases, except treason, felony, or breach of the peace, be privileged from arrest during their attendance at, going to, or returning from elections.

ART. 11. The Legislature shall provide by law, that the names and residence of all qualified electors of the City of New Orleans shall be registered, in order to entitle them to vote; but the registry shall be free of cost to the elector.

ART. 12. No soldier, seaman, or marine in the Army or Navy of the United States, no pauper, no person under interdiction, nor under conviction of any crime punishable with hard labor, shall be entitled to a vote at any election in this State.

ART. 13. No person shall be entitled to vote at any election held in this State, except in the parish of his residence, and in cities and towns divided into election precincts, in the election precinct in which he resides.

ART. 14. The members of the Senate shall be chosen for the term of four years. The Senate, when assembled, shall have the power to choose its officers.

ART. 15. The Legislature, in every year in which they shall apportion representation in the House of Representatives, shall divide the State into Senatorial districts. No parish shall be divided in the formation of a Senatorial district, the parish of Orleans excepted. And whenever a new parish shall be created, it shall be attached to the Senatorial district from which most of its territory was taken, or to another contiguous district, at the discretion of the Legislature; but shall not be attached to more than one district. The number of Senators shall be thirty-two, and they shall be apportioned among the Senatorial districts according to the total population contained in the several districts: *Provided*, That no parish shall be entitled to more than five Senators.

ART. 16. In all apportionments of the Senate, the population of the city of New Orleans shall be deducted from the population of the whole State, and the remainder of the population divided by the number twenty-seven, and the result produced by this division shall be the Senatorial ratio entitling a Senatorial district to a Senator. Single or contiguous parishes shall be formed into districts having a population the nearest possible to the number entitling a district to a Senator; and if, in the apportionment to be made, a parish or district fall short of or exceed the ratio one-fifth, then a district may be formed having not more than two Senators, but not otherwise. No new apportionment shall have the effect of abridging the term of service of any Senator already elected at the time of making the apportionment. After an enumeration has been made as directed in the eighth article, the Legislature shall not pass any law until an apportionment of representation in both houses of the General Assembly be made.

Art. 17. At the first session of the General Assembly after this Constitution takes effect, the Senators shall be equally divided by lot into two classes; the seats of the Senators of the first class shall be vacated at the expiration of the second year; of the second class, at the expiration of the fourth year; so that one-half shall be chosen every two years, and a rotation thereby kept up perpetually. In case any district shall have elected two or more Senators, said Senators shall vacate their seats respectively at the end of two and four years, and lots shall be drawn between them.

Art. 18. The first election for Senators shall be general throughout the State, and at the same time that the general election for Representatives is held; and thereafter there shall be biennial elections to fill the places of those whose time of service may have expired.

Art. 19. Not less than a majority of the members of each House of the General Assembly shall form a quorum to do business; but a smaller number may adjourn from day to day, and shall be authorized by law to compel the attendance of absent members.

Art. 20. Each House of the General Assembly shall judge of the qualification, election, and returns of its members; but a contested election shall be determined in such manner as shall be directed by law.

Art. 21. Each House of the General Assembly may determine the rules of its proceedings, punish a member for disorderly behaviour, and with the concurrence of two-thirds, expel a member, but not a second time for the same offence.

Art. 22. Each House of the General Assembly shall keep and publish a weekly journal of its proceedings; and the yeas and nays of the members on any question, shall, at the desire of any two of them, be entered on the journal.

Art. 23. Each House may punish by imprisonment, any person not a member, for disrespectful and disorderly behaviour in its presence, or for obstructing any of its proceedings. Such imprisonment shall not exceed ten days for any one offence.

Art. 24. Neither House, during the sessions of the General Assembly, shall, without the consent of the other, adjourn for more than three days, nor to any other place than that in which they may be sitting.

Art. 25. The members of the General Assembly shall receive from the public treasury a compensation for their services, which shall be four dollars per day during their attendance, going to and returning from the session of their respective Houses. The compensation may be increased or diminished by law; but no alteration shall take effect during the period of service of the members of the House of Representatives by whom such alteration shall have been made.—No session shall extend to a period beyond sixty days, to date from its commencement, and any legislative action had after the expiration of the said sixty days, shall be null and void. This provision shall not apply to the first legislature which is to convene after the adoption of this Constitution.

Art. 26. The members of the General Assembly shall, in all cases except treason, felony, breach of the peace, be privileged from arrest during their attendance at the sesssions of their respective Houses, and going to or returning from the same, and for any speech or debate in either House, they shall not be questioned in any other place.

Art. 27. No Senator or Representative shall, during the term for which he is elected, nor for one year thereafter, be appointed or elected to any civil office of profit under this State, which shall have been created, or the emoluments of which shall have been increased during the time such Senator or Representative was in office, except to such offices or appointments as may be filled by the elections of the people.

Art. 28. No person who at any time may have been a Collector of Taxes, whether State, Parish or Municipal, or who may have been otherwise entrusted with public money, shall be eligible to the General Assembly, or to any office of profit or trust under the State Government, until he shall have obtained a discharge for the amount of such collections, and for all public moneys with which he may have been entrusted.

Art. 29. No bill shall have the force of a law until on three several days it be read over in each House of the General Assembly, and free discussion allowed thereon, unless in case of urgency, four-fifths of the House where the bill shall be pending, may deem it expedient to dispense with this rule.

Art. 30. All bills for raising revenue shall originate in the House of Representatives, but the Senate may propose amendments as in other bills; provided they shall not introduce any new matter under color of an amendment, which does not relate to raising revenue.

Art. 31. The General Assembly shall regulate by law by whom, and in what manner writs of elections shall be issued to fill the vacancies which may happen in either branch thereof.

Art. 32. The Senate shall vote on the corfirmation or rejection of office, to be appointed by the Governor, with the advice and consent of the Senate, by yeas and nays, and the names of the Senators voting for and against the appointments respectfully, shall be entered on a journal to be kept for that purpose, and made public at the end of each session, or before.

Art. 33. Returns of all elections for members of the General Assembly shall be made to the Secretary of State.

Art. 34. In the year in which a regular election for a Senator of the United States is to take place, the members of the General Assembly shall meet in the Hall of the House of Representatives, on the Monday following the meeting of the Legislature, and proceed to the said election.

TITLE III.—EXECUTIVE DEPARTMENT.

Art. 35. The Supreme Executive power of the State shall be

vested in a Chief Magistrate, who shall be styled the Governor of the State of the Louisiana. He shall hold his office during the term of four years, and together with the Lieutenant Governor, chosen for the same term, be elected as follows: The qualified electors for Representatives, shall vote for a Governor and Lieutenant Governor, at the time and place of voting for Representatives; the returns of every election shall be sealed up and transmitted by the proper returning officer to the Secretary of State, who shall deliver them to the Speaker of the House of Representatives, on the second day of the session of the General Assembly, then next to be holden. The members of the General Assembly shall meet in the House of Representatives to examine and count the votes. The person having the greatest number of votes for Governor shall be declared duly elected, but if two or more persons shall be equal and highest in the number of votes polled for Governor, one of them shall immediately be chosen Governor by joint vote of the members of the General Assembly. The person having the greatest number of votes for Lieutenaut Governor shall be Lieutenant Governor; but if two or more persons shall be equal and highest in the number of votes polled for Lieutenant Governor, one of them shall be immediately chosen Lieutenant Governor by joint vote of the members of the General Assembly.

ART. 36. No person shall be eligible to the office of Governor or Lieutenant Governor who shall not have attained the age of twenty-eight years, and been a citizen and a resident within the State for the space of four years next preceding his election.

ART. 37. The Governor shall enter on the discharge of his duties on the fourth Monday of January next ensuing his election, and shall continue in office until the Monday next succeeding the day that his successor shall be declared duly elected, and shall have taken the oath or affirmation required by the Constitution.

ART. 38. The Governor shall be ineligible for the succeeding four years after the expiration of the time for which he shall have been elected.

ART. 39. No member of Congress or person holding any office under the United States, shall be eligible to the office of Governor or Lieutenant Governor.

ART. 40. In case of the impeachment of the Governor, his removal from office, death, refusal or inability to qualify, resignation or absence from the State, the powers and duties of the office shall devolve upon the Lieutenant Governor for the residue of the term, or until the Governor, absent or impeached, shall return or be acquitted. The Legislature may provide by law for the case of removal, impeachment, death, resignation, disability or refusal to qualify, of both the Governor and Lieutenant Governor, declaring what officer shall act as Governor, and such officer shall act accordingly, until the disability be removed, or for the residue of the term.

ART. 41. The Lieutenant Governor or officer discharging the duties of Governor, shall, during his administration, receive the same compensation to which the Governor would have been entitled had he continued in office.

ART. 42. The Lieutenant Governor shall, by virtue of his office, be President of the Senate, but shall have only a casting vote therein. Whenever he shall administer the Government, or shall be unable to attend as President of the Senate, the Senators shall elect one of their own members as President of the Senate for the time being.

ART. 43. While he acts as President of the Senate, the Lieutenant Governor shall receive for his services the same compensation which shall for the same period be allowed to the Speaker of the House of Representatives, and no more.

ART. 44. The Governor shall have power to grant reprieves for all offences against the State, and except in cases of impeachment, shall, with the consent of the Senate, have power to grant pardons and remit fines and forfeiture, after conviction. In cases of treason, he may grant reprieves until the end of the next session of the General Assembly, in which the power of pardoning shall be vested.

ART. 45. The Governor shall, at stated times, receive for his services a compensation, which shall neither be increased nor diminished during the term for which he shall have been elected.

ART. 46. He shall be Commander-in-Chief of the Army and Navy of this State and of the Militia thereof, except when they shall be called into the service of the United States.

ART. 47. He shall nominate, and by and with the advice and consent of the Senate, appoint all officers whose offices are established by this Constitution, and whose appointment is not therein otherwise provided for: *Provided*, however, that the Legislature shall have a right to prescribe the mode of appointment to all other offices established by law.

ART. 48. The Governor shall have power to fill vacancies that may happen during the recess of the Senate, by granting commissions which shall expire at the end of the next session, unless otherwise provided for in this Constitution; but no person who has been nominated for office and rejected by the Senate, shall be appointed to the same office during the recess of the Senate.

ART. 49. He may require information in writing from the officers in the Executive Department, upon any subject relating to the duties of their respective offices.

ART. 50. He shall, from time to time, give to the General Assembly information respecting the situation of the State, and recommend to their consideration such measures as he may deem expedient.

ART. 51. He may, on extraordinary occasions, convene the General Assembly at the Seat of Government, or at a different place, if that should have become dangerous from an enemy or from epidemic; and in case of disagreement between the two Houses as to the time of adjournment, he may adjourn them to such time as he may think proper, not exceeding four months.

ART. 52. He shall take care that the laws be faithfully executed.

ART. 53. Every bill which shall have passed both Houses, shall be presented to the Governor; if he approve, he shall sign it, if not, he shall return it, with his objections, to the House in which it originated, which shall enter the objections at large upon its journal and proceed to reconsider it. If, after such reconsideration, two-thirds of all the members elected to that House shall agree to pass the bill, it shall be sent, with the objections, to the other House, by which it shall likewise be reconsidered, and if approved by two-thirds of all the members elected to that House, it shall be a law; but in such cases the vote of both Houses shall be determined by yeas and nays, and the names of the members voting for or against the bill shall be entered on the journal of each House, respectively. If any bill shall not be returned by the Governor within ten days, (Sundays excepted,) after it shall have been presented to him, it shall be a law in like manner as if he had signed it, unless the General Assembly, by adjournment, prevent its return, in which case it shall be a law, unless sent back within three days after their next session.

ART. 54. Every order, resolution, or vote to which the concurrence of both Houses may be necessary, except on a question of adjournment, shall be presented to the Governor, and, before it shall take effect, be approved by him; or, being disapproved, shall be repassed by two-thirds of the members elected to each House of the General Assembly.

ART. 55. There shall be a Secretary of State, who shall hold his office during the time for which the Governor shall have been elected. The records of the State shall be kept and preserved in the office of the Secretary; he shall keep a fair register of the official acts and proceedings of the Governor, and, when necessary, shall attest them. He shall, when required, lay the said register, and all papers, minutes and vouchers relative to his office, before either House of the General Assembly, and shall perform such other duties as may be enjoined on him by law.

ART. 56. There shall be a Treasurer of the State who shall hold his office during the term of two years.

ART. 57. The Secretary of State and Treasurer of State, shall be elected by the qualified electors of the State. And in case of any vacancies caused by the death, resignation or absence of the Treasurer or Secretary of State, the Governor shall order an election to fill said vacancy.

ART. 58. All commissions shall be in the name and by the authority of the State of Louisiana, and shall be sealed with the State seal and signed by the Governer.

ART. 59. The free white men of the State shall be armed and disciplined for its defence; but those who belong to religious societies, whose tenets forbid them to carry arms, shall not be compelled so to do, but shall pay an equivalent for personal services.

ART. 60. The militia of the State shall be organized in such manner as may be hereafter deemed most expedient by the Legislature.

TITLE IV—JUDICIARY DEPARTMENT.

ART. 61. The Judiciary power shall be vested in a Supreme Court, in such Inferior Courts as the Legislature may, from time to time, order and establish, and in Justices of the Peace.

ART. 62. The Supreme Court, except in cases hereinafter provided, shall have appellate jurisdiction only, which jurisdiction shall extend to all cases when the matter in dispute shall exceed three hundred dollars; and to all cases in which the constitutionality or legality of any tax, toll, or impost whatsoever, or any fine, forfeiture or penalty imposed by a municipal corporation, shall be in contestation; and to all criminal cases, on questions of law alone, whenever the offence charged is punishable with death or imprisonment at hard labor, or when a fine exceeding three hundred dollars is actually imposed. The Legislature shall have power to restrict the jurisdiction of the Supreme Court in civil cases to questions of law only.

ART. 63. The Supreme Court shall be composed of one Chief Justice and four Associate Justices, a majority of whom shall constitute a quorum. The Chief Justice shall receive a salary of six thousand dollars, and each of the Associate Judges a salary of five thousand five hundred dollars, annually, until otherwise provided by law. The Court shall appoint its own Clerks; the Judges shall be elected for the term of ten years.

ART. 64. The Chief Justice shall be elected by the qualified elected of the State. The Legislature shall divide the State into four Districts, and the qualified electors ef each District shall elect one of the Associate Justices. The State shall be divided into the following Districts until the Legislature shall otherwise direct.

FIRST DISTRICT.

The Parishes of Plaquemines, St. Bernard, that portion of the Parish of Orleans on the right bank of the Mississippi River, and that portion of the City of New Orleans which lies below the line extending from the River Mississippi, along the middle of Julia street, until it strikes the New Orleans Canal, and thence down said Canal to the Lake.

SECOND DISTRICT.

That portion of the City of New Orleans which is situated above the line extending along the middle of Julia street until it stikes the New Orleans Canal, and thence down said Canal to the Lake, and the Parishes of Jefferson, St. John the Baptist, St. Charles, St. James, Ascension, Assumption, Lafourche Interior, Terrebonne, West Baton Rouge and Iberville.

THIRD DISTRICT.

The Parishes of St. Tammany, Washington, Livingston, St.

Helena, East Baton Rouge, East Feliciana, West Feliciana, Point Coupée, Avoyelles, Tensas, Concordia, Lafayette, Vermillion, St. Mary, St. Martin and St. Landry.

FOURTH DISTRICT.

The Parishes of Calcasieu, Rapides, Sabine, Natchitoches, De Soto, Caddo, Bossier, Claiborne, Bienville, Caldwell, Union, Ouachita, Morehouse, Jackson, Franklin, Catahoula, Madison, Carroll and Winn.

ART. 65. The office of one of the Associate Justices shall be vacated at the expiration of the second year, of another at the expiration of the fourth year, of a third at the expiration of the sixth year, and of the fourth at the expiration of the eighth year; so that one of the Judges of the Supreme Court shall be elected every second year.

ART. 66. The Secretary of State, on receiving the official returns of the first election shall proceed immediately, in the presence and with the assistance of two Justices of the Peace, to determine by lot among the four candidates having the highest number of votes in the respective districts, which of the Associate Justices elect shall serve for the term of two years, which for the term of four years, which for the term of six years, and which for the term of eight years, and the Governor shall issue commissions accordingly.

ART. 67. Any vacancy that may occur in the Supreme Court from resignation or otherwise, shall be filled by election for the remainder of the unexpired term, but if such remainder do not exceed one year, the vacancy shall be filled by Executive appointment.

ART. 68. The Supreme Court shall hold its sessions in New Orleans, from the first Monday of the month of November to the end of the month of June, inclusive. The Legislature shall have power to fix the sessions elsewhere during the rest of the year; until otherwise provided, the sessions shall be held as heretofore.

ART. 69. The Supreme Court, and each of the Judges thereof, shall have power to issue writs of *habeas corpus* at the instance of all persons in actual custody, under process, in all cases in which they may have appellate jurisdiction.

ART. 70. No judgment shall be rendered by the Supreme Court without the concurrence of a majority of the Judges comprising the Court. Whenever a majority cannot agree, in consequence of the recusation of any member or members of the Court, the Judges not recused shall have power to call upon any Judge or Judges of the Inferior Courts, whose duty it shall be, when so called upon, to sit in the place of the Judges recused, and to aid in determining the case.

ART. 71. All Judges, by virtue of their office, shall be conservators of the peace throughout the State. The style of all process shall be "The State of Louisiana." All prosecutions shall be carried on in the name and by the authority of the State of Louisiana, and conclude, against the peace and dignity of the same.

ART. 72. The Judges of all the Courts within this State shall, as often as may be possible so to do, in every definitive judgment, refer to the particular law in virtue of which such judgment may be rendered, and in all cases, adduce the reasons on which their judgment is founded.

ART. 73. The Judges of all Courts shall be liable to impeachment; but for any reasonable cause, which shall not be sufficient ground for impeachment, the Governor shall remove any of them on the address of three-fourths of the members present of each House of the General Assembly. In every such case, the cause or causes for which such removal may be required, shall be stated at length in the address and inserted in the journal of each House.

ART. 74. There shall be an Attorney General for the State, and as many District Attorneys as may be hereafter found nesessary. They shall hold their offices for four years; their duties shall be determined by law.

ART. 75. The Judges, both of the Superior and Inferior Courts, shall, at stated times, receive a salary, which shall not be diminished during their continuance in office; and they are prohibited from receiving any fees of office, or other compensation than their salaries, for any civil duties peformed by them.

ART. 76. The Legislature shall have power to vest in Clerks of Courts, authority to grant such orders and do such acts as may be deemed necessary for the furtherance of the administration of justice, and in all cases, the powers thus granted shall be specified and determined.

ART. 77. The Judges of the several Inferior Courts shall have the power to remove the Clerks thereof, for breach of good behavior; subject, in all cases, to an appeal to the Supreme Court.

ART. 78. The Jurisdiction of Justices of the Peace shall be limited in civil cases to cases where the matter in dispute does not exceed one hundred dollars, exclusive of interest, subject to appeal in such cases as shall be provided for by law. They shall be elected by the qualified electors of each Parish, District or Ward, for the term of two years in such manner, and shall have such criminal jurisdiction as shall be provided by law.

ART. 79. Clerks of the Inferior Courts in this State shall be elected for the term of four years, and should a vacancy occur subsequent to an election, it shall be filled by the Judge of the Court in which such vacancy exists, and the person so appointed shall hold his office until the next general election.

ART. 80. A Sheriff and a Coroner shall be elected in each parish, by the qualified voters thereof, who shall hold their offices for the term of two years, unless sooner removed. The Legislature shall have the power to increase the number of Sheriffs in any parish— Should a vacancy occur in either of these offices subsequent to an election, it shall be filled by the Governor; and the person so appointed shall continue in office until his successor shall be elected and qualified.

ART. 81. The Judges of the several Inferior Courts shall

be elected by the duly qualified voters of their respective Districts or Parishes.

ART. 82. It shall be the duty of the Legislature to fix the time for holding elections for all Judges at a time which shall be different from that fixed for all other elections.

ART. 83. The Attorney-General shall be elected by the qualified voters of the State, and the District Attorneys by the qualified voters of each District on the day of the election for the Governor of the State.

ART. 84. The Legislature may determine the mode of filling vacancies in the offices of the Inferior Judges, Attorney-General, District Attorneys, and all other officers not otherwise provided for in this Constitution.

TITLE V.—IMPEACHMENT.

ART. 85. The power of impeachment shall be vested in the House of Representatives.

ART. 86. Impeachments of the Governor, Lieutenant Governor, Attorney General, Secretary of State, State Treasurer, and of the Judges of the Inferior Courts, Justices of the Peace excepted, shall be tried by the Senate; the Chief Justice of the Supreme Court, or the senior Judge thereof, shall preside during the trial of such impeachment. Impeachments of the Judges of the Supreme Court shall be tried by the Senate. When sitting as a Court of Impeachment, the Senators shall be upon oath or affirmation, and no person shall be convicted without the concurrence of two-thirds of the Senators present.

ART. 87. Judgments in cases of impeachment shall extend only to removal from office and disqualification from holding any office of honor, trust or profit, under the State; but the convicted parties shall, nevertheless, be subject to indictment, trial and punishment, according to law.

ART. 88. All officers against whom articles of impeachment may be preferred, shall be suspended from the exercise of their functions during the pendency of such impeachment; the appointing power may make a provisional appointment to replace any suspended officer until the decision of the impeachment.

ART. 89. The Legislature shall provide by law for the trial, punishment and removal from office of all other officers of the State, by indictment or otherwise.

TITLE VI.—GENERAL PROVISIONS.

ART. 90. Members of the General Assembly, and all officers, before they enter upon the duties of their offices, shall take the following oath or affirmation:

I, (A. B.,) do solemnly swear (or affirm) that I will support the Constitution of the United States and of this State, and that I will faithfully and impartially discharge and perform all the duties incumbent on me as ——, according to the best of my abilities and understanding, agreeably to the Constitution and laws of the United States, and of this State; and I do further solemnly swear (or affirm) that since the adoption of the present Constitution, I, being a citizen of this State, have not fought a duel, with deadly weapons, within this State, nor out of it, with a citizen of this State, nor have I sent or accepted a challenge to fight a duel with deadly weapons with a citizen of this State, nor have I acted as second in carrying a challenge, or aided, advised, or assisted any person thus offending, so help me God."

Art. 91. Treason against the State shall consist only in levying war against it, or in adhering to its enemies, giving them aid and comfort. No person shall be convicted of treason, unless on the testimony of two witnesses to the same overt act, or his own confession in open court.

Art. 92. Every person shall be disqualified from holding any office of trust or profit in this State, who shall have been convicted of having given, or offered a bribe to procure his election or appointment.

Art. 93. Laws shall be made to exclude from office, and from the right of suffrage, those who shall hereafter be convicted of bribery, perjury, forgery, or other high crimes or misdemeanors. The privilege of free suffrage shall be supported by laws regulating elections, and prohibiting under adequate penalties, all undue influence thereon, from power, bribery, tumult or other improper practice.

Art. 94. No money shall be drawn from the Treasury but in pursuance of specific appropriation made by law, nor shall any appropriation of money be made for a longer term than two years. A regular statement and account of the receipts and expenditures of all public moneys shall be published annually, in such manner as shall be prescribed by law.

Art. 95. It shall be the duty of the General Assembly to pass such laws as may be proper and necessary to decide differences by arbitration.

Art. 96. All civil officers for the State at large, shall reside within the State, and all district or parish officers within their district or parishes, and shall keep their offices at such places therein as may be required by law.

Art. 97. All civil officers, except the Governor, and Judges of the Supreme and Inferior Courts, shall be removable by an address of a majority of the members of both Houses, except those the removal of whom has been otherwise provided for by this Constitution.

Art. 98. In all elections by the people the vote shall be by ballot, and in all elections by the Senate and House of Representatives, jointly or separately, the vote shall be given *viva voce.*

Art. 99. No member of Congress, nor person holding or exercising any office of trust or profit under the United States, or either of them, or under any foreign power, shall be eligible as a member of the General Assembly, or hold or exercise any office of trust or profit under the State.

ART. 100. The laws, public records, and the judicial and legislative written proceedings of the State, shall be promulgated, preserved and conducted in the language in which the Constitution of the United States is written.

ART. 101. The Secretary of the Senate and Clerk of the House of Representatives, shall be conversant with the French and English languages, and members may address either House in the French or English language.

ART. 102. No power of suspending the laws of this State shall be exercised, unless by the Legislature or by its authority.

ART. 103. Prosecutions shall be by indictment or information. The accused shall have a speedy public trial by an impartial jury of the vicinage: he shall not be compelled to give evidence against himself; he shall have the right of being heard by himself or counsel: he shall have the right of meeting the witnesses face to face, and shall have compulsory process for obtaining witnesses in his favor.

ART. 104. All prisoners shall be bailable by sufficient sureties, unless for capital offences, where the proof is evident, or presumption great, or, unless after conviction for any offence or crime punishable with death or imprisonment at hard labor. The privilege of the writ of *habeas corpus* shall not be suspended, unless when in case of rebellion or invasion the public safety may require it.

ART. 105. No *ex post facto* law, nor any law impairing the obligation of contracts, shall be passed, nor vested rights be divested, unless for purposes of public utility, and for adequate compensation previously made.

ART. 106. The press shall be free. Every citizen may freely speak, write and publish his sentiments on all subjects; being responsible for an abuse of this liberty.

ART. 107. The seat of Government shall be and remain at Baton Rouge, and shall not be removed without the consent of three-fourths of both Houses of the General Assembly.

ART. 108. The State shall not subscribe for the stock of, nor make a loan to, nor pledge its faith for the benefit of any corporation or joint stock company, created or established for banking purposes, nor for other purposes than those described in the following article.

ART. 109. The Legislature shall have power to grant aid to companies or associations of individuals, formed for the exclusive purpose of making works of internal improvement, wholly or partially within the State, to the extent only of one-fifth of the capital of such companies, by subscription of stock or loan of money or public bonds; but any aid thus granted shall be paid to the company only in the same proportion as the remainder of the capital shall be actually paid in by the stockholders of the company, and, in case of loan, such adequate security shall be required, as to the Legislature may seem proper. No corporation or individual association receiving the aid of the State, as herein provided, shall possess banking or discounting privileges.

ART. 110. No liability shall be contracted by the State as above mentioned, unless the same be authorized by some law for some single object or work to be distinctly specified therein, which shall be passed by a majority of the members elected to both Houses of the General Assembly, and the aggregate amount of debts and liabilities incurred under this and the preceding article shall never, at any one time, exceed eight millions of dollars.

ART. 111. Whenever the Legislature shall contract a debt exceeding in amount the sum of one hundred thousand dollars, unless in case of war to repel invasion or suppress insurrection, they shall, in the law creating the debt, provide adequate ways and means for the payment of the current interest and of the principal when the same shall become due. And the said law shall be irrepealable until principal and interest are fully paid and discharged, or unless the repealing law contains some other adequate provision for the payment of the principal and interest of the debt.

ART. 112. The Legislature shall provide by law for a change of venue in civil and criminal cases.

ART. 113. No Lottery shall be authorized by this State, and the buying and selling of lottery tickets within the State is prohibited.

ART. 114. No divorce shall be granted by the Legislature.

ART. 115. Every law enacted by the Legislature shall embrace but one object, and that shall be expressed in the title.

ART. 116. No law shall be revived or amended by reference to its title; but in such case, the act revived, or section amended, shall be re-enacted and published at length.

ART. 117. The Legislature shall never adopt any system or code of laws by general reference to such system or code of laws, but in all cases shall specify the several provisions of the laws it may enact.

ART. 118. Corporations with banking or discounting privileges may be either created by special acts, or formed under general laws; but the Legislature shall, in both cases, provide for the registry of all bills or notes issued or put in circulation as money, and shall require ample security for the redemption of the same in specie.

ART. 119. The Legislature shall have no power to pass any law sanctioning in any manner, directly or indirectly, the suspension of specie payments, by any person, association or corporation issuing bank notes of any description.

ART. 120. In case of insolvency of any bank or banking association, the bill holders thereof shall be entitled to preference in payment over all other creditors of such bank or association.

ART. 121. The Legislature shall have power to pass such laws as it may deem expedient for the relief or revival of the Citizens' Bank of Louisiana, and the acts already passed for the same purpose are ratified and confirmed, provided that the Bank is subject to the restrictions contained in articles 119 and 120 of this Constitution.

ART. 122. No person shall hold or exercise, at the same time more than one civil office of emolument, except that of Justice of the Peace.

ART. 123. Taxation shall be equal and uniform throughout the State. All property on which the taxes may be levied in this State shall be taxed in proportion to its value, to be ascertained as directed by law. No one species of property shall be taxed higher than another species of property of equal value, on which taxes shall be levied; the Legislature shall have power to levy an income tax, and to tax all persons pursuing any occupation, trade or profession.

ART. 124. The citizens of the city of New Orleans shall have the right of appointing the several public officers necessary for the administration of the police of the said city, pursuant to the mode of elections which shall be prescribed by the Legislature; *Provided*, that the Mayor and Recorders shall be ineligible to a seat in the General Assembly; and the Mayor, Recorders, Aldermen and Assistant Aldermen shall be commissioned by the Governor as Justices of the Peace, and the Legislature may vest in them such criminal jurisdiction as may be necessary for the punishment of minor crimes and offences, and as the police and good order of said city may require.

ART. 125. The Legislature may provide by law in what case officers shall continue to perform the duties of their offices until their successors shall have been inducted into office.

ART. 126. Any citizen of this State who shall, after the adoption of this Constitution, fight a duel with deadly weapons with a citizen of this State, or send or accept a challenge to fight a duel with deadly weapons, either within this State or out of it, with a citizen of this State, or who shall act as second, or knowingly aid and assist in any manner those thus offending, shall be deprived of holding any office of trust or profit, and of enjoying the right of suffrage under this Constitution; and the office of any State officer, member of the General Assembly, or of any other person holding office of profit or trust under this Constitution, and the laws made in pursuance thereof, shall be *ipso facto* vacated by the fact of any such person committing the offence mentioned in this article, and the Legislature shall provide by law for the ascertaining and declaration of such forfeiture.

ART. 127. The Legislature shall have power to extend this Constitution and the jurisdiction of this State over any territory acquired by compact with any State, or with the United States, the same being done by the consent of the United States.

ART. 128. None of the lands granted by Congress to the State of Louisiana for aiding it in constructing the necessary levees and drains, to reclaim the swamp and overflowed lands in this State, shall be diverted from the purposes for which they were granted.

ART. 129. The Constitution and Laws of this State shall be promulgated in the English and French languages.

TITLE VII.—INTERNAL IMPROVEMENTS.

ART. 130. There shall be a Board of Public Works to consist of four Commissioners. The State shall be divided by the Legislature into four districts, containing as nearly as may be an equal number of voters, and one Commissioner shall be elected in each district by the legal voters thereof for the term of four years; but, of the first elected, two, to be designated by lot, shall remain in office for two years only.

ART. 131. The General Assembly, at its first session after the adoption of this Constitution, shall provide for the election and compensation of the Commissioners and the organization of the Board. The Commissioners first elected shall assemble on a day to be appointed by law, and decide by lot the order in which their terms of service shall expire.

ART. 132. The Commissioners shall exercise a diligent and faithful supervision of all public works, in which the State may be interested, except those made by joint stock companies. They shall communicate to the General Assembly, from time to time, their views concerning the same, and recommend such measures as they may deem necessary, in order to employ to the best advantage and for the purposes for which they were granted, the swamps and overflowed lands, conveyed by the United States to this State. They shall appoint all officers engaged on the public works, and shall perform such other duties as may be prescribed by law.

ART. 133. The Commissioners may be removed by the concurrent vote of a majority of all the members elected to each House of the General Assembly; but the cause of the removal shall be entered on the Jourual of each House.

ART. 134. The General Assembly shall have power, by a vote of three-fifths of the members elected to each House, to abolish said Board, whenever in their opinion a Board of Public Works shall no longer be necessary.

TITLE VIII.—PUBLIC EDUCATION.

ART. 135. There shall be elected a Superintendent of Public Education, who shall hold his office for the term of two years. His duties shall be prescribed by law, and he shall receive such compensation as the Legislature may direct; provided, that the General Assembly shall have power, by a vote of the majority of the members elected to both Houses, to abolish the said office of Superintendent of Public Education whenever in their opinion said office shall be no longer necessary.

ART. 136. The General Assembly shall establish free Public Schools throughout the State, and shall provide for their support by general taxation on property or otherwise; and all moneys so raised or provided shall be distributed to each Parish in proportion to the number of free white children between such ages as shall be fixed by the General Assembly.

ART. 137. The proceeds of all lands heretofore granted by the United States to this State for the use or support of schools, and of all lands which may hereafter be granted or bequeathed to the State, and not expressly granted or bequeathed for any other purpose, which hereafter may be disposed of by the State, and the proceeds of the estates of deceased persons, to which the State may become entitled by law, shall be held by the State as a loan, and shall be and remain a perpetual fund, on which the State shall pay an annual interest of six per cent.; which interest, together with the interest of the trust funds deposited with this State by the United States, under the act of Congress, approved June 23, 1836, and all the rents of the unsold lands, shall be appropriated to the support of such schools, and this appropriation shall remain inviolable.

ART. 138. All moneys arising from the sales which have been or may hereafter be made of any lands heretofore granted by the United States to this State, for the use of a seminary of learning, and from any kind of donation that may hereafter be made for that purpose, shall be and remain a perpetual fund, the interest of which, at six per cent. per annum, shall be appropriated to the support of a seminary of learning for the promotion of literature and the arts and sciences, and no law shall ever be made diverting said fund to any other use than to the establishment and improvement of said seminary of learning.

ART. 139. The University of Louisiana in New Orleans as now established, shall be maintained.

ART. 140. The Legislature shall have power to pass such laws as may be necessary for the further regulation of the University, and for the promotion of literature and science; but shall be under no obligation to contribute to the support of said University by appropriations.

TITLE IX.—MODE OF REVISING THE CONSTITUTION.

ART. 141. Any amendment or amendments to this Constitution may be proposed in the Senate or House of Representatives, and if the same shall be agreed to by two-thirds of the members elected to each House, such proposed amendment or amendments shall be entered on their journals, with the yeas and nays taken thereon, and the Secretary of State shall cause the same to be published, three months before the next general election for Representatives of the State Legislature, in at least one newspaper in French and English, in every parish in the State in which a newspaper shall be published; and such proposed amendment or amendments shall be submitted to the people at said election; and if a majority of the voters at said election shall approve and ratify such amendment or amendments, the same shall become a part of the Constitution. If more than one amendment be submitted at a time, they shall be submitted in such manner and form, that the people may vote for or against each amendment separately.

TITLE X.—SCHEDULE.

ART. 142. The Constitution adopted in eighteen hundred and forty-five is declared to be superseded by this Constitution, and in order to carry the same into effect, it is hereby declared and ordained as follows:

Art. 143. All rights, actions, prosecutions, claims and contracts, as well of individuals as of bodies corporate, and all laws in force at the time of the adoption of this Constitution, and not inconsistent therewith, shall continue as if the same had not been adopted.

Art. 144. In order that no inconvenience may result to the public service from the taking effect of this Constitution, no office shall be superseded thereby: but the laws of the State relative to the duties of the several officers, Executive, Judicial and Military, shall remain in full force, though the same be contrary to this Constitution, and the several duties shall be performed by the respective officers of the State, according to the existing laws, until the organization of the Government under this Constitution, and the entering into office of the new officers to be appointed under said Government, and no longer.

Art. 145. Appointments to office by the Executive under this Constitution, shall be made by the Governor, to be elected under its authority.

Art. 146. The Legislature shall provide for the removal of all causes now pending in the Supreme or other Courts of the State under the Constitution of 1845, to Courts created by or under this Constitution.

Art. 147. The time of service of all officers chosen by the people, at the first election under this Constitution, shall terminate as though the election had been holden on the first Monday of November, 1851, and they had entered on the discharge of their duties at the time designated therein. The first class Senators designated in article 17 shall hold their seats until the day of the closing of the general elections in November, 1853, and the second class until the day of the closing of the general elections in November, 1855.

Art. 148. The first election for Judges of the Supreme Court shall be held on the first Monday of April next, (1853,) and they shall enter into office on the first Monday of May, 1853.

Art. 149. The first term of service of the District Attorneys and the Clerks of the Inferior Courts to be ordered and established under this Constitution, shall be regulated by the term of service of the first Governor, so that a new election for these officers shall be held on the first Monday of November, 1855.

TITLE XI.—ORDINANCE.

Art. 150. Immediately after the adjournment of the Convention, the Governor shall issue his proclamation, directing the several officers of this State authorized by law to hold elections for members of the General Assembly, to open and hold a poll in every parish of the State, at the places designated by law, upon the first Tuesday of November next, for the purpose of taking the sense of the good people of this State in regard to the adoption or rejection of this Constitution; and it shall be the duty of said officers to receive the votes of all persons entitled to vote under the old Constitution and under this Constitution. Each voter shall express his opinion by depositing in a separate box, kept for that purpose, a ticket, whereon shall be written "the Constitution accepted," or "the Constitution rejected," or some such word as will distinctly convey the intention of the voter. At the conclusion of said election, which shall be conducted in every respect as the general State election is now conducted, the Commissioners designated to preside over the same, shall carefully examine and count each ballot so deposited, and shall forthwith make due returns thereof to the Secretary of State, in conformity to the provisions of the existing law upon the subject of elections.

ART. 151. Upon the receipt of the said returns, or on the fifth Monday of November, if the returns be not sooner received, it shall be the duty of the Governor, the Secretary of State, the Attorney General and the State Treasurer, in the presence of all such persons as may choose to attend, to compare the votes given at the said poll for the ratification and rejection of this Constitution, and if it shall appear from said returns that a majority of all the votes given, is for ratifiying this Constitution, then it shall be the duty of the Governor to make proclamation of that fact, and thenceforth this Constitution shall be ordained and established as the Constitution of the State of Louisiana. But whether this Constitution be accepted or rejected, it shall be the duty of the Governor to cause to be published in the official paper of the Convention the result of the polls, showing the number of votes cast in each parish for and against the said Constitution.

ART. 152. Should this Constitution be accepted by the people, it shall also be the duty of the Governor forthwith to issue his proclamation, declaring the present Legislature, elected under the old Constitution, to be dissolved, and directing the several officers of the State authorized by law to hold elections for members of the General Assembly, to hold an election, at the places designated by law, upon the fourth Monday in December next, for Governor, Lieutenant Governor, members of the General Assembly, Secretary of State, Attorney General, Treasurer and Superintendent of Public Education; and the said election shall be conducted, and the returns thereof made, in conformity to the existing laws upon the subject of State elections.

ART. 153. The General Assembly elected under this Constitution shall convene at the State House, in Baton Rouge, upon the third Monday of January next after the elections, and the Governor and Lieutenant Governor elected at the same time, shall be duly installed in office during the first week of the session, and before it shall be competent for the said General Assembly to proceed with the transaction of business.

ART. 154. All the publications herein ordered shall be made in the official journal of the Convention.

ART. 155. This Constitution shall be published in French and English in the official journal of the Convention, from the period of its adjournment until the first Tuesday of November, 1852, one thousand eight hundred and fifty-two.

Done at Baton Rouge, July 31st, 1852.

(*Signed*) DUNCAN F. KENNER,
President of the Convention.

Attest:
J. B. WALTON,
Secretary of the Convention.

JAS. AKENHEAD,
WM. H. AVERY,
JOHN W. ANDREWS,
ROBERT ANDERSON, of Carroll.
E. S. ARMANT,
DANIEL ADDISON,
J. A. BRADFORD,
J. P. BENJAMIN,
SOLON BARTLETT,
CHAS. A. BULLARD,
C. L. BOUDOUSQUIE,
H. BERNARD,
ROBT. G. BEALE,
WM. BEARD,
CHAS. BIENVENU,
A. BROTHER,
JOHN H. BOYER,
FRED. BOUISSON,
DANIEL BYRNE,
T. WHARTON COLLENS,
HENRY C. CASTELLANOS,
A. G. CARTER,
J. G. CAMPBELL,
J. B. COTTON,
G. F. CONNELLY,
F. D. CONRAD,
C. DALFERES,
EDW. DELONY,
WM. R. DOUGLASS,
EDW. DUFFEL, JR.
CYPRIEN DUFOUR,
E. C. DAVIDSON,
F. DUGUE, JR.,
M. C. EDWARDS, of Orleans.
N. S. EDWARDS,
GEORGE EUSTIS, JR.,
H. B. EGGLESTON,
FERGUS GARDERE,
GEORGE S. GUION,
F. H. HATCH,
P. T. HARRIS,
JOHN B. LEEFE,
CHAS. J. LEEDS,
W. JONES LYLE,
DESIRÉ LE BLANC,
J. L. LOBDELL,
D. B. MCMILLEN,
L. MATTHEWS, of Orleans,
J. L. MATTHEWS,
ANT. MORENO,
GEORGE MATHER,
E. H. MARTIN,
EDWARD MONGE,
ALFRED MCILHENNY,
THO. C. NICHOLLS,
BENJ. P. PAXTON,
WM. PATTERSON,
WILLIAM PERKINS,
JOHN W. PRICE,
U. B. PHILLIPS,
WM. W. PUGH,
WM. S. PARHAM,
W. T. PALFREY,
ROBERT PREAUX,
H. H. PIERSON,
L. VINCENT REEVES,
G. RIXNER,
SAM. G. RISK,
D. D. RICHARDSON, of St. Mary.
R. W. RICHARDSON,
C. ROSELIUS,
A. B. ROMAN,
M. RONQUILLO,
JNO. M. SANDIDGE,
H. B. SHAW,
HENRY ST. PAUL,
E. STAES,
C. L. SWAYZE,
T. F. SCARBOROUGH,
JNO. M. SHELTON,
P. C. SMITH,
R. SMITH, of Winn,

R. A. Hargis,
M. Hernandez, Jr.,
Wade H. Hough,
R. Hodges,
Randall Hunt,
Andrew S. Herron,
P. O. Hebert,
Harry T. Hays,
A. J. Isaacks,
N. R. Jennings,
Aug. W. Jourdan,
Jesse R. Jones,
Peyton G. King,
Philip B. Key,
John E. King, of St. Landry.
J. M. Lapeyre,
R. H. Sibley,
B. B. Simms,
Wm. R. Stuart,
G. D. Tatman,
A. Talbot,
John R. Smart,
Hezek. Thompson,
Robert B. Todd,
A. Toulouse,
S. Van Wickle,
C. J. Villere,
J. P. Waddill,
J. S. Williams,
Wm. W. Whittintgon,
Henry H. Wilcoxon.

SKETCH OF LOUISIANA.

"Like all other European Colonies in America, Louisiana was composed of all the various elements that formed the parent stock. Adventurers from all ranks of society, many indigent and some criminal individuals entered into the mixture from which arose the present population.

Removed to distances the most remote from their native place, men may, for a time, retain many of their established customs; but local position so powerfully influences human action, that habits are acquired which give a distinct feature to society in all places. Something more than a century has elapsed since the colony began to be peopled from Europe; many opinions, the offspring of national or family pride, have been discarded and replaced by others better suited to the new position in which the posterity of the first settlers have been placed.

As the Valley of the Mississippi will for ages be the receptacle of emigrants from the eastern slope of that chain of mountains which divides our country, a developement of its resources, so favorable to agriculture and commerce, must claim no little part of our attention.

The comparative extent of surface, will, even at the present time, if carefully examined, enable the least discerning to trace the future migrations of wealth and power, and determine as far as human foresight can penetrate, the destiny of the United States.

Ferdinand De Soto, in 1539—40, was no doubt the first European who actually travelled the regions near the mouth of the Mississippi, whose adventures have been presented in literature. So extravagant, however, were the then projects of Spanish travellers in pursuit of the precious metals, and so little qualified to collect useful knowledge, that very few precise ideas of the countries through which they roamed, can be collected from their accounts.

We may, therefore, conclude of the voyage of Soto, like many others, that he travelled, but did not discover the countries over which he travelled.

After the voyage of Soto, one hundred and thirty-two years elapsed before further knowledge of Louisiana was obtained by any European nation.

In 1674 two French traders, Joliet and Marquette, reached the

Mississippi by penetrating from Canada through lakes Huron and Michigan, and through the Fort and Wisconsin Rivers.

In 1683, M. De La Salle, Father Louis Hennipen and the Chevalier Zonty, discovered the country now called Louisiana, and which included Arkansas, Missouri and Texas, and the course of the Mississippi.

These adventurers reached that river by the Illinois. M. De La Salle explored the river to the mouth. Hennipen surveyed it upwards above St. Anthony's Falls, went soon after to France, published an account of his discoveries, and named the country Louisiana.

In 1683, De La Salle returned to Canada, and from thence to France, when having assumed command of a small squadron, with which he landed on February 16, 1685, at the mouth of the Guadaloupe river, on the bay of Esperitu Santo, and built a fort.

The object of this expedition was to establish a colony on the Mississippi.

From the very defective knowledge then gained of the northern part of the Gulf of Mexico, De La Salle passed the mouth of the Mississippi, and entering a deep and wide bay, he landed his men and effects, thinking himself on the Mississippi, but soon found his fatal error—an establishment was made and a fort built.

The country was taken possession of in the name of the king of France, with the formalities usual on such occasions, practised by European nations in their American conquests.

In 1687, March 19th, De La Salle was murdered by two of his own men, on what is supposed the now Colorado river. Thus perished one of the most active, enterprising and illustrious discoverers that ever traversed the hills of the new world.

Shortly after the death of De La Salle, and the retreat of his brother, the residue of the colony was captured by a Spanish detachment sent from New Leon for that purpose, and the settlement broken up.

Twelve years again elapsed before another attempt was made by the French government to take possession of the regions contiguous to the Mississippi. At length, in 1698 a squadron was sent out to the Gulf of Mexico, commanded by D'Iberville and his brother Bienville.

The choice of the latter officer was fortunate; to his genius, talents and conciliating manners, France stood indebted for the success that crowned an expedition, with very inadequate means.

On January 26, 1699, M. D'Iberville and M. de Bienville arrived at Pensacola, and found the bay and shore occupied by a Spanish force under Don Andre de la Riole. On January 31, the squadron anchored before Dauphin Island.

In the course of the first four months of this year, the coast from Mobile to the efflux of the Manchac, the lakes Maurepas and Pontchartrain were successfully explored by the French. April 12th, Fort on Biloxi bay was founded.

In May, Iberville sailed for France, Leaving Bienville to command the colony, but returned the same year and resumed the government.

In May, 1700, Bienville, by order of Iberville, ascended Red River to Natchitoches, and on May 28th, Iberville sailed to Europe, leaving the command to Bienville.

Garrison built on the Mississippi, near where fort St. Philip, at the Plaquemine bend, now stands.

In 1712, The King of France, by letters patent, ceded the civil jurisdiction of Louisiana to Crozat.

In 1716, Bienville was appointed to command at the Mississippi. Hitherto, this truly estimable man had acted in a subordinate station, and, though his brother Iberville was nominally the founder of the Colony, the active operations were performed by Bienville. Vigilant, humane, and just, he conciliated the savages by his urbanity, and repelled their violence by his courage. In the spring of 1717, barracks were erected on the left bank of the Mississippi river, and a city laid out and named frem the then Regent of France, New Orleans.

Louisiana, as ceded by France to the United States, is bounded South, by the Gulf of Mexico; East, by the State of Mississippi and Perdido rivers; North, by the State of Mississippi, and an imaginary line connecting with the northernmost part of the 49th degree of north latitude, and Southwest by Mexican provinces, containing in the agregate 945,860 square miles of surface.

This immense surface is now divided into four sections:

The State of Louisiana, bounded by the Gulf of Mexico on the South; by the Sabine river and a meridian line from 32° to 33° North latitude, on the West, and by the States of Arkansas and Mississippi, North, and by the latter on the East.

The State contains, in round numbers, 46,000 square miles of area and is watered by the Mississippi, Red, Ouachita, Atchafalaya and Pearl rivers, together with the numerous other streams of lesser note.

The balance of the Province of Louisiana is included in Arkansas, Missouri and Texas, and the Indian Territories in the Northwest.

Louisiana is perhaps destined to be among the most remarkable upon which the happiness or misery of mankind have ever been or will be felt. It is the most extensive, unbroken, continuous body of productive soil on the globe. The climate the surface, and the animal and vegetable productions exhibit an endless variety.

The circumstances, however, which render the political and moral picture of this State peculiarly distinctive, is, that almost the total of the productions of the industry of its inhabitants, and that of the whole Valley of the Mississippi and its tributaries, must flow to one common centre.

New Orleans, alone, will be forever what it is now, the mighty mart of the merchandise brought from more than a thousand rivers. Unless prevented by some great accident or misrule in human affairs, this rapidly increasing city will, in no very distant time, leave the emporium of the East far behind.

With Boston, New York, Philadelphia and Baltimore, on the left, Mexico on the right, Cuba in front, the immense Valley of the

Mississippi in the rear, and California on the West; no other such a position for the accumulation of wealth and power ever existed.

By a careful and repeated admeasurement of the Mississippi river and its tributaries, we find that they drain a country of more than 1,400,000 square miles. If this wide expanse was peopled equal to many of the older States of the Union, which, according to the present progress of events, will, in less than two centuries hence, contain 100,000,000 of human beings, who will send the greater portion of the fruits of their lobor to New Orleans.

Few subjects have attracted more attention than the effects of local climate. The malignant fevers of the Southern States; their nature, origin, cure, and the certainty and uncertainty of their recurrence, have exercised the pens of the most scientific medical men of the age.

It is melancholy, however, to find that learning and the severest philosophical inquiries have failed to produce any certain or fixed facts as to the effect of climate in producing or perpetuating destructive malidies.

One will contend with great zeal for the contagious nature of yellow fever, whilst another with equal earnestness considers this disorder a severe type of billious complaint, aggravated by a morbid atmosphere; and we find that both parties produce the same evidence to probe the corrections of their antagonistical conclusions. Upon the subject of health all men are deeply concerned, and a knowledge, the want of which, has consigned many valuable lives to an early and premature death Whatever may be the difference of speculative science between the members of the Medical profession, upon malignant fevers, they fully agree that the best preventative, is temperance, cleanliness, and wholesome air and food.

That a great portion of the distempers of warm latitudes can be guarded against, I cannot entertain a single doubt.

Temperance, fresh air, good sound food in plenty, and above all, cleanliness of house and person, will contribute much more to secure cities and countries from pestilence, than all the sanitary regulations that were ever framed for that purpose.

An immense population must, in a few years be concentrated on the alluvial lands of the South, and as every facility is given by our form of government for the adoptian of a prodential system of Police, evils may be prevented, that have heretofore carried their ravages over cities and countries.

The importance of proper sanitary measures, ought to be constantly before the eyes of those who have the administration of Louisiana in their hands. The importance of these measures to the yet unborn millions of human beings should make us vigilant. We should not view future generations like distant nations, with whom we hold no intercourse. We should remember, that in proportion, as the present generation wisely provides for the happiness of its posterity, so will the reactive respect be from the latter to the former.

There cannot be any of the inhabitants who do not anticipate the rising greatness of our State. Yet we find but few who ever take into consideration the most suitable means to secure and accomplish that greatness. Robert Fulton has secured to himself immortality by perfecting and introducing to use the expansive power of steam. Jenner gained a name imperishable as literature, for disarming the virus of small-pox.

That man, who uniting energy of mind to political authority, who shall, in Louisiana, provide means to remedy the mischiefs now emanating from the annual inundation of the Mississippi, and widens the surface of arable land, and lessens the diseases of those who are to exist upon its surface—such a man would receive the spontaneous respect of his cotemporaries and the lasting gratitude of every succeeding generation.

There is nothing imaginary or delusive in this prospect. Everything is practicable to be accomplished with the resources of our people.

A glance at the map of the Mississippi and tributary streams, gives us full conviction of the importance of the City of New Orleans; but it demands deep reflection to foresee that it is necessary to preserve the lives of thousands and tens of thousands, who will daily visit this mighty and increasing emporium.

Immersed in their own present concerns, most men never bestow a thought upon any subject upon which they have no direct interest. This has been, and doubtless ever will be, the common routine of human affairs!

There are noble exceptions to this principles. Let us hope that Louisiana will add on more.

Let it not be considered useless or unprofitable to appeal to the wisdom of the administrators of our national or State Legislature, to call their attention towards a city, which, in the common course of events, must have a deep interest in the future progress of happiness, health, and power, in the United States; to a city whose name has become dear to the whole American people; as a scene where the nation gained—imperishable renown; and to a city, upon the prosperity of which, depends that of an immense number of the inhabitants of our Union.

The general Government is ever engaged in providing security against the attacks of invaders.

It should not be forgotten, that there are enemies who have carried death and ruin into cities, and against whose attacks, cannons or forts would be no defence.

It is against this insidious foe, whose approach is slow and silent, whose deadly weapons are aimed at youth and beauty, as well as age and decrepitude. That national precaution ought to be most carefully taken.

STATE GOVERNMENT.

GOVERNORS OF LOUISIANA.

W. C. C. Claiborne	1804 to 1812
W. C. C. Claiborne	1812 to 1816
James Villeré	1819 to 1820
Thomas Robinson	1820 to 1824
Henry Johnson	1824 to 1828
Peter Derbigny	1828 to 1829
A. Beauvais, acting	1229 to 1830
Jaques Duprè	1830 to 1831
A. B. Roman	1831 to 1835
E. D. White	1835 to 1839
A. B. Roman	1839 to h843
Alexander Mouton	1843 to 1846
Isaac Johnson	1846 to 1849
Joseph Walker	1849 to 1853
Paul O. Hebert	1853 to 1856

EXECUTIVE DEPARTMENT.

Paul O. Hébert, Governor, Salary	$4,000
T. B. R. Hatch, Governor's Private Secretary	1,000
James Cooper, Governor's Messenger	360
W. W. Farmer, Lieutenant Governor, and President of the Senate, $8 per day during the Session of the Legislature,	
Andrew S. Herron, Secretary of State	2,000
Augusté Duplantier, Clerk	1,000
C. E. Greneaux, Treasurer	2,500
George P. Briant, Clerk, "	2,000
Samuel F. Marks, Auditor of Public Accounts	4,000
H. Pearlata, Clerk, " " "	2,000
C. Metcalf, " " " "	1,200
Isaac E. Morse, Attorney General	3,500
S. Westmore, Adjutant and Inspector General	500
J. N. Carrigan, Superintendant of Public Education	2,000
G. W. Morse, State Engineer	3,000
J. C. Taylor, As't "	2,000
L. J. Sigur, Register of Land Office, fees, and	250
C. C. Biberon, Clerk, " " "	
Henry Droz, State Librarian	1,200
Louis Bringier, Surveyor General	600
A. F. Osborn, Register of Baton Rouge Land Office	
Thomas Cockerham, at Winnsborough, Receiver do	

SWAMP LAND COMMISSIONERS.

Donaldson C. Jenkins,	First District, Salary	$1,500
Griffin B. Miller,	Second " "	1,500
John W. Butler,	Third " "	1,500
E. B. Town,	Fourth " "	1,500

ENGINEER'S DEPARTMENT.

Charles Ritter,	First District, Salary,	$2,500
Hugh Grant,	Second " "	2,500
W. H. Osborne,	Third " "	2,500
W. H. Peck,	Fourth " "	2,500

T. B. R. Hatch, Secretary.

JUDICIARY—SUPREME COURT.

Thomas Slidell,	Chief Justice, Salary,	$,5000
A. M. Buchanan.	As't " "	5,000
A. W. Ogden,	" " "	5,000
W. H. Spofford,	" " "	5,000
Cornelius Voorhies,	" "	5,000

Eugene LeSere, Clerk, fees.
J. H. Randolph, Reporter, 2,500
R. Taylor, Clerk, Opelousas.
D. C. Goodwin, Clerk, Alexandria.
Henry H. Bry, Clerk, Monroe.

MEMBERS OF THE GENERAL ASSEMBLY FOR THE YEARS 1854 and '55.

HOUSE OF REPRESENTATIVES.

Avoyelles.—G. Berlin, L. Gauthier.
Assumption.—A. F. Williamson, A. Truxillo, W. W. Pugh.
Bienville.—B. W. Pearce.
Bossier.—J. M. Sandidge.
Carroll.—S. C. Floyd.
Calcasieu.—W. E. Gill.
Claiborne.—Jno. Kimball, J. W. McDonald.
Catahoula.—S. Y. Lacroix, F. Oliver.
Caldwell.—Thos. Morris.
Caddo.—A. Slaughter.
Concordia.—G. B. N. Wailes.
DeSoto.—J D. Wemple.
East Baton Rouge.—I. H. Boatner, Geo. C. McWhorter.
East Felciiana.—F. Hardesty.
Franklin.—A. Bonner.
Iberville.—E. D. Woods, E. W. Robertson.
Jefferson.—S, Green.
Jackson.—I. H. Stevens.
Lafourche.—Chas. W. Armitage, J. S. Williams.
Lafayette.—V. Bertrand, V. Comier.

Livingston.—T. G. Davidson.
Madison.—Lafayette Jones.
Morehouse.—I. B. R. Jones.
Natchitoches.—B. H. Baird, Chas. A. Bullard, A. Sompayrac.
Orleans.—D. L. Beecher, J. H. Caldwell, W. S. Campbell, Dennis Corcoran, Dennis Cronan, F. M. Crozat, W. Deacon, Geo. W. Dirmeyer, Jas. Drummond, S. P. Farge, H. R. Grandmont, R. W. James, R. M. Kearney, F. H. Loze, J. J. McCormack, Thos. McKeon, Jno. Newman, J. W. Nixon, Benj. Olney, W. J. A. Roberts, A. Scates, Chas. Seuzeneau, Th. Thayer, J. E. Trémé, P. K. Wagner, W. Weisheimer.
Ouachita.—C. H. Morrison.
Pt. Coupee.—A. D. M. Haralson.
Plaquemines.—E. Lawrence, C. J. Villere.
Rapides. A. Tanner, G. Labatt.
St. Mary.—A. W. Baker, P. C. Bethel.
St. John Baptist.—Jos. Bossier.
St. Martin.—J. Etié, H. J. Heard.
St. Tammany.—A. F. Cooper.
St. Landry.—E. N. Cullom, A. Dejean, J. D. Gardner, O. A. Guedry.
St. Helena.—F. H. Hatch.
St. James.—T. Lagroue, E. Locoul.
St. Bernard.—E. Duballen.
Sabine.—I. Rains, J. R. Smart.
St. Charles.—F. B. Trepagnier.
Terrebonne.—R. D. Jordan.
Tensas.—H. McCullough.
Union.—Ths. Van Hook.
Vermillion.—P. O. Broussard.
West Baton Rouge.—H. M. Favrot.
West Feliciana.—U. B. Phillips.
Washington.—Jeff. Roberts.
Winn.—F. Waddell.

W. H. Higgins, Chief Clerk.
J. H. Rhineheart, Minute Clerk.
I. H. Peralta, Sergeant-at-Arms.
David Martin, Reporter.

SENATE.

W. W. Farmer, Lieut. Gov. and President of the Senate.
Assumption, Lafourche and Terrebonne.—P. B. Key, E. E. Kittridge.
Catahoula, Franklin and Caldwell.—M. Boatner.
Claiborne, Bossier and Bienville.—J. R. Evans.
Caddo, DeSoto and Sabine.—B. L. Hodge.
Concordia and Tensas.—D. L. Rivers.
East Baton Rouge.—G. S. Lacey.
East Feliciana.—G. W. Munday.
Iberville and West Baton Rouge.—Louis Hebert, N. Lauve.

Jefferson aad St. Charles.—W. R. Taylor, R. Trudeau.
Lafayette and Vermillion.—D. Pellerin.
Madison and Carroll.—W. S. Scott.
Natchitoches and Winn.—G. L. DeRussey.
Orleans.—W. W. King, J. R. McMurdo, Thos. McCay.
Ouachita, Morehouse, Union and Jackson.—B. L. Dufrees.
Point Coupee.—C. W. Clifton.
Plaquemines, St. Bernard and Orleans Right Bank.—C. Lacoste.
Rapides and Avoyelles.—W. F. Griffin, M. Ryan.
St. Landry and Calcasieu.—A. Dupré, B. A. Martel.
St. John Baptist, St. James and Ascension.—D. F. Kenner, W. C. Lawes.
St. Martin.—John Moore.
St. Mary.—W. T. Palfrey.
Washington, St. Helena and St. Tammany.—H. Richardson.
West Feliciana.—R. C. Wickliffe.

W. H. Wagner, Secretary.
A. Levison, Assistant Secretary.
Durant Duponte, Reporter.
Berlin Childres, Sergeant-at-Arms.

SENATORS AND REPRESENTATIVES IN CONGRESS.

SENATORS.

Judah P. Benjamin, of New Orleans.
John Slidell, " "

HOUSE OF REPRESENTATIVES.

William Dunbar, First District.
T. G. Hunt, Second "
John Perkins, jr., Third "
Roland Jones, Fourth "

DISTRICT COURTS OF LOUISIANA.

First Judicial District—Parish of Orleans.

	Name			Office		SALARY.
1.	J. B. Robertson,	New	Orleans,	Judge,	1857	$3,500
	D. Scully,	"	"	Clerk,	"	6,000
2.	J. N. Lea,	"	"	Judge,	"	3,500
	A. Derbés,	"	"	Clerk,	"	fees.
3.	T. M. Kennedy,	"	"	Judge,	"	3,500
	W. J. Castell,	"	"	Clerk,	"	
4.	M. M. Reynolds,	"	"	Judge,	"	3,500
	W. C. Auld,	"	"	Clerk,	"	
5.	D. Augustin,	"	"	Judge,	"	3,500
	W. A. Nott,	"	"	Clerk,	"	
6.	J. A. Cotton,	"	"	Judge,	"	3,500
	S. Newberger,	"	"	Clerk,	"	
	B. S. Tappan,	"	"	Dis't Att'y.		2,500
	M. Marigny,	"	"	Sheriff, fees		

Second District.—St. Bernard and Plaquemines.

O. Rousseau, St. Bernard, Judge, 1857........................ 2,500
L. Lombard, " Dis't Att'y, "........................ 800

Third District—Jefferson and St. Charles.

Victor Burthe, Jefferson, Judge, 1857........................ 2,500
E. Dreux, " Dis't Att'y, " 800

Fourth District—St. John the Baptist, Ascension and St. James.

A. Duffel, Donaldsonville, Judge, 1857........................ 2,500
E. Legendre, " Dis't Att'y " 800

Fifth District—Assumption, Lafourche and Terrebonne.

James Cole, Thibodeaux, Judge, 1857........................ 2,500
I. J. Roman, " Dis't Att'y, "........................ 800

Sixth District—East Baton Rouge, West Baton Rouge and Iberville.

W. B. R bertson, W. B. Rouge, Judge, 1857........................ 2,500
R. G. Beale, E. B. Rouge, Dis't Att'y "........................ 800

Seventh District—East and West Feliciana.

Judge, 1857........................ 2,500
W. F. Kernan, Clinton, Dis't Att'y, " 800

Eighth District—St. Tammany, Washington, St. Helena and Livingston.

G. Watterson, Livingston, Judge, 1857........................ 2,500
G. H. Penn, St. Tammany, Dis't Att'y, " 800

Ninth District—Pt. Coupee and Concordia.

T. J. Cooly, Point Coupee, Judge, 1857........................ 2,500
P. A. Roy, " " Dis't Att'y, "........................ 800

Tenth District—Tensas, Madison and Carroll.

A. Snyder, Madison, Judge, 1857........................ 2,500
J. Nolan, Madison, Dis't Att'y, " 800

Eleventh District—Catahoula, Franklin and Caldwell.

E. Barry, Catahoula, Judge, 1857........................ 2,500
W. H. Hough, Caldwell, Dis't Att'y, " 800

Twelfth District—Ouachita, Morehouse, Union and Jackson.

R. W. Richardson, Ouachita, Judge, 1857........................ 2,500
R. T. Caldwell, " Dis't Att'y, " 800

Thirteenth District—Rapides and Avoyelles.

R. Cushman, Rapides, Judge, 1857........................ 2,500
J. H. C. Barlow, " Dis't Att'y, "........................ 800

Fourteenth District—St. Mary, St. Martin and Vermillion.

A. Voorhies, St. Martin, Judge, 1857........................ 2,500
S. H. McGill, " Dis't Att'y, " 800

Fifteenth District—Lafayette, St. Landry and Calcasieu.

L. Dupree, Opelousas, Judge, 1857........................ 2,500
P. D. Hardy, " Dis't Att'y " 800

Sixteenth District—Natchitoches, Sabine and Winn.

C. Chaplin, Natchitoches, Judge, 1857........................ 2,500
W. J. Hamilton, " Dis't Att'y, " 800

Seventeenth District—Bossier, Bienville and Claiborne.

H. A. Drew, Minden, Judge, 1857........................ 2,500
J. D. Watkins, " Dis't Att'y, " 800

Eighteenth District—DeSoto and Claiborne.

Judge, 1857........................ 2,500
G. Williamson, DeSoto, Dis't Att'y, " 800

MILITIA.

Quarter Master General, C. Lacoste.
Surgeon General, R. Hagan, M. D.

FIRST DIVISION.

John L. Lewis, Major General.
E. L. Tracy, Brigadier General.
D. Cronan, " "

SECOND DIVISION.

C. W. Clifton, Major General.
G. S. Rosseau, Brigadier General.
[Vacancy.]

THIRD DIVISION.

R. C. Wickliffe, Major General.
G. W. Munday, Brigadier General.
[Vacancy.]

FOURTH DIVISION.

L. G. DeRussy, Major General.
Alfred Mouton, Brigadier General.
T. J. Wells, " "

FIFTH DIVISION.

Jacob Humble, Major General.
Mark Boatner, Brigadier General.

JOINT COMMITTEE.

Senate Committee.—Hon. Mark Boatner, Hon. B. L. Hodge.

House of Representatives.—Hon. Thos. Green Davidson, D. L. Beecher, Chas. A. Ballard.

Commissioner.—Hon. U. B. Philips, of West Baton Souge.

BOARD OF CURRENCY.

A. S. Herron, *Secretary.* Chas. E. Greneaux, *Treasurer.*

LOUISIANA PENITENTIARY—B. ROUGE.

McHatton, Ward & Co., Lessees.

Board of Directors.—Timothy Fay, V. Blanchard, Levi Spillers, E. Hiriart.

William Hubbs, Clerk.
J. W. Williams, M. D., Physician.
No. of Convicts, January, 1854......................................283

Board Administrators Deaf and Dumb and the Blind Asylum.

Dr. B. F. Harney, President.
Wm. S. Pike, Secretary and Treasurer.
Dr. Thos. J. Buffington, Physician.
August Duplantier, Andrew S. Herron, James N. Brown, T. B. R. Hatch.
James S. Brown, General Superintendent.

General Statement of the Debt of Louisiana on the 1st of January, 1854:

Bonds of the State, loaned the Consolidated Bank, due in June, 1854, 1857, 1860, 1863 and 1866, in equal amounts,..................		$1,376,000
Bonds of the State, loaned the Citizens' Bank,	6,468,000	
Bonds outstanding for interest,.	577,888	7,045,888
Bonds to the second municipality,...............		198,240
State debts proper, of which trust fund due on demand,...		1,221,809
Due 1st June, 1855, bonds to Draining Company,..		50,000
Due 1st June, 1857, to Citizens' Bank for Loans,.........		250,000
Due 1st Dec., 1867, to old New Orleans and Nashville Railroad,.............................		483,000
Due Dec. 1869, and March and May, 1870, to Mexican Gulf Railroad,......................		100,000
Due 21st March, 1872, for purchase ground Charity Hospital,................................		125,000

Due 18th July, 1893, for relief of treasury, being the loan of 1853, taken by Corning & Co.,	750,000
Due July and August 1893, Bonds to Jackson and Opelousas Railroads,	302,000
Total,	$11,901,939

CULTIVATION OF SUGAR IN LOUISIANA.

The quantity of sugar raised in Louisiana for the past six years was as follows :

1848—220,000 hhds.
1849—247,923 hhds.; increase over 1848, 30,874 per cent.
1850—211,203 hhds.; decrease from 1849, 14.81 per cent.
1851—236,547 hhds.; increrse over 1850, 12 per cent.
1852—321,934 hhds.; increase over 1d51, 36.097 per cent.
1853—449,324 hhdr.; increase over 1852, 39.570 per cent.

Value of Property Subject to Taxation, for 1853.

PARISHES,	PROPERTY.
Concordia,	9,547—600
Tensas,	8,219—648
W. Feliciana,	6,369—992
E. B. Rouge,	6,671—032
Calcasieu,	1,066—540
St. Bernard,	2,012—675
Avoyelles,	3,750—868
Plaquemines,	5,112—875
St. Helena,	1,552—659
Sabine,	980—217
Carroll,	6,693—678
Terrebonne,	5,775—000
Lafayette,	2,356—238
Catahoula,	2,919—985
Winn,	467—369
St. Tammany,	1,724—937
W. B. Rouge,	4,840—610
Washington,	833—400
Point Coupée,	6,348—010
Madison,	6,596—746
Ascension,	6,441—364
St. Mary,	10,595—050
Caddo,	4,578—139
Iberville,	9,407—950
St. Landry,	7,877—840
Franklin,	1,319—257
De Soto,	3,513—816
Bienville,	2,212—182
St. James,	7,256—510

Morehouse,	1,659—852
Assumption,	6,998—850
Rapides,	10,371—381
Jackson,	2,359—683
E. Feliciana,	7,099—318
Caldwell,	909—450
Ouachita,	2,566—136
St. John the Baptist,	3,754—040
Natchitoches,	4,748—225
St. Martin,	4,622—500
Union,	1,944—996
Bossier,	4,255—695
Livingston,	835—138
Claiborne,	2,748—200
Lafourche,	5,661—700
Jefferson,	3,009—168
Vermillion,	No Returns.

PARISH OF ORLEANS.

Real Estate,	66,350—260
Negroes,	4,342—300
Capital,	12,895—495
	83,588—055

State Tax, 16⅔ per $100	158,313 42
Mill Tax for Schools	83,588 05
State Licenses,	163,115 00
Poll Tax for Public Schools,	9,709 00
	395,725 47

CITY TAXES.

New Orleans and Jackson Rail Road, 50 c. per $100	331,751 30
" " " Opelousas " 33⅓ c. " "	221,167 53
Consolidated debt,	697,677 73
Current Expenses, 75c. per $100,	530,194 20
Total Tax,	$1,779,790 70

Estimated Revenue for the present Fiscal Year from all sources, 1854.

State Taxes proper on an assessment of 300,000,000, as the total taxable property of the State at 16⅔c. per $100,	$500,000 00
Licenses,	140,000 00
Auction duties,	25,000 00
School Lands and Rents,	30,000 00
Arrears of Taxes,	40,000 00
Miscellaneous Sources,	30,000 00
For general objects,	$765,000 00

CITY AND PARISH OF ORLEANS.

John L. Lewis, Mayor.
W. H. Garland, Treasurer.
O. Debuys, Comptroller.
L. Pilie, Surveyer.
John Forshee, Coroner.
R. M. Sumners, Recorder, First District.
Clement Ramos, " Second "
P. Suzeneau, " Third "
Henry Jackson, " Fourth "
W. H. James, Chief of Police.
Samuel Powers, Keeper of City Prison.

JUSTICES COURT.

L. U. Gaennie, 1st Justice.
Chas. V. Jonte, 2nd Justice.
R. Richardson, 3d Justice.
F. Calonge, 4th Justice.
Geo. Lugenbuhl, 5th Justice.
J. McGarey, 6th Justice.
John G. Haynes, 7th Justice.

J. J. Hoppe, Constable.
J. J. Agaisse, Constable.
J. Delarue, Constable.
C. Lange, Constable.
Charles Grandpré, Constable.
J. H. Shelling, Constable.
John D. Norris, Constable.

STATE TAX ASSESSORS.

First District.—John Farrell.
Second " —J. C. Kathman.
Third " —A. Pellerin.
Fourth " —Peter Kayser.
Algiers.—N. Bernody.

STATE TAX COLLECTORS.

First District.—Thomas Asken.
Second " —M. Esnard.
Third " —D. Farrar.
Fourth " —R. McDonnell.
Algiers.—John Brunet.

Recorder of Mortgages.—Bernard Avegno.

Register of Conveyances.—Bernard Marigny.

Recorder of Births and Deaths.—N. Trepagnier.

Administrators of Charity Hospital.—Dr. A. Mercer, The. O. Stark, R. W. Adams, Dr. P. Durel, John Pemberton, P. E. Bonford, D. L. Beecher.

Port Wardens.—David Martin, Master Warden; G. Hilliman, B. Beauregard, Horatio Davis, John Deniger.

Marine and River Inspectors.—R. L. Robertson, Richard Swain Capt. Cooper.

Fire Inspector.—John Adams.

New Orleans Chamber of Commerce.—John Woodruff, President; Chas. Briggs, First Vice President; J. M. Lapayre, Second Vice President; J. A. Mansoni, Secretary and Treasurer.

Committee of Appeals.—G. W. Holt, R. B. Sumner, W. S. Pickett, S. H. Kennedy, J. W. Carroll, Jas. Greenleaf.

Harbor Masters.—David Adams, Jas. A. Lusk, John M. Scott, Peter M. Peterson, John Denigre.

Armourer State Arsenal.—Francis Garcia.

Post Office.—W. G. Kendall, Post Master; W. P. Reyburn, Assistant Post Master; G. Levasseur, Head of City Post; George Whiteman, Special Mail Agent; F. Dentzel, Local Agent.

Custom House.—T. C. Porter, Collector; Joseph Genois, Naval Officer; W. E. Stark, Surveyor; D. O. Hinks, Deputy Collector; J. W. Hinks, Deputy Collector; R. W. Adams, Appraiser; A. G. Penn, G. T. Beauregard, Commissioners New Custom House.

Branch of U. States Mint.—Charles Bienvenu, Superintendent; James Brewer, Treasurer; M. F. Bonzano, Melter and Refiner; A. J. Guizot, Coiner: H. Millspaugh, Assayer; J. D. Gilmore, Chief Clerk; M. G. Kennedy, Weigher.

Howard Association.—V. Boullement, President; G. Kursheidt, Treasurer; D. J. Ricardo, Secretary.

Mechanics' Institute.—Newton Richards, President; A. W. Scates, Secretary and Librarian.

RAIL ROAD COMPANIES.

New Orleans, Jackson and Great Northern Rail Road Company. —W. S. Campbell, President; John Calhoun, Secretary.

New Orleans, Opelousas and Great Western Rail Road Company. —J. H. Overton, President; B. F. Flanders, Secretary.

Rail Road Officers not known.—New Orleans and Carrollton Rail Road; Jefferson and Lake Pontchartrain Rail Road; Pontchartrain Rail Road; Mexican Gulf Rail Road.

ASSESSED VALUE OF PROPERTY—PARISH OF ORLEANS.

REP. DIST.	REAL EST.	NEGROES.	CAPITAL.	LICENSES.
First	5,653,260	680,000	213,155	6,475
Second	7,251,415	676,150	586,360	9,730
Third	20,157,175	537,750	6,882,030	76,235
Fourth	9,150,730	376,800	2,630,800	24,115
Fifth	6,886,340	551,900	851,100	16,960
Sixth	4,356,760	549,900	492,600	7,980
Seventh	2,538,615	255,800	317,800	6,990
Eighth	1,669,175	117,400	406,900	3,670

Ninth.........	1,880,790	234,100	266,050	3,710
Tenth.........	6,806,000	362,500	198,700	7,250
Real Estate...	66,350,260	4,342,300	12,895,495	163,115
Negroes........	4,342,300			
Capital.........	12,895,495			
	83,588,055			

State Tax 16⅔c. per $100....................................	159,313 42
Mill Tax for the support of Public Schools..............	83,588 05
State Licenses..	163,115 00
Poll Tax for the support of Public Schools..............	9,709 00
Total..	395,725 47

CITY TAXES, ETC.

Jackson Rail Road Company	50c.	per $100	...............331,751 30
Opelousas " "	33⅓	"	...............221,167 53
Consolidated debt,	105c.	"	...............696,677 73
Current Expenses,	75c.	"	...............530,194 20
			1,779,790 76

BANKING COMPANIES.

Bank of Louisiana.—Capital, $4,000,000. W. W. Montgomery, President; R. M. Davis, Cashier.

Branch of the Louisiana State Bank.—W. H. Avery, President; R. J. Palfrey, Cashier.

Canal Bank.—Capital, $4,000,000. H. A. Rathbone, President; Samuel C. Bell, Cashier.

Citizens Bank.—Capital, $1,500,000. J. D. Denegre, President; Eug. Rousseau, Cashier.

Louisiana State Bank.—Capital, $2,000,000. Samuel J. Peters, President; R. Relf, Cashier.

Mechanics and Traders Bank.—Capital, $1,000,000. U. H. Dudley, President; Gustave Cruzat, Cashier.

Bank of New Orleans.—Capital, $1,000,000. W. P. Converse, President; W. P. Grayson, Cashier.

Consolidation of Planters.—In liquidation.

Southern Bank.—Capital, $1,000,000. John Egerton, President; James L. Wibray, Cashier.

Union Bank of Louisiana.—Capital, $1,000,000. Alfred Penn, President; P. N. Wood, Cashier.

PRIVATE BANKERS.

James Robb & Co.; Louisiana Savings Bank, W. H. Garland, President; Benoit, Shaw & Co.; Matthews Finley & Co.; Samuel Nicholson; Judson & Co.; Thos. H. Barker; Bank of Commerce; Brown Johnston & Co.; Samuel Smith & Co; City Bank of

Cochrane & Co.; Agency of Commercial and Agricultural Bank of Texas; Agency of the Bank of Charleston, S. C.; Horace Bean & Co.; H. B. Merrill & Co.; Pickett, McMurdo & Co.; Insurance and Banking Agency; C. C. Lathrop.

INSURANCE COMPANIES.

Louisiana Mutual Insurance Company, Charles Briggs, President; Liverpool and London Fire and Life Insurance Company, Charles Briggs, Agent; Merchants' Mutual Insurance Company, John Robertson, President; New York Life Insurance Company, C. C. Lathrop, Agent; Tennessee Marine and Fire Insurance Company, Perkins, Campbell & Co.; Granite Insurance Company, New York, C. C. Lathrop, Agent; The Royal Insurance Company, Liverpool, James Magee, Agent; Crescent Mutual Insurance Company, Thos. A. Adams, President; Home Mutual Insurance Company, A. Brother, President; The Mutual Life Insurance Company, New York, Thos. A. Adams, Agent.

PROMINENT AUCTIONEERS.

J. A. Beard, George May, Gardner Smith, Bernard Turpin, Geo. Pardon, George Palfrey, Louis Florence, Joseph Depas, R. B. Sykes, N. Vigné, M. Barnett, P. E. Tricou, D. E. Morphy, W. E. Vincent, H. J. Domingon, F. Hernandez, G. Leaumont, J. L. Carman, Thos. J. Spear, R. M. Montgomery.

NOTARIES PUBLIC.

Jas. Gauthier, E. G. Gottschalk, D. J. Ricardo, John Craig, A Roman, A. Robert, P. W. Robert, Wm. Christy, J. A. Lusk, Guy Duplantier, A. Abat, P. C. Cuvillier, A. Mazereau, H. Keating, J. R. Rareshide, Theodore Gengol, John Claiborne, J. R. Vanduslieu, Dennis Prieur, A. Chipella, P. E. Laresche, J. L. Lisbony, H. Remy, J. Cuvillier, R. J. Kerr, A. Ducatel, G. Drouet, A. E. Bienvenue, C. L. Kernion, R. Brenan, P. Condrain, M. Gernon, C. A. Tallarie, C. C. Porter, O. De Armas, G. Lugenbuhl, A. A. Baudoin, Y. O. Stark, Thos. Bayton, J. Graham, W. Shannon, P. Lacoste, H. P. Caire, H. B. Cenas, Thomas J. Beck, A. Boudesquie, P. B. Phelps, P. E. Theard, John Molly, E. Barnett, M. G. Kennedy, Jos. Cohn, John G. Poindesster, A. Dreyfous, Jacob Soria, W. L. Poole, H. Pedesclaux, George Rareshide, J. F. Coffy, E. Floyd, Wm. Monaghan, W. H. Peters, J. Agaisse, Th. H. Bartlett, Philip Prendergast, C. C. Ladeyere, Clement Brown, Edwin L. Lens, A. Doricourt, Jas. Fulhouse.

CHURCHES IN NEW ORLEANS.

Catholics, 17; Christian 1; First Congregrational, 1; Episcopal, 4; Hebrew, 2; Lutherian, 1; Methodist, 11; Presbyterian 6; Presbyterian Mission, 2; German Evangelical, 1; Unitarian, 4. Total, 30.

Value of Church Property, $1,203,500.

Aggregate Church accommodations, 27,350.

CHARITABLE INSTITUTIONS.—NEW ORLEANS.

Female Orphan Asylum; Poydras Female Asylum; St. Anna's Asylum for destitute widows and children of all denominations; Institute for colored orphans; Orphan Boys Asylum, 4th District; Institute for indigent widows; Orphans Home; Charity Hospital.

MEDICAL COLLEGE, NEW ORLEANS.

Faculty.—Dr. Stone, Dr. Jones, Dr. Wedderburn, Dr. Holt, Dr. Cenas, Dr. Hunt and Dr. Riddell.

UNIVERSITY OF LOUISIANA.

Law Department.—Christian Roselius, Esq., *Prof. of Civil Law.* Hon. Theodore McCaleb, *Admiralty and Maritine Law.* Randall Hunt, Esq., *Commercial and Criminal Law.* Hon. T. B. Monroe, *Common Law, Constitutional Law, &c.*

Collegiate Department.—Hon. Theodore McCaleb, LLD. *President.* J. D. B. DeBow, M A. *Professor of Political Economy.* J. Lawrence Smith, M. D., *Professor of Chemistry and Mineralogy.* Richard H. Chilton, *Professor of Geology.* Claudius W. Sears, *Professor of Mathematics and Natural Philosophy.* W. C. Duncan, M. A. *Professor of Greek and Latin Languages and Literature.* M. MacRoux, *Professor of French Literature.* Herman Kohlmayer, Ph. D., *Professor of German and Hebrew Languages.* DeYomas, *Professor of the Spanish Language and Literature.*

ACADEMIES AND INSTITUTES, NEW ORLEANS.

Young Ladies' Institute, Miss S. S. Hull Principal, 150 Carondelet Street.

New Orleans Female Seminary, Miss C. Gardner, Principal, Tivoli Circle.

Orleans Academy, M. D. Dimitry, Principal, Tivoli Circle.

Jefferson Academy, G. J. Lord, Principal, 53 Bourbon Street.

St. Louis Institute, Mme. Deron, Principal, 313 Dauphin Street.

Young Ladies' Boarding School, Madam Desrayaux, Principal, Burgundy Street.

G. Blackman's Academy, Calliope Street.

Young Ladies' Academy, Madam Parent, Principal, Corner Rampart Street.

St. Charles Institute, Mme C. Mace, Principal, Greenville.

PARISH OF ASCENSION.

J. L. Comstock, Sheriff; L. D. Nichols, Clerk of Court; John F. Ayraud, Recorder; J. B. Hebert, Assessor; Sothene Moliere, Coroner.

Justices of the Peace.—A. W. Warren, J. B. Hebert, Octave Terrio, Wm. C. Lawes, Simeon J. Arnold, Pierre Rougeau.

Notaries Public.—Henry F. Duffel, Macolm H. Nichols, P. H. Harbour.

Seat of Justice.—Donaldsonville.

Charitable Institutions.—St. Vincents, Hospital and Asylum.

PARISH OF ASSUMPTION.

A. F. Hickman, Sheriff; A. De Blanc, Recorder; Edward Vives, Assessor; E. Bergerson, Coroner.

Justices of the Peace.—Antoine Martinez, Traismond Trahant, C. Sinosser, Ed. Cotey, D. Himel, Amedeé Bourg, Amedeé Domas, Amdeé Morel, F. Haybet, Pierre Theriot.

Notaries Public.—Francis A. Tete, Amedeé Morel, Traismon Truhan, C. L. Mayor, Antonio Martinez.

Seat of Justice.—Napoleonville.

PARISH OF AVOYELLES.

A. D. Coco, Sheriff; J, H. Barbin, Clerk of Court; A. Barbin, Recorder; A. G. Morrow, Assessor; ——— Coroner.

Justices of the Peace.—Jos. Guellot, Joseph H. Bordelon, F. M. Haygood, Joseph Coppel, V. Roy.

Notaries Public.—B. W. Kimball, S. H. Cuvillion, R. J. Taliafero.

Seat of Justice—Marksville.

Schools.—Young Ladies Institute, Jeannie Hazletine, Principal; Marksville Male and Female Academy, John McDonnell, Mary McDonnell, Principals.

PARISH OF BIENVILLE.

James Upshaw, Sheriff; John F. Stephens, Clerk of Court; John G. Noles, Recorder; Moses Hurley, Assessor; John Rice, Coroner.

Justices of the Peace.—Jacob Pearce, R. J. Wharton, Jesse Smith, William Wimberly, J. M. Looney, Isaac Melton.

Notaries Public.—W. B. Stuart, Jacob Pearce, Richard Pickett, James H. Head.

Seat of Justice.—Sparta.

Schools.—Mount Lebanon University; Mount Lebanon Female Institute.

PARISH OF BOSSIER.

L. F. Steele, Sheriff; A. A. Abney, Clerk of Court; Austin Miller, Recorder; C. Snindle, Assessor; J. S. Briggs, Coroner.

Justices of the Peace.—Arthur Yarborough, Vincent Walker, C. R. Hereing, J. M. Canfield, Andrew Lawrence, W. J. Dellafield.

Notaries Pablic.—John W. Mahle, Vincent Walker, E. R. Herring.

Seat of Justice.—Bellveue.

Schools.—Female Academy, Pineville.

PARISH OF CADDO.

H. Watson, Sheriff; W. G. Kerly, Clerk of Court; R. T. Buckner, Recorder; F. R. Simpson, Assessor; A. F. Clark, Coroner.

Justices of the Peace.—M. H. Erwin, E. M. Jenkins, E. R. Bugby; H. W. Allen, John W. Jones, John L. Fitzpatrick, S. P. McCall.

Notaries Public.—John M. Landrum, David J. Hooks, H. J. G. Battle, John Maley, W. H. Erwin.

Seat of Justice.—Shreveport.

Schools.—Collegiate Institute, Rev. S. P. Helme, Principal; Shreveport Female High School, J. Franklin Ford, Principal.

PARISH OF CALCASIEU.

J. H. Cole, Sheriff; Jos. V. Moss, Clerk of Court; J. W. Parsons, Recorder; Nath. Clifton, Assessor; A. Salier, Coroner.

Justices of the Peace.—Louis Vallin, Chas. A. Handy.

Notaries Public.—Alexander Dessessart, Traismond Trahan.

PARISH OF CATAHOULA.

Timothy Spann, Sheriff; C. C. Duke, Clerk of Court; W. E. Gaulden, Recorder; James A. Holiday, Assessor; T. W. Graves, Coroner.

Justices of the Peace.—J. P. Markham, Wm. C. Finley, John B. Heard, Henry Tussler, George W. Magee, A. Young, Robt. J. Newsom, S. P. Stone, John Ballew, Isaac W. Davis.

Notaries Public.—Felix Robb, R. H. Cuney.

Seat of Justice.—Harrisonburg.

PARISH OF CALDWELL.

C. J. Mandeville, Sheriff; R. Duckworth, Clerk of Court; John C. Hill, Recorder; J. J. B. Everett, Coroner; James A. Royal, Assessor.

Justices of the Peace.—Elias Adams, James M. Meredith, John C. Hill, A. W. Faulkner, R. Sluckworth.

Notaries Public.—J. J. Stringer.

Seat of Justice.—Columbia.

Schools.—Sweet Gum Ridge Academy, Mrs. M. P. Wood, Preceptress.

PARISH OF CARROLL.

W. L. Knox, Sheriff; P. W. Defrance, Clerk of Court; S. D. Oliver, Recorder; Thos. Shadduck, Assessor; George W. McCarrell, Coroner.

Justices of the Peace.—E. Terry, R. McCain, L. C. G. Henry, W. F. Oliver, James P. Mebane.

Notaries Public.—E. Harris, H. Hilliman, J. W. Draughorn, W. J. Oliver, R. H. Dollarhide.

Seat of Justice.—Lake Providence.

PARISH OF CLAIBORNE.

R. Warren, Sheriff; D. H. Dyer, Clerk of Court; J. W. Harrison, Recorder; J. S. Burnham, Coroner; E. B. D. Johnson, Assessor.

Justices of the Peace.—Jas. A. Millican, James A. Williams, John Cook, R. A. Green, John S. Wise, James W. Miller, James Killbourne, James A. Barker, Arthur McFarland.

Notaries Public.—Thomas L. Terry, R. A. Green, Henry S. Martin, James M. Thomasson, Nelson J. Scott.

Seat of Justice.—Homer.

Schools.—Minden Female College, at Minden.

PARISH OF CONCORDIA.

W. R. C. Vernon, Sheriff; Thomas Edwards, Clerk of Court; A. C. Hunter, Recorder; A. G. Tyler, Assessor; A. White, Coroner.

Justices of the Peace.—Elisha Knight, D. D. Miller, George W. Green, Thomas Edwards, B. C. S. Guice, J. A. McPheeters, M. A. Scott, Henry Tooley, R. W. Prater, E. Young.

Notaries Public.—Samuel C. Scott, Zebulon York, G. W. Miller,

Seat of Justice.—Vidalia.

PARISH OF DE SOTO.

James H. Dillard, Sheriff; J. H. Sutherlin, Clerk of Court; Samuel F. Smith, Recorder; F. P. Prudhomme, Assessor; Jesse G. Steel, Coroner.

Justices of the Peace.—George Hendrick, Wm. E. North, R. Munday, Wiley White, J. B. Norman, G. Franklin, E. H. Hare, W. Chaluser, R. B. Fuerson, A. R. Mitchell.

Notaries Public.—F. L. Armstead, A. R. Mitchell, J. D. Brown, J. W. Parson, R. B. Fuerside, R. Burns.

Seat of Justice.—Mansfield.

PARISH OF EAST BATON ROUGE.

H. V. Babin, Sheriff; Manuel Moreno, Clerk of Court; Samuel Skolfield, Recorder; Samuel Bates, Coroner; H. M. Pearce, Assessor.

Justices of the Peace.—P. A. Walker, F. B. Sans, Jesse Edward, Wm. Campbell, John A. Messugh, Jos. Heard.
John R. Dufrocq, Mayor of Baton Rouge.

Notaries Public.—P. A. Walker, Wm Gil, A. W. Bell, John F. McCaa, John A. McHugh, L. Grandpré.
J. M. Haliday, Parish Surveyor.

Bank.—Branch of the Louisiana State Bank, J. B. Kleinpeter, President; W. S. Pike, Cashier.

Colleges and Schools.—College of St. Peter and St. Paul; Convent of the Sacred Heart; Catholic Male School; Catholic Female School; Female School, Mrs. L. M. Philips; Female School, Mrs. M. W. Read; Female Institute, Rev. S. H. Slosson; Female Institute, Mrs. Guion; Boys School, R. D. Wilson.

Benevolent Institutions.—Deaf and Dumb and Blind Asylum; Female Orphan Asylum; Benevolent Association of Catholic Ladies of Baton Rouge.

Churches in the City of Baton Rouge.—Methodist, 1; Episcopalian, 1; Presbyterian, 1; Catholic, 1; Christian, 1.

Seat of Justice.—Baton Rouge.

PARISH OF EAST FELICIANA.

A. J. Law, Sheriff; H. Skipwith, Clerk of Court; J. C. White, Recorder; Joseph Drawdy, Assessor; L. L. Magee, Coroner.

Justices of the Peace.—R. C. Carman, Wm. H. Carter, Edmund Story, James C. Jackson, J. H. Hansey, Henry Hawford, J. N. Delee, George W. Catlett, George C. Green.

Notaries Public.—Thomas F. Noone, James C. Jackson, Henry Hawford, A. Robinson, B. D. Roberts, Edmund Story.

Colleges, Schools, &c.—Centenary College, Jackson; Female Academy, Jackson; Female Academy, Clinton; Feliciana Female Institute, Jackson; Southern Institute, Jackson; Insane Asylum, Jackson.

Seat of Justice.—Clinton.

PARISH OF FRANKLIN.

William Hampton, Sheriff; H. T. Earle, Clerk of Court; A. N. Moore, Recorder; J. E. Abell, Assessor; M. G. Jones, Coroner.

Justices of the Peace.—Thomas Cockerham, Samuel G. Cloun, Benj. A. Hallock, John D. Thompson, R. E. Johnson, E. J. Walton.

Notaries Public.—M. E. J. Walton.

Seat of Justice.—Winnsborough.

PARISH OF IBERVILLE.

Josoph A. Erwin, Sheriff; M. A. Estevan, Clerk of Court; G. S. Rosseau, Recorder; Pierre Gillesseau, Assessor; S. M. Rils, Coroner.

Justices of the Peace.—J. L. Webb, W. B. Thomas, A. Hébert, Joseph Pardo, P. J. Cole.

Notaries Public.—Adolphe Hébert, Joseph Walsh, J. L. Webb, J. H. Balch.

Seat of Justice.—Plaquemine.

College.—Parochial College.

PARISH OF JACKSON.

M. Johnson, Sheriff; B. Sanders, Clerk of Court; S. Frank, Recorder; A. Hightower, Assessor; William Mathews, Coroner.

Justices of the Peace.—J. M. Morris, Richard Jacobs, Walker Brown, Lewis S. Markham.

Notaries Public.—J. B. Otis, Isaac N. Bills.

Seat of Justice.—Vernon.

PARISH OF JEFFERSON.

P. Labarre, Sheriff; Ed. Buisson, Clerk of Court; J. B. G. Arnault, Recorder; E. Megell, Assessor; V. Munch, Coroner.

Justices of the Peace.—W. Forshey, R. K. Cutler, E. B. Robinson, Guy Dreux, J. Casimer Ortis.

Notaries Public.—Dennis McAffee.

State Tax Collector.—John D. Harper.

Seat of Justice.—Carrollton.

Schools.—Bell Grove Academy, Carrollton, J. M. Everett, Principal.

PARISH OF LAFAYETTE.

B. V. Voorhies, Sheriff; E. Mouton, Clerk of Court; William Brands, Recorder; O. Mouton Assessor; John A. Requis, Coroner.

Justices of the Peace.—Pierre S. Arceneaux, John Campbell, C. H. Eastin, Asa Foreman.

Notaries Public.—Gustave Lauvent, D. Breaux, E. M. Girard.

Seat of Justice.—Vermillionville.

PARISH OF LAFOURCHE.

Mathurin Bourg, Sheriff; L. L. Allain, Clerk of Court; J. K. Gourdain, Recorder; E. B. Robichaux, Assessor; J. B. Laisure, Coroner.

Justices of the Peace.—James Bellin, E. D. Richardson, Pierre Thibodaux, Edmund Savoie, John L. Seely, V. Terbonne, A. B. Rugan, Emile Flagont, B. F. Barker, Aug. Cretine.

Notaries Public.—Jona C. White, Joseph Nichols.

Seat of Justice.—Thibodaux.

PARISH OF LIVINGSTON.

Samuel Peterson, Sheriff; D. T. Settoon, Clerk of Court; P. F. Stairns, Recorder; Adam Lobell, Assessor; J. P. Wall, Coroner.

Justices of the Peace.—John W. Stilly, Jacob J. Watts, Nicholas George, Sanford R. Terry, P. H. Spear.

Notaries Public.—Jefferson Lee, Wm. H. Wilder, William Acres, Jacob J. Watts, Chas. C. Kennedy, Rufus Felder.

Seat of Justice.—Springfield.

PARISH OF MADISON.

James L. Crandall, Sheriff; John S. Mason, Clerk of Court; L. M. Bozer, Recorder; A. F. Shelton, Assessor; F. Kelch, Coroner.

Justices of the Peace.—Alva Frisby, A. A. S. Newton, John M. Karr, John Castleman, John A. Nolly, Thomas Montgomery, E. B. Loun, J. W. Robeson, Wm. Fetherston, John Neely, Serpand Kilzen.

Notaries Public.—Jos. W. Williams, Jacob C. Seal, A. J. Lowry, Jas. A. Fleetwood, F. M. Dawson.

Seat of Justice.—Richmond.

PARISH OF MOREHOUSE.

A. J. Bobo, Sheriff; James Bussey, Clerk of Court; John Howe, Assessor; Jacob M. Heard, Recorder; Elias Miller, Sr., Coroner.

Justices of the Peace.—Daniel B. Douglas, Andrew Cain, Wm. Furlow, G. C. Martin, Milton B. Holt, R. L. Knox, Henry Curtis, L. N. Harrison, Wm. R. Ward, John M. Carr, Joel R. Cameron.

Notaries Public.—W. M. Lee, J. R. Cameron, Wm. McFee.

Seat of Justice.—Bastrop.

Schools.—Bastrop Academy, John W. Allen, Principal; Isaac T. Naff, Assistant.

PARISH OF NATCHITOCHES.

F. Vienne, Sheriff; W. P. Morrow, Clerk of Court; Thomas P. Jones, Recorder; L. G. DeRussey, Assessor; Th. Bossier, Coroner.

Justices of the Peace.—A. P. Sisson, B. D. Owen, Clinton Berry.

Notaries Public.—Frederick Williams, Joseph M. Compere, Valery B. Shultz, Charles Sers, B. H. Baird.

Seat of Justice.—Natchitoches.

Convent.—Convent of the Sacred Heart; 9 Teachers; 64 Pupils.

PARISH OF PLAQUEMINES.

R. Johnson, Sheriff; J. L. Marciacq, Recorder; A. Lartigue, Clerk of Court; Stephen Dolese, Assessor; Villere Deusse, Coroner.

Justices of the Peace.—George Garr, John C. DeSavine, Simeon Martin.

Notaries Public.—Oscar Arroyo, Chas. Dutilet, F. G. Schmidt.

Seat of Justice.—Pt. L'Hache.

PARISH OF POINT COUPEE.

Jas. A. Morgan, Sheriff; A. Bondy, Clerk of Court; Valery Ledoux, Recorder; Alexander Chutz, Assessor; George Fernandez, Coroner.

Justices of the Peace.—Thomas Mabins, A. W. Carruth, Elijah Eastwood, U. Harrison, S. Pourieaux, Ovide Barras.

Notaries Public.—Homer Bouis, W. G. Bozeman, A. O. LeBlanc, A. S. Carruth, William Beatty, Narcisse Bauvais.

Seat of Justice.—New Road, Maysville.

Schools.—Poydras College, Fusse River.

PARISH OF RAPIDES.

J. C. Wise, Sheriff; M. R. Araial, Clerk of Court; R. M. Kilpatrick, Recorder; Louis Gossen, Assessor; G. C. Wood, Coroner.

Justices of the Peace.—Guinn Harris, E. C. Leekie, William Randolph, Rosemond Legras, F. B. Armsden, G. Labat, A. C. Lewis.

Notaries Public.—John W. Pearce, R. Legras, Thos. F. Scott, F. A. Biossat, E. C. Leekie, Guinn Harris.

Seat of Justice.—Alexandria.

Schools.—State Seminary of Learning, near Alexandria; Boy's Institute, L. F. Parker, Principal.

Trnstees of State Seminary.—M. R. Aarial, R. C. Hynson, S. Smith, George M. Graham, Orin Mayo, J. P. Waddell, J. C. Goodwin.

PARISH OF SABINE.

R. A. Sibley, Sheriff; E. F. Presley, Clerk of Court; John Baldwin, Recorder; L. B. Gray, Assessor; W. H. Turner, Coroner.

Justices of the Peace.—A. Wright, W. C. Beddingfield, F. Bendridge, W. H. McLemon, Benj. Biles, W. Darnell, R. K. McDonald, Jas. Weeks, W. W. Sibley, M. R. Spreight.

Notaries Public.—Nathaniel Sanders, E. C. Davidson.

Seat of Justice.—Manny.

PARISH OF ST. BERNARD.

A. Morales, Sheriff; P. Jorda, Clerk of Court; Philip Toca, Recorder; Martial Verrett, Assessor; Valery Veillon, Coroner.

Justices of the Peace.—P. V. Rosseau, Philip Toca, D. S. Morales, Pierre Prejols, jr., P. A. Rosseau.

Notaries Public.—Victor DeBouchel.

Seat of Justice.—Terre Aux Bœuffs.

PARISH OF ST. CHARLES.

Noel St. Martin, Sheriff; C. St. Martin, Clerk of Court; E. Tastet, Recorder; J. B. Trepagnier, Assessor; Pierre Roux, Coroner.

Justices of the Peace.—Emile Tastet, B. D. LaBranche.

Notaries Public.—Francis Chaix.

PARISH OF ST. HELENA.

T. G. Watson, Sheriff; J. B. McClenden, Clerk of Court; H. K. George, Recorder; P. Easley, Assessor; Charles Hughes, Coroner.

Justices of the Peace.—William Dennis, Jr., S. B. Draughon, E. B. Carey, Z. G. Horwood, R. F. Hodges, Wm. J. Huitt, W. W. Watson, J. H. George, A. B. Quinlin.

Notaries Public.—Thomas Bennett.

Seat of Justice.—Greensburg.

Schools.—Female Seminary, Greensburg, Mrs. J. P. Gookin.

PARISH OF ST. JAMES.

John B. Ory, Sheriff; T. S. Gaudett, Clerk of Court; John B. Ferchand, Recorder; J. V. Armant, Assessor; Joseph Landry, Coroner.

Justices of the Peace.—O. Melancon, J. V. Cantrelle, Gideon Subra.

Notaries Public.—Henry Remy, A. Roman.

Seat of Justice.—Right Bank, opposite the Convent.

Schools.—Convent of the Sacred Heart; Louisiana College.

PARISH OF ST. JOHN THE BAPTIST.

Jean F. Brucand, Sheriff; L. Perret, Clerk of Court; Adolphe Sorapuro, Recorder; Placide Barré, Assessor; Z. Duhé, Coroner.

Justices of the Peace.—Theophile Desgrais, Emile Rigault, Lucien Soncher.

Seat of Justice.—Near Church St. John.

PARISH OF ST. LANDRY.

J. B. David, Sheriff; Adolphe Garriques, Clerk of Court; T. D. Avy, Recorder; Pierre Monille, Assessor; O. Matté, Coroner.

Justices of the Peace.—Guy H. Bell, S. D. Allis, William Cushman, T. S. Robin, J. P. Smith, John P. Hudson, William Elkins, Joseph Chenier, Henry S. Dunbar, James M. Moore, James Mayes.

Notaries Public.—John J. Morgan, A. G. Thornton, A. M. Perault, F. C. Kauffman, Joseph Bacon, W. D. Collins, John F. Smith.

Seat of Justice.—Opelousas.

Schools.—St. Charles College; Convent of the Sacred Heart.

PARISH OF ST. MARTIN.

J. A. DeBlanc, Sheriff; V. A. Fournett, Clerk of Court; C. M. Olivier, Recorder; John G. Harry, Assessor; Th. Bienvenu, Coroner.

Justices of the Peace.—John M. Terrell, Saml. A. Bunch, Wm. Robertson, Chas. D. Arby, Alex Dumo, Edmund Morgi, Gilbert Hébert, T. Richard, E. Patin, Philip Wiltz, Antoine Bruno.

Notaries Public.—A. DeBlanc, A. D. Miner, Antoine Bruno, G. Ratier, A. Condroy.

Seat of Justice.—St. Martinsville.

Schools.—Attakapas College, St. Martinsville, A. Renoudet, Principal.

PARISH OF ST. MARY.

W. F. Harfliegh, Sheriff; Jas. V. Fourney, Clerk of Court; J. A. Dumartrait, Recorder; Wilson McKendall, Assessor; W. B. McNamar, Coroner.

Justices of the Peace.—A. L. Tucker, W. P. Allen, L. R. Curtis, Daniel Fisher, B. Delahussey.

Notaries Public.—James W. Crapen, D. Agt. Delahoussage,

E. M. Seagrave, L. R. Curtis, R. W. McMillon, W. A. Langly, Jas. R. Dally.

Seat of Justice.—Franklin.

PARISH OF ST. TAMMANY.

C. Morgan, Sheriff; W. B. Hosmer, Clerk of Court; John J. Mortée, Recorder; A. L. Carpenter, Assessor; W. H. Meritt, Coroner.

Justices of the Peace.—Geo. L. B. Miller, Alex. W. Weens, August Guibert, J. Blocker, Geo. H. Gilbert, Wm. S. Barker.

Notaries Public.—A. M. Bowie, Paris Childress.

Seat of Justice.—Covington.

PARISH OF TENSAS.

G. W. Williams, Sheriff; Julius Aroni, Clerk of Court; R. Lewis, Recorder; N. Murphy, Coroner; Wm. Bantz, Assessor.

Justices of the Peace.—William Bell, B. Mason, J. H. Armat, E. W. Hicks, W. F. Lynch, Eben Miller, Reeve Lewis.

Notaries Public.—Ebenezer Miller.

Seat of Justice.—St. Joseph.

PARISH OF TERREBONNE.

J. A. Gagné, Sheriff; J. Aycock, Clerk of Court; Joseph A. LeBlanc, Recorder; Eugene Engersan, Assessor; M. Fields, Coroner.

Justices of the Peace.—Thomas Buford, Joseph Toupes, C. C. Wallis, E. Hoton, P. H. Darcé, O. F. Aycock, Aubin Bourg, J. C. Potts, R. D. Jordan.

Notaries Public.—F. S. Goode, Solomon Friend.

Seat of Justice.—Houma.

PARISH OF UNION.

A. G. Taylor, Sheriff; C. T. Barton, Clerk of Court; W. C. Smith, Recorder; R. G. Pleasants, Assessor; Solomon Treagle, Coroner.

Justices of the Peace.—H. D. Hays, Stephen Wood, H. H. Ramsey, W. B. Cooper, W. J. Rainey, Daniel Pucket, N. D. Mayes, W. A. Darley, Chas. C. McDonald, H. W. Hamilton, Jas. A. Martin, T. W. Wilson, Benj. Ford, S. S. Heard, Spencer Evans.

Notaries Public.—Daniel Pucket, C. L. Norman, Jesse F. Fuller, Thomas Whithoix, D. M. Harris.

Seat of Justice.—Farmersville.

PARISH OF VERMILLION.

Leo N. Hébert, Sheriff; A. J. Kearney, Clerk of Court; John B. Theall, Recorder; Treville Stelly, Assessor; Chas. H. Wagner, Coroner.

Justices of the Peace.—Andrew J. Kearney, V. Veazy, M. McCall, Elijah Erwing.

Notaries Public.—Elijah Erwing.

Seat of Justice.—Perry's Bridge.

PARISH OF WASHITA.

A. T. Norwood, Sheriff; B. F. Cauthom, Clerk of Clerk; B. D. Shepherd, Recorder; W. W. Patrick, Assessor; John H. Butt, Coroner.

Justices of the Peace.—M. H. Butler, Jas. G. Richardson, Paul McEnery, A. Carman, H. Young, J. S. Greenlee, J. Newsom, T. Goodlet, John F. Shepherd, John F. Huey.

Notaries Public.—C. P. Cosby, Wm. Earle, Thomas L. Simpson.

Seat of Justice.—Monroe.

PARISH OF WASHINGTON.

T. C. Bickham, Sheriff; Stephen Aldrich, Clerk of Court; Jas. A. Erwin, Recorder; J. R. McElwin, Assessor; H. Jones, Coroner.

Justices of the Peace.—Joseph M. Simonds, Henry Z. Jenkins, John Lewis, Step. Albritton, Alfred Richardson, Jas. F. Ard.

Seat of Justice.—Franklinton.

PARISH OF WEST BATON ROUGE.

N. W. Pope, Sheriff; W. B. Chamberlin, Clerk of Court; O. Bernard, Recorder; Joseph Braud, Assessor; O. Hébert, Coroner.

Justices of the Peace.—Valmont Hébert, Rose Hébert, Chas. Smith, John T. Nolan.

Notaries Public.—None commissioned.

Seat of Justice.—Opposite the City of Baton Rouge.

Schools.—Male and Female Institute, under charge of St. John's Church.

PARISH OF WEST FELICIANA.

Seymour H. Lurty, Sheriff; Chas. B. Collins, Clerk of Court; B. Haralson, Recorder; Wm. B. Clugston, Assessor; Edwin Leet, Coroner.

Justices of the Peace.—Edwin Leet, Henry Hinch, Fred. Fisher, F. V. D. Hagaman, Thomas Dawson, C. G. Hale, J. R. Marks.

Notaries Public.—DeWitt Jones, R. C. Wederstrand, George Cook.

Seat of Justice.—St. Francisville.

PARISH OF WINN.

Asa Emanuel, Sheriff; A. C. Banks, Clerk of Court; W. R. Bingham, Recorder; R. D. Hall, Assessor; Josiah Allen, Coroner.

Justices of the Peace.—Austin C. Banks, Timothy F. Smith, William Peters, Luther Barnes, J. H. Lacey, J. W. Bingham, James Roberts.

Notaries Public.—Robt. H. Williams, Abram G. Hardie.

Seat of Justice.—Winfield.

COMMISSIONERS TO TAKE TESTIMONY IN OTHER STATES.

J. B. Jones, New York; D. B. Birney, Philadelphia; C. R. Haws, Philadelphia; H. H. Baker, Charleston, S. C.; W. B. Wiggins, Wilmington, Del.; A. M. Hart, New York; Leonard Meyer, Philadelphia; A. W. Campbell, Jackson, Tenn.; Chas. McKenstry, New York; J. C. Starkweather, Milwaukie; E. R. Newhall, Cincinnati; J. L. Kazer, Alexandria, Va.; L. Hermann, San Francisco; Wiley Williams, Columbus, Ga.; John Bissell, New York; T. S. Crombarger, Philadelphia; James Wade, Jr., Cleveland, O.; T. R. Westmore, St. Louis; D. Mumma, Jr., Harrisonburg; J. D. Pratt, Baltimore; E. H. Cushing, Columbia, Tex.; Saml. J. Hall, Charleston, S. C.; J. H. Lawrence, New York; W. S. Leland, Boston; S. P. Montgomery, Philadelphia; R. D. Hopkins, Mobile; R. A. Watkins, New York; Edward Armstrong, Philadelphia; J. P. Montgomery, Philadelphia; John Handy, Canton, Miss.; Charles De Selding, Washington City; G. C. Thomas; Washington City; J. R. Strother, Greenville, Miss.; C. M. Chamberlin, San Francisco; Chas. C. Tucker, Washington City; E. Duzenbury, New York; J. L. A. Andrews, Boston; H. J. Labatt, San Francisco; Ira Floyd, New York,; James E. Sickles, New York; A. F. Cushman, New York; C. McClure Hays, Pittsburg, Pa.; Josh Abraham, Cincinnati; Florence McCarty, New York; L. D. Marks, Henderson C'ty., Tex.; J. H. Smoot, Mobile; Jas. J. Dozier, Louisville; John Livingston, New York; N. G. Bryson, Vicksburg; James Abbott, Baltimore; J. S. Byrne, Vicksburg; Henry Palmer, Philadelphia; J. P. Haven, San Francisco; James A. Baker, Florence, Ala.; T. P. Lockwood, Charleston, S. C.; F. J. Shaffer, Charleston, S. C.; F. A. Sawyer, San Francisco; Joseph Grant, San Francisco; Sylvester Lacey, New York; H. C. Banks, New York; E. F. Corey, New York; W. H. Browne, New York; G. L. Brent, Richmond, Va.; Jas. Todd, Philadelphia; J. K. Lee, Richmond, Va.; Saml. S. Bailey, Richmond, Va.; F. H. Davidge, Washington City; S. Coolidge, Boston; S. A. Atchinson, Louisville; Charles Halsey, San Francisco; M. B. McCay, New York; William N. Stogdile, New York; Abel U. Mayo, Richmond, Va.; A. M. Benton Philadelphia; Danl. Seixas,

New York; R. H. Stanley, Sacramento, Cal.; James L. Autry, Holly Springs, Miss.; K. M. Loudon, Port Lavaca, Tex.; Wm. C. Betts, New York; Joseph Simpson, San Francisco; Chas. B. F. Adams, Boston; Chas C. Nutter, Boston; Sydney Abel, Marysville, Cal.; Montgomery Gibbs, New York; C. W. Downing, Washington City.

STATE CENSUS—1853.

NAMES OF PARISHES.	Qualified Electors.	No. of free white People.	No. of free people of color.	Number of Slaves.	No. of free white males between 18 and 45 yrs.	Total Population.
Plaquemines...........	608	2,045	377	3,926	623	6,348
St. Bernard............	323	1,447	78	1,794	369	4,011
Orleans, Right Bank.....	280	2,312	128	964	631	3,404
" 1st Rep. Dist....	1,251	11,290	435	1,732	2,639	13,457
" 2d do	2,623	16,374	228	2,077	3,733	18,679
" 3d do	2,750	20,183	824	2,236	5,629	23,243
" 4th do	2,021	12,681	1,200	1,172	4,000	15,053
" 5th do	1,167	10,356	2,214	1,845	3,056	14,415
" 6th do	1,793	11,795	2,441	1,669	1,479	15,905
" 7th do	1,007	7,239	3,011	2,201	1,560	12,451
" 8th do	1,453	10,100	1,286	373	3,032	17,769
" 9th do	798	8,252	196	1,001	1,731	9,449
" 4th Lafayette...	1,885	16,615	441	1,530	3,929	18,586
Jefferson..............	1,074	9,254	791	4,580	3,004	14,625
St. Charles............	209	971	136	4,628	.....	5,734
St. John the Baptist.....	388	2,336	288	4,050	350	6,674
St. James..............	628	3,440	92	8,930	719	12,462
Ascension..............	673	3,520	203	6,889	660	10,622
Assumption............	1,107	6,095	70	6,407	1,080	12,572
Lafourche..............	1,219	6,423	110	5,600	1,346	12,134
Terrebonne..............	578	4,409	349	5,195	808	9,963
St. Mary...............	827	3,670	585	10,846	767	15,101
St. Martin..............	1,074	5,573	731	6,673	985	12,977
Iberville...............	860	5,426	169	9,517	1,092	15,112
West Baton Rouge.....	381	1,782	106	4,178	325	6,060
East Baton Rouge......	905	7,895	700	7,320	2,200	15,916
Livingston.............	649	2,799	19	916	577	3,734
St. Helena.............	494	2,621	4	2,487	484	5,105
Washington............	502	2,397	0	1,094	365	3,491
St. Tammany..........	498	2,588	447	1,374	382	4,409
East Feliciana.........	880	3,796	39	9,990	724	13,825
West Feliciana........	560	2,331	70	10,278	523	12,679
Point Coupée..........	720	3,042	695	8,000	865	11,737
Avoyelles.............	803	4,264	121	5,468	786	9.853
Madison...............	402	1,361	16	7,351	429	8,726
Tensas................	313	1,078	13	9,142	323	10,233
Concordia.............	376	1,221	14	8,559	348	9,784
Carroll................	606	2,499	1	7,859	590	10,359
Catahoula.............	702	3,090	37	3,834	588	5,96[illegible]
Calcasieu..............	441	2,367	280	853	386	3,500
Natchitoches...........	1,131	5,141	982	7,670	982	13,793
Ouachita..............	570	2,531	7	3,237	499	5,775
Bossier................	656	3,130	14	5,648	588	3,792
Caldwell...............	389	1,906	0	1,460	357	3,366
Lafayette..............	720	3,767	215	3,649	682	7,631
St. Landry............	1,888	10,003	2,298	10,783	1,437	22,084
Morehouse............	734	2,701	27	2,698	672	5,426
Franklin..............	393	1,703	10	1,728	376	3,441
DeSoto................	864	3,764	0	5,416	832	9,180
Sabine................	717	3,472	2	1,218	624	4,692
Bienville..............	865	4,451	18	3,020	727	7,489
Union.................	1,236	5,863	0	3,530	1,080	9,392
Winn..................	354	2,032	33	567	360	2,632
Claiborne..............	1,221	6,709	0	3,890	1,000	10,599
Rapides...............	976	5,641	260	12,701	.....	18,548
Caddo.................	459	4,073	44	5,833	.....	9.950
Jackson...............	857	4,662	2	2,911	858	7,575
Vermillion.............	458	2,607	16	1,195	.....	3,818
	50,376	301,103	28,820	261,692	....	585,312

REVENUE FOR THE YEAR 1853.

Amount deposited by Union Bank of Louisiana, to secure the State against liabilities on account of bonds missing,	$21,000 00
Amount paid by R. C. Nichols, State Superintendent, on account of school moneys remaining in his hands,	80,413 97
Amount borrowed by the State from the Louisiana State Bank,	100,000 00
Amount paid by Jos. A. Aiklen for the purchase of the land of Mrs. Thompson on the Raccourci Cut-off, ...	237 70
Amount overpaid for the contingent expenses of the Legislature,	12 00
Amount refunded to the State for interest on bonds of the Third Municipality, paid by the State,	11,070 00
Amount received from the Union Bank of Louisiana, on account of the profits accruing to the State in settlement with said Bank,	47,000 00
Amount refunded to the State by the U. S. Government for advances made for equiping regiments during the Mexican war,	7,325 86
Amount of State taxes received from the following Parishes:	
Ascension,	6,929 00
Assumption,	7,351 70
Avoyelles,	2,786 47
Bossier,	499 50
Bienville,	2,058 14
Claiborne,	3,110 23
Caddo,	5,046 98
Calcasieu,	951 06
Caldwell,	578 86
Carroll,	7,133 93
Catahoula,	5,259 57
Concordia,	8,680 87
De Soto,	3,502 95
E. B. Rouge,	7,033 72
E. Feliciana,	9,340 00
Franklin,	1,322 19
Iberville,	9,457 65
Jackson,	2,054 30
Jefferson,	17,023 82
Lafayette,	2,303 59
Lafourche Interior,	6,182 05
Livingston,	895 57
Madison,	6,248 98
Morehouse,	1,517 68
Natchitoches,	4,818 79
Orleans, Right Bank,	1,879 07
First District, New Orleans,	43,266 84

Amount of State taxes received from the following Parishes :—*Continued.*

Second District, New Orleans,	$26,743 79
Third " "	7,468 76
Fourth " "	
Plaquemines,	5,144 60
Point Coupée,	4,074 02
Rapides,	7,765 94
Sabine,	939 36
St. Bernard,	2,346 51
St. Charles,	3,867 39
St. Helena,	1,600 05
St. James,	7,519 29
St. John the Baptist,	4,403 20
St. Landry,	
St. Martin,	5,153 74
St. Mary,	10,963 80
St. Tammany,	1,752 24
Tensas,	8,634 95
Terrebonne,	6,027 23
Union,	2,000 99
Vermillion,	729 13
Washington,	848 39
Washita,	2,585 68
W. B. Rouge,	5,185 91
W. Feliciana,	8,500 00
Winn,	466 25
Balance Contingent Fund of the Secretary of State's Office, paid by Chas. Gayarre, late Secretary of State,	526 20
Balance Contingent Fund of the Attorney General's Office, paid by Isaac Johnson, late Attorney General,	40 90
Duties on sales at Auction,	25,422 17
Dividend received from the Union bank of Louisiana,	108,529 27
Excess on appropriation to procure a block of marble for the Washington Monument paid in the Treasury,	150 00
Fines paid for the use of the Charity Hospital,	1,060 87
Interest paid by the Third Municipality of New Orleans on amount disbursed by the State, for payment of coupons of interest on bonds issued by the State to said Municipality,	1,854 70
Interest paid on redemptions of property adjudicated to the State,	208 12
Licences on trades, professions, &c., for 1852,	1,555 10
Leases of 16th sections of land,	107 06
Loan effected by the State Treasury,	750,000 00
Lease of the La. Penitentiary,	4,000 00
Money received for Overplus Bonds,	1,253 57
Mill Tax for 1850,	125 89

Mill Tax of 1851,	$5,796 32
Mill Tax of 1852,	242,699 63
Mill Tax of 1849,	1,758 11
Money deposited in the Treasury to reimburse taxes paid by purchasers of lands sold for taxes,	420 00
Poll Tax of 1850,	75 00
Poll Tax of 1851,	2,202 00
Proceeds of the sale of certain slaves for the year 1852,	2,061 15
Poll Tax for the year 1852,	36,406 00
Proceeds of the sale of public property in New Orleans,	4,698 12
Principal paid on redemptions of lands adjudicated to State,	655 28
Payments made on redemptions of lands adjudicated to individuals,	385 19
Proceeds of vacant estates paid into the Treasury,	938 82
Road and Levee funds,	5,765 73
Redemption of lands forfeited to the State, general fund paid,	1,863 04
Redemption of lands forfeited to the State, Mill Tax fund paid,	1,811 44
Sales of Reports of the Supreme Court,	1,577 69
Sales of Internal Improvement lands at Winnsboro',	4,330 11
Sales of 16th Sections of Land,	14,440 21
Sales of School Lands,	14,530 22
Sales of Lake Lands,	1,973 43
Sales of Seminary Lands,	3,695 82
Sales of Internal Improvement Lands at Baton Rouge,	12,941 92
Sales of Swamp and Overflowed Lands,	207,197 53
School Funds paid into the Treasury,	8,894 95
Taxes on Trades, Professions, &c., for 1853,	103,697 30
Taxes received from public officers, paid by fees,	19 10
Taxes levied on successions accruing to foreigners,	12,775 33
Amount balance on hand on the 31st December, 1852,	354,470 61
	$2,502,938 26

Said balance being composed of

General Fund,	$647,363 75
Mill Tax,	173,910 84
Poll Tax,	27,392 47
Internal Improvement Fund,	27,110 75
Levee and Drainage Fund,	273,988 84
Road and Levee Fund,	12,360 65
	$1,162,127 30

Payments during 1853, *as follows:*

For Free Public Schools, under Act No. 2, of 1853,	75,458 66
Under Act No. 8, of 1853,	58,694 85
Salaries of Public School Superintendents,	332 50

Acts Nos. 65, 158, 234 and 322 of 1853, ...	895 18	
Under Act No. 265 of 1852, for fiscal year, 1853, ...	119,671 05	
Under Act 326 of 1853, for account of fiscal year, ending March 31st, 1854,	87,276 94	
Collectors for deductions and commissions, and compensation to Assessors,	51,121 31—	$393,450 48
Internal Improvement Fund, ...		35,631 34
Levee and Drainage Fund, ...		11,543 73
General Funds, ...		899,817 75
		$1,340,443 30

STATEMENT Showing the number of Educable Children in 1851 and '53 as per Assessor's Returns, and the gross amount of Mill and Poll Tax for the year 1852.

PARISHES.	Number of educable children in 1851.	Number of educable children in 1853.	Male.	Female.	Gross amount of Mill Tax for the year 1852.	Gross amount of Poll Tax for the year 1852.
Ascension	869	882	425	457	$6329 00	$ 678 00
Assumption	1396	....	....	....	6687 73	1219 00
Avoyelles	918	1270	661	609	3436 22	842 00
Bienville	1248	1382	718	664	1871 22	126 00
Bossier	808	924	495	429	333 72	126 00
Caddo	1047	1218	667	351	4166 00	913 00
Calcasieu	723	772	401	891	837 71	377 00
Caldwell	484	569	300	269	194 70	136 00
Catahoula	1010	765	385	380	2417 62	759 00
Carroll	301	606	414	292	5983 50	750 00
Claiborne	1553	1933	1041	912	2800 90	1257 00
Concordia	297	335	187	168	7339 50	259 00
De Soto	1036	1210	628	582	3309 25	756 00
East Baton Rouge	1259	1481	771	710	6443 20	850 00
East Feliciana	993	1008	520	488	8209 81	866 00
Franklin	356	455	241	212	1024 45	359 00
Iberville	781	855	453	402	8599 78	947 00
Jackson	948	....	....	....	1862 75	924 00
Jefferson	927	999	521	478		
Jefferson City	597	551	267	284	2795 15	2010 00
Carrollton	495	450	214	236		
Lafayette	1000	1032	559	473	2086 45	698 00
Lafourche	1671	1850	928	922	5620 95	1285 00
Thibodaux	135	....	....	....	.... ..	.... ..
Livingston	684	....	....	....	797 84	570 00
Madison	283	323	175	148	5818 38	375 00
Morehouse	549	....	....	....	1425 29	681 00
Natchitoches	1446	1370	740	630	4380 67	1155 00
Orleans, Right Bank	345	302	146	156	1708 25	472 00
" First District	5055	4282				
" Second "	3430	4523				
" Third "	3073	3253	....	....	70198 32	7507 00
" Fourth "	3263	3284				
Plaquemines	381	273	....	....	4677 01	417 00
Point Coupée	945	742	....	....	1000 00	... ..
Rapides	1787	....	....	....	2604 50	... ..
Sabine	930	1099	579	520	782 09	716 00
St. Bernard	361	402	228	178	2044 55	281 00
St. Charles	266	....	....	....	3524 90	210 00
St. Helena	731	785	430	355	1454 51	555 00
St. James	977	1035	510	515	6855 81	713 00
St. John Baptist	704	....	....	....	3694 82	617 90
St. Landry	2632	2333	1276	1057	.... ..	... ..
St. Martin	1167	1356	....	....	4685 82	999 00
St. Mary	899	....	....	....	9987 55	821 00
St. Tammany	818	780	396	384	1617 32	571 00
Tensas	224	264	137	127	7128 00	386 00
Terrebonne	1042	1234	666	568	5479 30	754 00
Union	1604	1720	911	809	1834 03	1180 00
Vermillion	764	....	....	....	667 80	256 00
Washington	704	....	....	....	769 54	592 00
Washita	630	966	396	270	2346 43	615 00
West Baton Rouge	520	476	....	....	4665 38	366 00
West Feliciana	514	579	317	362	6695 01	534 00
Winn	371	630	348	282	423 84	394 00
	58,524	52,457	17,951	16,360	249,827 75	38,683 00

STATEMENT Showing Amount Appropriations to each Parish from March 31st to December 31st, 1853.

NAMES OF PARISHES.	Apport. March 31st. 1853.	Apport. June 30th, 1853.	Apport. Sept. 30th, 1853.	Apport. Dec'r 31st, 1853.
Ascension	$1230 31	$ 745 59	$ 938 52	$ 938 52
Assumption	1664 20	1369 36	1723 68	1723 68
Avoyelles	931 27	848 56	1068 12	1068 12
Bienville	976 44	1070 78	1347 84	1347 84
Bossier	819 70	693 36	872 64	872 64
Caddo	888 87	898 32	1130 76	1130 76
Calcasieu	569 46	620 33	780 84	780 84
Caldwell	532 18	415 27	522 72	522 72
Catahoula	1770 97	866 58	901 80	901 80
Carroll	863 72	429 85	541 08	541 08
Claiborne	1427 40	1332 47	1677 24	1677 24
Concordia	988 79	254 92	320 76	320 76
De Soto	931 41	888 88	1118 88	1118 88
East Baton Rouge	1398 70	1077 22	1359 72	1359 72
East Feliciana	1317 35	850 99	1072 44	1072 44
Franklin	740 3	305 04	384 48	384 48
Iberville	2062 69	670 09	843 48	843 48
Jackson	779 53	8[illegible]3 38	1023 84	1023 84
Jefferson	971 01	797 08	1001 16	1001 16
Jefferson City	394 02	511 12	446 76	644 76
Carrollton	326 70	426 71	534 60	534 60
Lafayette	872 74	858 00	1080 00	1080 00
Lafourche	1695 32	1433 71	1804 68	1804 68
Thibodaux	89 10	115 83	.... ..	.... ..
Livingston	521 16	586 87	738 72	738 72
Madison	762 09	242 81	305 64	305 64
Morehouse	489 37	471 04	592 92	392 92
Natchitoches	1425 35	1240 66	1561 68	1561 68
Orleans, Right Bank	366 72	296 01	372 60	372 60
" 1st District	4026 84	4337 19	.... ..	.... ..
" 2d "	3726 28	2942 94	16006 68	16006 68
" 3d "	2239 35	2636 63	.... ..	....
" 4th "	2153 58	27[illegible]9 65	.... ..	....
Plaquemines	746 41	326 89	411 48	411 48
Point Coupée	1123 52	800 81	1020 60	1020 60
Rapides	1759 61	1533 24	1939 96	1939 96
Sabine	669 93	797 94	1004 40	1004 40
St. Bernard	449 38	309 73	389 88	389 88
St. Charles	556 30	231 22	287 08	287 08
St. Helena	550 06	627 19	789 48	789 48
St. James	1028 06	838 26	1055 16	1055 16
St. John Baptist	634 26	404 03	760 32	60 32
St. Landry	1737 12	2258 25	2842 56	2842 56
St. Martin	1091 57	1087 08	1368 36	1368 36
St. Mary	1629 30	771 34	970 92	970 92
St. Tammany	713 55	701 84	883 44	883 44
Tensas	885 78	192 19	241 92	241 92
Terrebonne	1210 10	694 03	1125 36	1125 36
Union	1206 03	1376 23	1732 32	1732 32
Vermillion	835 64	655 51	825 12	825 12
Washington	541 07	604 03	760 32	760 32
Washita	636 74	540 54	680 40	680 40
West Baton Rouge	784 90	447 16	561 60	561 60
West Feliciana	910 17	441 01	555 12	555 12
Winn	244 86	318 32	589 68	589 68
	59917 18	50203 98	63067 76	63067 76

STATEMENT Showing the amount of School funds paid out during the year 1853.

PARISHES.	Amounts paid out of moneys returned by State Superintendent, under No. 2, of Acts of 1853, to Teachers up to June 30th, 1853.	Amounts paid out of moneys returned by State Superintendent to Parish Treasurers, subsequent to June 30th, 1853.	Amounts paid out of moneys returned by Parish Superintendents from February 2nd, to June 30th, 1853, to Teachers.	Amounts paid out of money returned by Parish Superintendents to Parish Treasurers, subsequent to June 30th, 1853.	Amount paid to Teachers out of the apportionment of March 31st, 1853, ending June 30th, 1854.	Amount of money paid to Parish Treasurers, out of the apportionment of March 31st, 1853.	Amount paid to Parish Treasurers, out of the apportionment of June 30th 1853.	Amounts paid out of the apportionment of Sept. 30th, 1853, up to January 1st, 1854.	Amounts paid by Tax Collectors out of the apportionment of December 31st, 1853, and subsequent to 31st of December, 1853.	Amounts paid by Tax Collectors on the apportionment of March 31st, 1854.	Amount paid out of moneys returned by Parish Superintendents by R. C. Nicholas.
Ascension	$1105 81	$ 42 13	$1815 36	$1732 78	$ 857 87	$ 475 43	$ 745 59	$ 938 52	$	$	$1635 64
Assumption	1964 21		1431 37	127 62	971 25	673 00	1369 36	1723 68			762 75
Avoyelles	1131 49	1148 83	305 50	951 97	151 47	778 25	848 56	1068 12	1068 12	1068 12	
Bienville	299 50	2327 29			91 10	854 44	1070 78				
Bossier	645 46	2426 08			12 30		693 36				
Caddo	692 49				205 86						
Calcasieu	85 65		205 60		333 05						
Caldwell	191 61	639 21		55 02	59 67	463 87	415 27				
Catahoula	220 09				427 81						
Carroll	417 22		1582 61		151 06						575 74
Claiborne	1206 79	990 83			412 20		1332 47	1677 24	1192 29		
Concordia	432 68	843 64	733 95	1791 58	117 15	893 08	254 82				
DeSoto	509 57				146 25		888 88	1116 88	1118 88	1113 88	
East Baton Rouge	628 61		244 73	539 79	916 76	191 17	1078 22	1359 72	1359 72		741 80
East Feliciana	1292 28	728 23	1140 18	966 83	257 74	844 98	850 99				393 86
Franklin	119 97	221 40			114 34	637 32	305 04				
Iberville	1633 84	1044 96	111 51	4790 29	916 45	1129 09	670 09				

STATEMENT *Showing amount of School Funds paid out during the year* 1853.—*Continued.*

PARISHES.	Am. paid out of moneys returned by S. S., under No. 2, of Acts of '53 to Teachers, up to June 30, 1853.	Am. paid out of moneys returned by S. S. to Parish Treasurers, subsequent to June 30, 1853.	Am. paid out of moneys returned by P. S., from Feb. 2, to June 30, 1853, to Teachers.	Amts. paid out of money returned by P. S., to Parish Treasurers, subsequent to June 30th, 1853.	Amts. paid to Teachers out of the apportionment of March 31st, 1853, ending June 30th, 1853.	Amount of money paid to Parish Treasurers, out of the apportionment of March 31st, 1853.	Amounts paid to Parish Treasurers out of the apportionment of June 30, 1853.	Amounts paid out of the apportionment of Sept. 30th, 1853, up to January 1st, 1853.	Amounts paid by Tax Collectors out of apportionment of Dec. 31, 1853, and subsequent to 31st of Dec. 1853.	Amounts paid by Tax Collectors on the apportionment of March 31st, 1854.	Amount paid out of moneys returned by Parish Superintendents by R. C. Nicholas.
Jackson	735 68	334 72	259 79	187 38	309 71	371 22	813 38	1023 84	1023 84	132 57	418 11
Jefferson	1228 69	....	....	....	971 01	....	797 08	....	....	....	....
Jefferson City	1282 55	....	....	....	394 02	....	511 12	....	....	....	....
Carrollton	....	....	....	....	326 70	....	426 71	....	....	....	....
Lafayette	199 75	140 37	....	....	642 30	57 14	858 00	1080 00	....	....	....
Lafourche	969 22	....	3972 08	5766 57	172 69	1370 11	1433 71	1804 68	1804 68	....	1253 03
Thibodeaux	229 50	....	....	....	89 10	....	115 83	....	....	....	....
Livingston	537 71	533 01	19 22	235 52	170 49	309 32	586 87	738 72	738 72	....	112 66
Madison	91 80	....	1734 80	2768 39	....	600 56	242 81	....	....	....	268 83
Morehouse	724 87	39 45	....	....	408 86	62 67	471 04	592 92	592 92	540 12	....
Natchitoches	795 46	1901 28	115 33	1205 66	146 50	1246 02	1240 66	1561 68	1561 68	1561 68	17 23
Orleans, R. Bank	994 79	....	....	....	366 72	....	296 01	....	....	....	....
" 1st Dist.				....	....	....	4337 19	....	....	....	....
" 2d "	10951 47			....	12146 05	....	2942 94	16006 68	16006 68	....	....
" 3d "				....	....	....	2636 63	....	....	....	....
" 4th "				....	....	....	2799 65	....	....	....	....
Plaquemines	1217 52	....	1652 72	....	233 21	....	....	....	....	....	....
Point Coupee	925 06	729 74	....	434 32	297 65	685 83	800 80	1020 60	9 72	....	545 23
Rapides	2432 52	738 95	....	....	718 69	884 90	1533 24	....	....	....	....
Sabine	501 39	....	700 60	....	....	....	797 94	1004 40	287 21	....	349 30

STATEMENT Showing amount of School Funds paid out during the year 1853.—Continued.

PARISHES.	Amts. paid out of moneys returned by S. S., under No. 2, of Acts of 1853, to Teachers, up to June 30, 1853.	Amounts paid out of moneys returned by S. S., to Parish Treasurers, subsequent to June 30, 1853.	Amounts paid out of moneys returned by Parish Superintendents from Feb. 2, to June 30, 1853, to Teachers.	Amounts paid out of money returned by P. S., to Parish Treasurers, subsequent to June 30, 1853.	Amts. paid to Teachers out of the apportionment of March 31st, 1853, ending June 30th, 1853.	Amount of money paid to Parish Treasurers out of the apportionment of March 31st, 1853.	Amounts paid to Parish Treasurers out of the apportionment of June 30, 1853.	Amounts paid out of the apportionment of Sept. 30th, 1853, up to Jan. 1st, 1854.	Amounts paid by Tax Collectors out of the apportionment of Dec. 31st, 1853, and subsequent to 31st of Dec., 1853.	Amounts paid by Tax Collectors on the apportionment of March 31st, 1854.	Amount paid out of moneys returned by Parish Superintendents by R. C. Nicholas.
St. Bernard......	197 10	363 07	....	....	....	447 64	309 73	389 88	389 88	389 88	....
St. Charles........	....	....	1571 56	....	....	....	....	....	....	....	252 68
St. Helena........	1056 07	433 60	64 44	116 70	251 33	316 29	627 19	789 48	789 48	....	....
St. James.........	887 02	163 90	29 63	20 86	898 94	156 45	838 26	1055 16	1055 16	1055 16	....
St. John Baptist.	516 40	565 06	....	....	278 78	286 20	604 05	....	....	....	....
St. Landry.......	3116 16	....	....	....	1075 66	....	....	....	....	....	....
St. Martin........	808 06	115 23	....	....	886 50	305 07	1087 08	1368 36	1368 36	1368 36	....
St. Mary..........	1334 00	2034 31	2417 24	2316 55	....	1629 71	771 34	970 92	970 92	970 92	....
St. Tammany....	652 25	431 84	627 91	1853 41	53 15	556 54	701 84	....	....	....	....
Tensas............	768 45	1958 55	377 26	1022 74	30 00	854 80	192 19	241 92	241 92	241 92	....
Terrebonne.......	880 59	663 10	2160 32	2507 59	67 28	1134 08	894 03	....	....	241 92	446 27
Union.............	1651 55	....	573 97	....	398 72	806 06	1376 23	1732 32	....	....	172 51
Vermillion........	56 06	....	617 41	....	578 51	604 03	....	....	....	....	431 11
Washington......	449 62	....	....	43 94	339 00	....	....	....	....	....	....
Washita...........	408 40	....	....	....	163 62	....	....	680 40	....	....	....
W. Baton Rouge.	155 99	129 80	669 77	....	726 44	48 96	446 16	561 60	561 60	....	526 88
West Feliciana...	536 65	615 04	2068 10	1878 39	379 90	518 80	441 01	....	....	....	1069 32
Winn.............	168 74	....	....	....	192 19	196 95	318 32	589 68	167 54	....	....
	51008 37	22313 42	27202 76	33313 90	29908 15	20659 21	43376 50	41099 40	32309 32	8447 61	9972 95

Apportionment of Representation in the House of Representatives by the Legislature of 1854.—Representative Number 7,000.

PARISHES AND DISTRICTS.	Population.	No. of Representatives,	Fractions under.	Fractions over.
Plaquemines,	6,348	1	652	....
St. Bernard,	4,011	1	2,989	....
Orleans, Right Bank,	3,404	1	3,596	....
" 1st Representative Dist.	13,457	2	143	......
" 2d do	18,679	3	2,321	....
" 3d do	23,243	3	......	2,243
" 4th do	15,053	2	......	1,053
" 5th do	14,415	2	......	415
" 6th do	15,905	2	......	1,905
" 7th do	12,451	2	1,549	....
" 8th do	11,769	2	2,231	....
" 9th do	9,449	1	......	2,449
Fourth District, Lafayette,	18,586	3	2,418	....
Jefferson,	14,625	2	......	625
St. Charles,	5,734	1	1,268	......
St. John the Baptist,	6,674	1	326	......
St. James,	12,464	2	1,536	......
Ascension,	10,622	2	3,378	......
Assumption,	12,572	2	1,428	......
Lafourche Interior,	12,134	2	1,866	......
Terrebonne,	9,963	1	......	2,963
St. Mary,	15,101	2	......	1,101
St. Martin,	12,977	2	1,023	......
Iberville,	15,112	2	......	1,112
West Baton Rouge,	6,060	1	940	......
East Baton Rouge,	15,916	2	......	1,916
Livingston,	3,734	1	3,266	......
St Helena,	5,105	1	1,895	......
Washington,	3,491	1	3,509	......
St. Tammany,	4,409	1	2,591	......
East Feliciana,	13,825	2	175	......
West Feliciana,	12,679	2	1,321	......
Point Coupée,	11,739	2	2,261	......
Avoyelles,	9,853	1	......	2,853
Madison,	8,726	1	......	1,726
Tensas,	10,253	1	......	3,233
Concordia,	9,794	1	......	2,794
Carroll,	10,359	1	......	3,359
Catahoula,	6,961	1	39	......
Calcasieu,	3,500	1	3,500	......
Natchitoches,	13,793	2	290	......
Ouashita,	5,775	1	1,225	......
Bossier,	8,792	1	......	1,792
Caldwell,	3,366	1	3,634	......
Lafayette,	7,631	1	......	631

Apportionment of Representation in the House of Rep.—Continued.

PARISHES AND DISTRICTS.	Population.	No. of Representatives.	Fractions under.	Fractions over.
St. Landry,	22,084	3	......	1,084
Morehouse,	5,426	1	1,574	......
Franklin,	3,451	1	3,559	......
De Soto,	9,180	1	......	2,180
Sabine,	4,692	1	2,308	......
Bienville,	7,489	1	......	489
Union,	9,393	1	......	2,373
Claiborne,	10,599	2	3,401	......
Winn,	2,632	1	4,368	......
Rapides,	18,548	3	2,452	......
Caddo,	9,950	1	......	3,950
Jackson,	7,575	1	......	575
Vermillion,	3,818	1	......	3,182
		88		

SENATORIAL RATIO, 16,011.

No. of Districts	Senatorial Districts.	Population.	No. of Senat'rs
No. 1	Plaquemines......	6,348	
	St. Bernard.......	4,011	
	Orleans, Right Bank	3,404	
		13,763	1
2	City of New Orleans	153,007	5
3	Jefferson.........	14,625	1
4	St. Charles........	5,734	
	Lafourche........	12,134	
		17,868	1
5	St. John the Baptist	6,674	
	St. James.........	12,462	
		19,136	1
6	Ascension........	10,622	
	Assumption.......	12,574	
	Terrebonne........	9,963	
		33,159	2
7	Iberville..........	15,122	1
8	East Baton Rouge.	15,916	1
9	West Baton Rouge.	6,060	
	Point Coupée	11,737	
	West Feliciana....	12,679	
		30,476	2
10	East Feliciana....	13,825	1
11	Washington........	3,491	
	St. Tammany......	4,409	
	St. Helena........	5,105	
	Livingston........	3,734	
		16,739	1
12	Concordia........	9,794	
	Tensas...........	10,233	
		20,027	1

No. of Districts	Senatorial Districts.	Population.	No. of Senat'rs
13	Madison..........	8,726	
	Carroll...........	10,359	
		14,085	1
14	Morehouse	5,426	
	Ouachita.........	5,775	
	Jackson..........	7,575	
	Union...........	9,393	
		28,169	2
15	Catahoula........	6,961	
	Caldwell.........	3,366	
	Franklin.........	3,441	
		13,768	1
16	Claiborne........	10,599	
	Bossier	8,792	
	Bienville.........	7,489	
	Winn............	2,632	
		29,512	2
17	DeSoto..........	9,180	
	Caddo...........	9,950	
	Sabine..........	4,692	
	Natchitoches......	13,793	
		37,615	2
18	St. Landry	22,084	
	Lafayette	7,631	
	Calcasieu	3,500	
		33,215	2
19	St. Martin........	12,977	
	Vermillion	3,818	
		16,795	1
20	St. Mary	15,101	1
21	Rapides..........	18,548	
	Avoyelles	9,853	
		28,601	2

CHUCHES IN LOUISIANA.

Parish	Number of	Churches,		—Value,	
Ascension,	Number of	Churches,	3	—Value,	$60,000
Assumption,	"	"	3	"	31,000
Avoyelles,	"	"	3	"	5,000
East Baton Rouge,	"	"	4	"	25,000
West Baton Rouge,	"	"	2	"	8,000
Bienville,	"	"	12	"	2,370
Bossier,	"	"	5	"	3,200
Caddo,	"	"	8	"	......
Calcasieu,	"	"	–	"	......
Caldwell,	"	"	7	"	600
Carroll,	"	"	4	"	6,120
Catahoula,	"	"	14	"	4,700
Claiborne,	"	"	10	"	6,600
Concordia,	"	"	1	"	500
De Soto,	"	"	6	"	3,200
East Feliciana,	"	"	9	"	11,900
West Feliciana,	"	"	7	"	9,500
Franklin,	"	"	3	"	200
Iberville,	"	"	7	"	24,050
Jackson,	"	"	12	"	2,400
Jefferson,	"	"	11	"	102,000
Lafayette,	"	"	1	"	2,000
Lafourche,	"	"	3	"	17,800
Levingston,	"	"	14	"	2,400
Madison,	"	"	5	"	1,580
Morehouse,	"	"	1	"	1,200
Natchitoches,	"	"	13	"	20,275
Orleans,	"	"	30	"	1,205,500
Ouachita,	"	"	1	"	500
Plaquemines,	"	"	2	"	7.000
Point Coupée,	"	"	2	"	4,000
Rapides,	"	"	4	"	12,250
Sabine,	"	"	16	"	1,500
St. Bernard,	"	"	1	"	5,000
St. Charles,	"	"	1	"	10,000
St. Helena,	"	"	14	"	4,475
St. James,	"	"	2	"	18,000
St. John the Baptist,	"	"	1	"	8,000
St. Landry,	"	"	6	"	93,000
St. Martin,	"	"	4	"	28,000
St. Mary,	"	"	6	"	11,000
St. Tammany,	"	"	14	"	10,000
Tensas,	"	"	3	"	1,400
Terrebonne,	"	"	3	"	6,800
Union,	"	"	11	"	3,150
Termillion,	"	"	8	"	500
Washington,	"	"	9	"	1,900
				Total Value,	$1,782,470

Aggregate Church accommodations, for 109,615 persons.

NEWSPAPERS IN THE STATE.

IN NEW ORLEANS.—*Bee, Commercial Bulletin, Crescent, Delta, Louisiana Courier, Orleanian, Picayune, True Delta, Prices Current, DeBow's Commercial Review, German Gazette, Medical and Surgical Journal, Creole, Southern Organ, Statesman, Spectator, Southern Journal, Republican, Propath Catholique, Coup D' Oeil, L. Semaine, German Paper.*

IN OTHER PORTIONS OF THE STATE.—*Vigilant*, Donaldsonville; *Pioneer*, Napoleonville; *Villager*, Marksville; *Advocate*, Baton Rouge; *Gazette*, Baton Rouge; *Comet*, Baton Rouge; *Capitolian Vis-a-Vis*, West Baton Rouge; *Bienville Times*, Mt. Lebanon; *Gazette*, Shreveport; *Democrat*, Shreveport; *Southwestern*, Shreveport; *Herlad*, Lake Providence; *Courier*, Opelousas; *Herald*, Waterproof; *Advocate*, Trinity; *Independent*, Harrisonburg; *Herald*, Minden; *Advocate*, Homer; *Intelligencer*, Vidalia; *Advertiser*, Mansfield; *Mirror*, Jackson; *State Paper*, Clinton; *Whig*, Clinton; *Ledger*, Bayou Sara; *Chronicle*, Bayou Sara; *Gazette*, Plaquemine; *Sentinel*, Plaquemine; *Carrollton Star*, Carrollton; *The Echo*, Vermillionville; *Register*, Monroe; *Banner*, Franklin; *Chronicle*, Natchitoches; *Independent*, Abbeville; *Courier*, St. Martinsville; *Gazette*, Opelousas; *Whig*, Opelousas; *Minerva*, Thibodeaux; *Piny Woodsman*, Livingston; *Journal*, Richmond; *North Louisianian*, Bastrop; *Echo*, Point Coupee; *Democrat*, Alexandria; *Republican*, Alexandria; *Meschacebe*, St. Charles; *Messenger*, St. James; *Advocate*, Covington; *Inquirer*, Farmersville; *New Orleans Medical News and Hospital Gazette*, New Orleans; *Coast Journal*, Donaldsonville.

MORTALITY OF THE YELLOW FEVER IN 1853.

New Orleans, from May to Dec. 30		12,151
Ascension,	" "	50
Assumption,	" "	50
Caddo,	" "	250
Carroll,	" "	166
Concordia,	" "	40
East Baton Rouge,	" "	250
East Feliciana,	" "	50
Lafourche,	" "	160
Madison,	" "	35
Point Coupee,	" "	150
Natchitoches,	" "	130
Rapides,	" "	90
St. Charles,	" "	150
St. John Baptist,	" "	250
St. James,	" "	400
St. Landry,	" "	90
Iberville,	" "	50
West Feliciana,	" "	90
Total		14602

No returns of other Parishes.

POPULATION OF THE STATE OF LOUISIANA, FROM 1810 to 1850 INCLUSIVE.

Parishes.	Whites.					Free Colored.					Slaves.					Aggregate Population.				
	1810.	1820.	1830.	1840.	1850.	1810.	1820.	1830.	84 0.	1850.	1810.	1820.	1830.	1840.	1850.	18 10.	1820.	1330.	1840.	1850.
Ascension,	1,141	1,495	1,725	2,255	3,340	47	104	134	143	146	1,031	2,129	3,567	4,553	7,266	2,219	3,728	5,426	6,951	10,752
Assumption,	1,915	2,409	3,760	4,103	5,170	10	18	28	50	27	547	1,149	1,881	2,988	5,341	2,472	3,576	5,669	7,141	10,538
Avoyelles,	783	1,438	2,114	3,066	4,059	22	25	35	78	106	404	782	1,335	3,472	5,161	1,209	2,245	3,484	6,616	9,326
Baton Rouge, East,	706	3,012	3,168	3,750	5,347	82	132	182	182	279	675	2,076	3,348	4,206	6,351	1,463	5,220	6,698	8,138	11,977
Baton Rouge, West,		908	1,004	1,371	1,815		124	148	120	105		1,303	1,932	3,147	4,350		2,335	3,084	4,638	6,270
Bienville,					3,623					21					1,895					5,539
Bossier,					2,507										4,455					6,962
Caddo,				2,416	3,634				29	42				2,837	5,208				5,282	8,884
Calcasieu,				1,349	2,718				226	239				482	957				2,057	3,914
Caldwell,				1,354	1,584				14					649	1,231				2,017	2,815
Carroll,				1,146	2,336				9	10				3,082	6,443				4,237	8,789
Catahoula,	808	1,524	1,643	2,935	3,585	8	12	18	22	19	348	751	920	1,998	3,528	1,164	2,287	2,581	4,955	7,132
Claiborne,			1,539	3,846	4,949			10	44				215	2,295	2,522			1,764	6,185	7,471
Concordia,	1,279	827	1,025	1,380	823	35	12	20	31	1	1,581	1,787	3,617	8,003	6,934	2,895	2,626	4,662	9,414	7,758
DeSoto,					3,549					24					4,450					8,023
Feliciana, East,			3,571	3,992	4,060			24	30	24			4,652	7,871	9,514			8,247	11,893	13,598
Feliciana, West,		5,499	2,019	2,064	2,473		69	94	91	106		7,164	6,345	8,755	10,666		12,732	9,629	10,910	13,245
Franklin,					1,664					14					1,573					3,251
Iberville.	1,429	2,019	2,380	2,523	3,568	45	16	161	85	104	1,205	2,279	4,508	5,887	8,606	2,679	4,414	7,049	8,495	12,278
Jackson,					3,406					2					2,158					5,566
Jefferson			1,596	4,866	18,046			343	618	851			4,907	4,986	6,196			6,846	10,470	25,094
Lafayette,			3,177	4,474	3,390			109	134	160			2,367	3,233	3,170			5,653	7,841	6,720
Lafourche,	1,691	2,659	3,310	3,986	5,142	15	128	40	71	22	289	968	2,153	3,246	4,368	1,995	3,755	5,503	7,303	9,532
Livingston,				1,533	2,524				43	19				739	842				2,315	3,385
Madison,				1,210	1,416				9	4				3,923	7,353				5,142	8,773
Morehouse,					1,877					30					2,006					3,913
Natchitoches,	1,213	4,745	3,802	7,042	5,466	181	415	532	657	881	1,476	2,326	3,571	6,651	7,881	2,870	7,486	7,905	14,350	14,228
Orleans,	8,001	19,244	21,281	59,519	91,431	5,727	7,161	11,906	19,226	9,961	10,824	14,946	16,639	23,448	18,068	24,552	41,351	49,826	102,193	119,460
Ouachita,	784	2,016	2,938	2,188	2,292	9	44	57	14	8	284	836	2,145	2,438	2,708	1,077	2,896	5,140	4,640	5,008
Plaquemines,	557	637	1,082	1,351	2,221	239	151	219	324	390	753	1,566	3,188	3,385	4,779	1,549	2,354	4,489	5,060	7,390
Point Coupee,	1,248	1,092	1,471	2,087	2,968	104	190	255	381	560	3,187	3,630	4,210	5,430	7,811	4,539	4,912	5,936	7,898	16,339
Rapides,	996	2,491	2,133	3,243	5,037	123	85	113	378	184	1,081	3,489	5,329	10,511	11,340	2,200	6,065	7,575	14,132	11,561
Sabine,					3,347										1,168					4,515
Carried forward,	20,860	42,095	62,644	128,849	209,457	6,647	8,686	14,428	23,010	14,623	23,685	47,081	66,829	128,215	175,289	52,883	107,982	156,034	280,283	399,905

POPULATION OF THE STATE OF LOUISIANA, FROM 1810 TO 1850, INCLUSIVE.—*Concluded.*

Parishes.	Whites.					Free Colored.					Slaves.					Aggregate Population.				
	1810.	1820.	1830.	1840.	1850.	1810.	1820.	1830.	1840.	1850.	1810.	1820.	1830.	1840.	1850.	1810.	1820.	1830.	1840.	1850.
Brought forward,	20,860	42,095	62,644	128,849	209,457	6,647	8,686	14,428	23,010	14,628	23,685	47,081	66,829	128,215	175,289	52,883	107,982	156,034	280,283	399,905
St. Bernard,	628	667	780	1,035	1,406	10	45	57	65	73	382	1,923	2,519	2,137	2,323	1,020	2,635	3,356	3,237	3,802
St. Charles,	820	727	871	874	867	150	148	158	104	121	2,321	2,987	4,118	3,722	4,132	3,291	3,862	5,147	4,700	5,120
St. Helena,		2,164	2,624	1,945	2,354		32	45	7	11		830	1,359	1,573	2,196		3,026	4,028	3,525	4,561
St. James,	1,962	2,522	2,557	2,762	3,285	41	52	60	75	62	1,952	3,086	5,029	5,711	7,751	3,955	5,660	7,646	8,548	11,098
St. John Baptist,	1,402	1,532	1,980	2,141	2,586	70	113	204	191	191	1,518	2,209	3,493	3,444	4,540	2,990	3,854	5,677	5,776	7,317
St. Landry,			6,712	7,179	10,140			909	925	1,242			4,970	7,129	10,871			12,591	15,233	22,253
St. Martin,			2,810	3,549	4,743			408	484	529			3,987	4,641	6,489			7,205	8,674	11,761
St. Mary,			1,912	2,366	3,423			226	298	424			4,304	6,286	9,850			6,442	8,950	13,697
St. Tammany,		1,053	1,318	2,353	3,642		39	186	305	359		631	1,360	1,940	2,363		1,723	2,864	4,598	6,364
Tensas,					900					2					8,138					9,040
Terrebonne,			1,063	2,075	3,305			25	35	91			1,033	2,300	4,328			2,121	4,410	7,724
Union,				1,273	4,778				2					563	3,425				1,838	8,203
Vermillion,					2,328					14					1,067					3,409
Washington,		1,957	1,695	1,856	2,367		1	4	2	4		559	587	791	1,037		2,517	2,286	2,649	3,408
Winn,																				
Attakapas,	3,959	5,862				278	494				3,132	5,707				7,369	12,063			
Opelousas,	2,989	5,368				389	766				1,670	3,951				5,048	10,085			
Total,	34,311	73,867	89,231	158,457	255,491	7,585	10,476	16,710	25,502	17,462	34,660	69,064	109,588	163,452	244,809	76,556	153,407	215,739	352,411	517,762

It appears that of the Frce Population of Louisiana in 1850, amounted to 272,953, something over one half are natives of this State, more than one fifth natives of other States of the Union, and nearly one fourth foreign born.

As follows:

Natives of Louisiana,	145,474
Natives of the other States of the Union,	60,447
Foreign born,	66,413
Places of birth unknown,	679
	272,953

Of the 66,413 foreign born, there are—

English,	2,550
Irish,	24,266
Scotch,	1,196
Welsh,	48
Germans,	17,507
French,	11,552
Spanish,	1,417
Partuguese,	157
Belgian,	115
Hollanders,	112
Turks,	48
Italians,	915
Austrians,	156
Swiss,	723
Russians,	65
Norwegians,	64
Danes,	288
Swedes,	249
Prussians,	380
Sardinians,	9
Greeks,	23
Chinese,	33
Asiatics,	17
Africans,	90
British Americans,	499
Mexicans,	405
West Indians,	1,337
Other foreign countries,	1,192
Total foreign born,	66,413

Of the natives of the other States of the Union, there are—

Marylanders,	1,440
Virginians,	3,216
North Carolinians,	2,923
South Carolinans,	4,583
Georgians,	5,917
Floridians,	372

Alabamians, ... 7,346
Mississippians, ... 10,913
Texans, ... 864
Arkansians, ... 803
Tennesseeans, ... 3,352
Kentuckians, ... 2.968

The true valuation of the real and personal estate within the United States, exclusively the District of Columbia and the Territories, by the Census of 1850, was, ... $7,067,157,179
That of Louisiana was, ... 233,998,764

The number of Slave owners in the State is about 20,670. In tho following ratio

Those owning one slave, is........ 4,797
" " one and under five........ 6,072
" " five and under ten........ 4,327
" " ten and under twenty........ 2,652
" " twenty and under fifty........ 1,774
" " fifty and under one hundred........ 728
" " one hundred and under two hundred........ 274
" " two hundred and under three hundred........ 36
" " three hundred and under five hundred........ 6
" " five hundred and under one thousand........ 4

Making a total of slave owners........ 20,670

The State of Louisiana contains area of 46,631 square miles, or about 29,615,840 acres.

The value of land in farms, in the whole State is estimated at $75,814,398.

The returns of births and deaths among the whites and free colored of the State for 1850, show

Births, ... 7,292
Deaths, ... 6,083

Adults in the State who cannot Read nor Write, according to the Census of 1850.

White Males, ... 9,842
" Females, ... 11,379

Total, ... 21,221

Free Colored Males, ... 1,038
" " Females, ... 2,351

Total, ... 3,389

Native, ... 18,339
Foreign, ... 6,271

Aggregate, ... $24,610

Births, White and Free Colored,	7,292
Slaves,	494
Total Births,	12,232
Marriages, Whites,	2,890
Deaths, White and Free Colored,	6,083
" Slaves,	5,873
Total,	11,956

Professions, Occupations, and Trades, of the Male Population of Louisiana.—Census of 1850.

Occupation	Number	Occupation	Number
Actors,	48	Coppersmiths,	69
Agents,	86	Cordweiners,	1,102
Apothecaries and druggists,	205	Cotton packers,	31
Architecrs,	30	Cutlers,	7
Artists,	59	Daguerreotypists,	3
Astronomical instrument makers,	6	Dairymen,	63
Anctioneers,	37	Dealers,	29
Bakers,	591	Dentists,	62
Bankers,	25	Drivers,	295
Bank officers,	23	Dyers,	21
Barbers,	315	Editors,	58
Barkeepers,	747	Engineers,	538
Basket makers,	25	Engravers,	53
Black and white smiths,	989	Farmers,	11,697
Block and pump makers,	8	Farriers,	5
Boarding-house keepers,	123	Fire-work makers,	5
Boat builders,	5	Fishermen,	477
Boatmen,	1,383	Foundrymen,	37
Boiler makers,	29	Fruiterers,	187
Bookbinders,	30	Furriers,	5
Booksellers and stationers,	27	Gardeners and florists,	471
Bottlers,	15	Gas makers,	9
Brass founders,	14	Gate-keepers,	5
Brewers and distillers,	47	Gold and Silver Smiths,	27
Brick makers,	76	Grocers,	755
Brokers,	306	Gunsmiths,	98
Brush makers,	5	Hair-workers,	5
Builders,	90	Hat and cap manufacturers,	79
Butchers,	548	Horse dealers,	17
Cabinet and chair makers,	336	Insurance company officers,	9
Carpenters,	4,571	Ice dealers,	13
Carpet makers,	5	Inn keepers,	358
Carriers,	36	Inspectors,	31
Carters and draymen,	1,076	Jewellers,	122
Carvers and gilders,	33	Joiners,	181
Cattle dealers,	11	Laborers	12,978
Caulkers,	110	Lath makers,	3
Chandlers,	30	Lawyers,	622
Charcoal burners,	34	Lithographers,	9
Chemists,	4	Livery-stable keepers,	49
City, county, and town officers,	285	Locksmiths,	45
Civil engineers,	8	Lumbermen,	106
Clergymen,	229	Machinists,	28
Clerks,	4,881	Manufacturers not specified,	36
Clock makers,	7	Mariners,	2,203
Clothiers,	19	Marketmen,	206
Coach makers,	62	Masons and plasterers,	968
Coffee-house keepers,	288	Mechanics not specified,	543
Collectors,	119	Merchants,	3,958
Confectioners,	126	Milkmen,	208
Coopers,	906	Millers,	76

Professions, Occupations and Trades,—Continued.

Occupation	Number	Occupation	Number
Millwhights	30	Shingle Makers	43
Miners	10	Ship Carpenters	46
Moulders	29	Slaters	47
Musicians	167	Soldiers	45
Music Sellers	2	Stevedores	175
Music Teachers	41	Stewards	126
Newsmen	19	Stone and Marble Cutters	71
Ostlers	94	Store Keepers	188
Overseers	1,808	Students	598
Oystermen	37	Sugar Manufacturers	95
Painters and Glaziers	865	Surgeons	2
Paper Dealers	5	Surveyors	34
Pattern Makers	12	Tailors	1,160
Pavers	66	Tanners and Curriers	35
Pedlers	292	Tar Makers	7
Perfumers	10	Teachers	791
Physicians	912	Teamsters	22
Piano Forte and Musical Instrument Makers	12	Telegraph Operators	3
		Tinsmiths	300
Pilots	162	Tobacconists and Segar Makers	386
Planters	6,471	Traders	258
Plumbers	9	Trunk Makers	38
Polishers and Finishers	15	Turners	37
Potters	10	Umbrella Manufacturers	10
Printers	317	Undertakers	22
Produce Dealers	39	Upholsterers	50
Professors	47	United States and State Officers	233
Publishers	2	Vinegar Makers	2
Rag Collectors	60	Warehousemen	75
Railroad Men	6	Watchmakers	155
Refrectory Keepers	171	Watchmen	228
Refiners	9	Weavers	16
Reporters	3	Weighmasters	34
Riggers	29	Wheelwrights	270
Rope Makers	26	Wine and Liquor Dealers	37
Saddle and Harness Makers	214	Wood Corders	15
Sail Makers	82	Wood Cutters	306
Sash Makers	2	Wood Dealers	62
Sawyers	44	Wool Dealers	14
Scale Makers	3	Woolen Manufacturers	5
Sculptors	3	Other Occupations	362
Servants	508		
Sextons	20	Total	77,168

PRESIDENTS OF THE UNITED STATES,
From the Adoption of the Constitution to the present time.

No.	Name	Term Began.	Term Ended.
1.	George Washington, Virginia,	April 30, 1789,	March 3, 1797
2.	John Adams, Massachusetts,	March 4, 1797,	March 3, 1801
3.	Thomas Jefferson, Virginia,	March 4, 1801,	March 3, 1809
4.	James Madison, Virginia,	March 4, 1809,	March 3, 1817
5.	James Monroe, Virginia,	March 4, 1817,	March 3, 1825
6.	John Q. Adams, Massachusetts,	March 4, 1825,	March 3, 1829
7.	Andrew Jackson, Tennessee,	March 4, 1829,	March 3, 1837
8.	Martin Van Buren, New York,	March 4, 1837,	March 3, 1841
9.	William Henry Harrison, Ohio,	March 4, 1841,	April 4, 1841
10.	John Tyler, Virginia,	April 4, 1841,	March 3, 1845
11.	James Knox Polk, Tennessee,	March 4, 1845,	March 3, 1849
12.	Zachary Taylor, Louisiana,	March 4, 1849,	July 9, 1850
13.	Millard Fillmore, New York,	July 9, 1850,	March 3, 1853
14.	Franklin Pierce, N. Hampshire,	March 4, 1853,	

EXECUTIVE DEPARTMENT UNITED STATES.

Franklin Pierce, New Hampshire President,..........Salary, $25,000
William L. Marcy, New York, Secretary of State,................ 8,000
James Gruther, Kentucky, Secretary of the Treasury,........... 8,000
Jefferson Davis, Mississippi, Secretary of War,.................... 8,000
James C. Dobbins, North Carolina, Secretary of the Navy,..... 8,000
Robert McClelland, Michigan, Secretary of the Interior,........ 8,000
James Campbell, Pennsylvania, Post Master General,............ 8,000
Caleb Cushing, Massachusetts, Attorney General, ... 8,000

SUPREME COURT.

Roger B. Taney, Maryland, Chief Justice,...............Salary, $5,000
John McLean, Ohio, Ass't " 4,500
James W. Wayne, Georgia, " " 4,500
John Catron, Tennessee, " " 4,500
Peter Y. Daniel, Virginia, " " 4,500
Samuel Nelson, New York, " " 4,500
R. C. Grier, Pennsylvania, " " 4,500
B. R. Curtis, Massachusetts, " " 4,500
Jas. A. Campbell, Alabama, " " 4,500
Benjamin Howard, Baltimore, Reporter.
W. T. Carroll, Washington, D. C. Clerk.

UNITED STATES COURTS.

United States Circuit Court for Louisiana.—Theo. H. McCaleb, Associate Judge; E. W. Moise, District Attorney; J. W. Gurly, Clerk; J. M. Kennedy, Marshall.

United States District Court.—Theo. H. McCaleb, Judge; N. R. Jennings, Clerk.

Western District—District Court.—Henry Boyce, Judge; Peter Alexander, District Attorney; W. M. Smoot, Marshall; R. J. Wilson, Clerk.

UNITED STATES AND OFFICERS.

Surveyor General's Office, Donaldsonvile; W. J. McCulloch, Surveyor General; Thos. H. Weightman, Chief Clerk.

Greensburg District—Greensburg.—C. C. Strickland, Register; John M. Vernon, Receiver.

South Eastern Disirict—New Orleans.—Louis Palmes, Register; W. H. Palfrey, Receiver.

Southwestern District—Opelousas.— ——— ———, Register; Eugene Wartelle, Receiver.

Southwestern District—Natchitoches.—J. B. Cloutier, Register; J. B. O. Bruart, Receiver.

Ouachita District.—Monroe.—W. Shannon, Register, P. G. King, Receiver.

MINISTERS PLENIPOTENTIARY.

James Buchannan, of Pennsylvania, Great Britain; Thos. H. Seymour, of Connecticut, Russia; John Y. Mason, of Virginia, France; Pierre Soule, of Louisiana, Spain; Peter D. Vroom, of New Jersey, Prussia; James Gadsden, of South Carolina, Mexico; Wm. Trousdale, of Tennessee, Brazil; D. Starkweather, of Ohio, Chili; John R. Clay, of Pennsylvania, Peru.

MINISTERS RESIDENT.

Carroll Spence, of Maryland, Turkey; Theodore S. Fay, of Massachusetts, Switzerland; John H. Wheeler, of North Carolina, Nicaragua

REISDENT COMMISSIONERS.

Robert McLane, of Maryland, China; David L. Gregg, of Illinois, Sandwich Islands.

CHARGES D'AFFAIRES.

August Belmont, of New York, Netherlands; John M. Daniels, of Virginia, Sardinia: Henry Bedinger, of Virginia, Denmark; Henry R. Jackson, of Georgia, Austria; J. J. Seibels, of Alabama, Belgium; Robert Dale Owen, of Indiana, Naples; Francis Shroeder, of Rhode Island, Sweden; John L. O. Sullivan, of New York, Portugal; Lewis Cass, jr., of Michigan, Rome; John W. Dana, of Maine, Bolivia; Philo White, of Wisconsin, Ecuador; James S. Green, of Missouri, New Grenada; J. Nevitt Steele, of Maryland, Venezuala.

FOREIGN CONSULS RESIDENT IN NEW ORLEANS.

Austria and Baden, F. H. Ermer, 17 Carondelet St.;
Brazil, B. Valls, 73 Magazine St.;
Bremen, Fred. Rodewald, 17 CommonPlace St.;
Denmark, F. F. C. Fles, 53 Carondelet St.;
France, Aimé Roger, 123 Royal St.;
Great Britain, William Mure, 118 Common St.;
Hamburg, Wm. Vogle, 57 St. Charles St.;
Hanover, A. Reichard, 57 St. Charles St.;
Mecklenburg, William Prehn, 121, Common St.;
Mexico, J. P. Oropesa, Durean's Buildings;
Montivedo, B. Valls, 73 Magazine St.
Nassau, F. W. Fredenthal, 31 Gravier, St.;
New Grenada, J. P. Beyelle, 31 Gravier St.;
Oldenburg, Wm. Vogle, 57 St. Charles St.;
Portugal, G. A. Barralli, 61 Common St.;
Prusia, Wm. Vogle, 57 St. Charles St.;
Rome, C. J. Daron, 93 Common St.;
Russia, E. Johns, 20 Carondelet St.;
Sardinia, J. Lanata, 11 Jefferson St.;
Saxony, F. F. C. Fles, 53 Carondelet St.;

Spain, A. M. Segovia,
Sweden and Norway, Ambrose Lanfear, 93 Common St.;
Switzerland, J. B. Fach, 17 Carondelet St.;
Two Scicilies, G. A. Barrelli, 61 Common St.;
Venezula, A. D. Dieter, 13 Gravier St.;
Wurtemburg, C. Honold, 2 Royal St.;
Guatemala, E. J. Gomez.

OUTSTANDING STATE BONDS.

Maine,	$471,500
New Hampshire,	75,899
Vermont,	None
Massachutetts,	6,445,000
Rhode Island,	None
Connecticut,	None
New York,	24,323,837
New Jersey,	None
Pennsylvania,	40,021,445
Delaware,	None
Maryland,	15,356,224
Virginia,	12,089,382
North Carolina,	2,224,000
South Carolina,	1,025,893
Georgia,	2,802,472
Florida,	None
Alabama,	4,497,000
Louisiana,	9,589,207
Arkansas,	2,488,839
Mississippi,	7,271,907
Tennessee,	3,363,856
Kentucky,	5,571,297
Missouri,	802,000
Illinois,	17,000,000
Indiana,	7,712,850
Ohio,	15,542,549
Michigan,	2,389,550
Wisconsin,	100,000
Iowa,	88,000
Texas,	5,351,628
California,	2,097,428

Churches and Church Property in the United States.

	NUMBER.	VALUE.
Methodist,	12,467	$14,636,671
Baptist,	9,791	10,900,382
Presbyterian,	4,584	14,369,898
Congregational,	1,316	7,970,962
Episcopalion,	1,474	11,251,960
Roman Catholic,	1,112	8,973,848

Amount of Land unsold in the United States, up to the year ending June, 1853.

	ACRES.
Ohio,	244,499,08
Indiana,	246,339,41
Illinois,	4,115,969,97
Missouri,	22,722,801,41
Alabama,	15,049,693,70
Mississippi,	9,083,654,94
Louisiana,	9,134,143,81
Michigan,	16,142,293,48
Arkansas,	15,725,388,33
Florida,	29,262,674,50
Iowa,	22,773,175,57
Wisconsin,	23,678,486,19
California,	113,682,436,00
Total.	281,861,254,48

Revenue and Expenditures of the Postoffice Department, for the Year ending June, 1853.

FREE.	COLLECTED	EXPENDED
Maine,	$125,194	$112,654
New Hampshire,	81,708	67,310
Vermont,	78,638	96,860
Massachusetts,	453,969	999,362
Rhode Island,	47,377	30,817
Connecticut,	146,364	121,368
New York,	1,175,516	729,421
New Jersey,	89,074	109,913
Pennsylvania,	488,308	414,042
Ohio,	375,759	531,396
Michigan,	96,757	182,872
Indiana,	137,339	174,361
Illinois,	175,346	264,223
Iowa,	40,980	55,336
Wisconsin,	73,570	78,605
California,	123,153	242,043
Oregon,	9,797	52,282
Minnesota,	3,529	3,845
	$3,722,369	$8,661,701

Surplus, $60,668.

SLAVE.		
Delaware,	$16,310	$16,357
Maryland,	152,158	239,953
District of Columbia,	37,832	33,006
Virginia,	183,472	398,769
North Carolina,	60,751	204,806
South Carolina,	82,985	157,573
Georgia,	142,800	279,441

Revenue and Expenditures of Postoffice—Continued.

Florida,	16,878	45,050
Alabama,	86,091	223,520
Mississippi,	73,108	151,422
Arkansas,	25,105	103,692
Texas,	47,164	161,149
Tennessee,	85,701	134,009
Kentucky,	112,542	191,114
Missouri,	98,781	188,041
Louisiana,	128,170	141,953
	$1,359,848	$2,671,755

Deficiency, $1,359,907.

UNCERTAIN WHETHER TO BE FREE OR SLAVE.

New Mexico,	$517	$10,925
Utah,	955	3,633
Nebraska,	—	237
	$1,472	$23,795

Deficiency, $22,323.

Total deficiency, aside from ocean mail service, $1,273,562.

INSANE AND IDIOTIC.

The last Census furnishes the whole number of Insane and Idiotic persons in the various States of the Union. The aggregate number is 31,494. The proportion of each State and Territory is as follows:

	INSANE.	IDIOTIC.
Main,	561	577
New Hampshire,	373	353
Vermont,	560	299
Massachusetts,	1680	791
Rhode Island,	217	116
Connecticut,	470	287
New York,	2521	1665
New Jersey,	379	419
Pennsylvania,	1914	1467
Delaware,	68	92
Maryland,	546	394
District of Columbia,	23	12
Virginia,	970	1182
North Carolina,	510	794
South Carolina,	249	348
Georgia,	224	664
Florida,	11	36
Alabama,	233	476
Louisiana,	200	174
Mississippi,	129	222
Texas,	37	104
Arkansas,	63	115

Insane and Idiotic—Continued.

Tennesee,	407	468
Kentucky,	528	907
Missouri,	262	257
Illinois,	238	363
Indiana,	563	928
Ohio,	1317	1361
Michigan,	133	189
Wisconsin,	54	94
Iowa,	42	94
California,	2	7
Minnesota,	1	1
New Mexico,	11	44
Oregon,	5	4
Utah,	5	1
Total,	15,768	15,706

Of the insane persons enumerated, 14,972 were white, and 638 colored; and of the idiotic, 14,257 were white, and 1,530 colored.

Amount of Coinage of the United States.

The entire coinage at the several mints, from the time they commenced operations, is as follows:

Mint at	Philadelphia,	established	1793	$322,228,868
Do	New Orleans,	do	1838	50,497,665
Do	Charlotte, N. C.,	do	1838	3,790,038
Do	Dahlonega, Ga.,	do	1838	5,280,728
	Total at all the Mints,			$381,797,299

A recent publication in London, by Mr. Wesgarth, states that when the California mines were discovered the gold in the world was worth £500,000,000, one-fourth of which was coin. The silver was worth £1,200,000, one.fifth of which was coin. Since the discovery, Mr. W. estimates each year's supply in pounds sterling as follows:

YEARS	CALIFORNIA	AUSTRALIA	ELSEWHERE	TOTAL
1848	Unimporlant	....	£8,000,000	£8,000,000
1849	£2,000,000	....	8,000,000	10,000,000
1850	9,000,000	....	8,000,000	17,000,000
1851	13,000,000	£ 1,000,000	8,000,000	22,000,000
1852	15,000,000	14,000,000	8,000,000	37,000,000
1853	20,000,000	20,000,000	8,000,000	48,000,000

Forty-eight millions pounds sterling is supposed to be the supply of gold for the past year, say in Federal currency value $232,320,000 Then, according to Mr. Wesgarth's estimate, there ought to be in the world at this time £634,000,000 sterling, over one-fourth of which should be coin, say, $651,000,000, of which we have in the city of

New Orleans the small amount of $7,000,000. If there is any pleasure in consolation, we can console ourselves with the thought that if we have not got any more of the vast amount, we ought to have it.

The manufacture of iron in the world is divided as follows by the *London Chronicle*:—In Great Britain, 2,380,000 tons; United States, 400,000; France, 348,000; Russia, 189,000; Austria, 160,000; Sweden, 132,500; Prussia, 112,000; making a total of 3,723,300 tons of iron manufactured annually. In 1850 there were 450 iron furnaces in Great Britain, and of the 2,380,000 tons which these produced, about 809,000 were exported. In 1786 but 125,000 tons were manufactured in Great Britain, and the total exports were about 408 tons. During the ten months ending November 5, 1853, Great Britain exported $75,000,000 worth of iron, and by far the largest portion of this enormous mass of exports were taken by the United States. Of pig iron the United States received 57.000 tons, and Holland, which comes next upon the list, took 13,000. Of bar, bolt and rod iron, the United States took 263,530 tons, or nearly six times as much as Canada, which received the next largest amount.

VOTE FOR PRESIDENT OF U. S. IN LOUISIANA, 1852.

DISTRICT I.	PIERCE.	SCOTT.
Orleans,	4,682	4,663
DISTRTCT II.		
Ascension,	360	296
Assumption,	552	511
Iberville,	426	318
Jefferson,	943	928
Lafourche,	135	676
Orleans, R. B.,	161	67
Plaquemines,	372	151
St. Bernard,	120	130
St. Charles,	39	101
St. John B.,	160	202
St. James,	158	321
Terrebonne,	97	197
West Baton Rouge,	148	220
DISTRICT III.		
Avoyelles,	387	300
Concordia,	86	121
East Baton Rouge,	485	484
East Feliciana,	443	342
Lafayette,	277	117
Livingston,	337	159
Point Coupee,	364	242
St. Helena,	246	209
St. Landry,	568	692
St. Martin,	298	479
St. Mary,	243	390
St. Tammany,	208	254
Tensas,	107	120
Vermillion,	126	136
Washington,	258	125
West Feliciana,	302	190
DISTRICT IV.		
Bienville,	313	172
Bossier,	248	180
Calcasieu,	221	34
Caddo,	342	344
Catahoula,	310	280
Caldwell,	158	54
Carroll,	261	219
Claiborne,	506	330
De Soto,	288	241
Franklin,	192	110
Jackson,	241	174
Madison,	147	171
Morehouse,	137	196
Natchitoches,	407	289

Ouachita,	240	190
Rapides,	623	401
Sabine,	251	237
Union,	465	435
Winn,	138	57
Total,	18,647	17,255

Majority for Pierce, ...1,392

Majority for Taylor, (1848,) 2,847.

Deaths, Resignations, and Vacancies Filled.

JUDGES.

E. T. Merrick, of Clinton, Judge of the 7th Judicial District.

T. T. Land, of Shreveport, Judge of the 18th Judicial District.

NOTARIES.

Fergus Fusilier, Notary Public, Parish of St. Martin, in place of A. Deblanc, resigned.

E. Miller, Notary Public, Last Island, Parish of Terrebonne.

Elisha Eastwood, Notary Public, Point Coupee, *vice* W. C. Bozeman, resigned.

John Halsey, Notary Public, Ascension, *vice* M. H. Nichols.

Michael Heahn, Notary Public, New Orleans, *vice* Herman Lucas,

John C. Potts, Notary Public, Terrebonne, *vice* E. D. Burgard.

REPRESENTATIVE TO GENERAL ASSEMBLY.

B. B. Sims, Point Coupée.

PENITENTIARY.

L. C. Morris, Director, in place of G. W. Christine, deceased.

T. J. Buffington, Physician.

LAND OFFICE.

Robt. Bengurel, Register, in place of Fitzgerald, deceased.

DEATHS AND RESIGNATIONS.

W. W. Farmer, Lt. Governor, deceased.

A. W. Baker,	Representative to	Gen'l Ass'y,	St. Mary,	deceased.
J. B. R. Jones,	do.	do.	Morehouse,	do.
J. A. Ranaldson,	do.	do.	E. Feliciana,	do.
H. M. Summers,	do.	do.	N. Orleans,	resig'd.
P. P. Briant,	do.	do.	St. Martin,	do.
Thos. McKeon,	do.	do.	N. Orleans,	do.
J. H. Boatner,	do.	do.	E. B. Rouge,	do.
J. A. Braud, Senator,			N. Orleans,	do.

Progress of the United States.

BY J. B. D. DeBOW.

When the revolution handed over to us the republic, won by the blood and the sword of our ancestors, it embraced a territory little greater than that of our possessions on the Pacific at the present moment. Exposed on its frontiers to the attacks of numerous tribes of remorseless savages—cut off in its western limits from the ocean by the possessions of a power hostile to us in feeling, and different from us in language—the republic has advanced in its course, dealing with the savage with justice and magnanimity, and obtaining only by fair concessions what was necessary to its development; and in passing the boundaries of the Mississippi, and sweeping across the great mountains to the Western ocean, it has violated no law of good neighborhood, but relied upon those of negotiation and purchase, or the results of a just war, undertaken in maintenance of the integrity of the national domain. From a territory of less than 900,000 square miles the republic has swelled into nearly *three* millions of miles, being nearly one-half of the whole of North America. This vast domain is nearly ten times as large as that of Great Britain and Ireland and France combined—three times as large as the whole of France, Great Britain and Ireland, Austria, Prussia, Spain, Portugal, Belgium, Holland, and Denmark together—one and a half times as large as the Russian empire in Europe—one-sixth less only than the area covered by the fifty-nine or sixty empires, States, and republics of Europe—of equal extent with the Roman empire, or that of Alexander, neither of which is said to have exceeded three millions of square miles.

Already does our empire extend over domain wider than that of the Romans in their proudest days of conquest. From the island of Brazos, in the Gulf of Mexico, to the straits of Fuca, on the Northern Pacific; from the Arostook valley to the bay of San Diego, the Union extends its leviathan proportions. The inhabitants of these extreme points, more distant than the shores of the Old and New World apart, on the usual routes of travel, are brothers and fellow-citizens under common laws and with a common destiny. It is as though the Shetland islands and the Bosphorus, Siberia and the gates of Hercules, were made the outports of an empire which embraced the whole of Europe. For such an empire Alexander and Cæsar sighed in vain, and Napoleon deluged Europe in blood.

Viewed in its great geographical divisions, the portions which are watered by rivers falling into the Atlantic and the Pacific are respectively of very nearly equal areas; whilst the great interior valley has an extent but little less than the Pacific and Atlantic regions combined.

Considered in less geographical divisions, the area of the northwestern States is nearly two and a half times as large as that of the northern—twice as large as the southwestern—four times as large as the southern—eight times as large as the middle States—fifteen times as large as New England.

Divided as slave territory and free territory, exclusive of unformed territorial governments, the slave States have one and a third times the territory of the free States.

The shore line of this great empire, including the indentures of bays, &c., is 12,609 miles, equal to one-half the circumference of the earth; or if we follow the irregularities of islands and enter the rivers as far as tide extends, the total shore line of the United States will be found to be 33,069 miles, or one and one-third the circumference of the earth.

The area of the great western valley has been calculated as follows:

Ohio valley . . .	200,000	square miles.
Mississippi proper . .	180,000	"
Missouri	500,000	"
Lower Mississippi . .	330,000	"
Total . .	1,210,000	"

Its outline is 6,100 miles, and this portion of the Union included, embraces western New York, Pennsylvania, and Virginia; Kentucky, Tennessee, Alabama, Mississippi, Louisiana, Arkansas, and Missouri; Illinois, Indiana, and Ohio; Michigan, Iowa and Wisconsin, whose total population may be estimated at 10,000,000 or 12,000,000. From 1800 to 1810 the population of the valley doubled. In half a century its popution has increased twenty-fold—an average duplication every 12 years. The average density to the square mile is now but 10 or 12. If as densely populous as Britain, there is space enough in our interior empire for 300,000,000 of people.

Mr. Calhoun, in his great report on the Memphis convention (1846), kindled with the magnificent theme which was presented before him—a population pressing upon the limits of the Rocky mountains—a tonnage augmented thirty-fold in thirty years—a trade already equalling the whole foreign exports and imports of the United States together—three hundred millions of dollars—and this but in the beginning:

"Looking beyond to a not very distant future, when this immense valley, containing within its limits one million two hundred thousand square miles, lying in its whole extent in the temperate zone, and occupying a position midway between the Atlantic and the Pacific oceans, unequalled in fertility and the diversity of its productions, intersected in every direction by the mighty stream, including its tributaries, by which it is drained, and which supply a continuous navigation of upwards of ten thousand miles, with a coast, including both banks, of twice that length, shall be crowded with population, and its resources fully developed; imagination itself is taxed in the attempt to realize the magnitude of its commerce."

After these tedious details, let us rise to some calculation which must become of exciting interest. What may we reasonably calculate as the increase of the population of the United States in the next hundred years? If its increase be as great as in the last sixty years, we shall have 497,000,000; if as great as between 1840 and 1850, deducting foreigners that have come in and formed a part of the population, it would be 252,000,000; if it were no greater than the increase of Delaware, which has increased the least of all the States, it would be 48,000,000. At a mean of this ratio and that of the Union in sixty years, we shall have in 1900, 75,000,000, and in 1950, 125,000,000. This calculation will no doubt be nearer the truth than any other.

A probable distribution of the population of the United States in 1950 would be, the Atlantic States 30,000,000, the Mississippi valley 75,000,000, the Pacific coast 20,000,000.

But these are idle dreamings. Those who have prophesied before have proved such indifferent prophets that we cannot but be considered on dangerous ground. Who shall dare to compute what waves from the ocean of eternity shall come rolling in year, and year, and year again, in a whole century which is before us? What wars, what pestilences, what famine, what social or political convulsions, what breaking up and building up of dynasties, what territories gained, what territories lost! Will the liberties of our people subsist then, and their vital energies be preserved? In a hundred years nations have risen to glory, or have perished and been lost. In a hundred years the whole face of the earth has been changed. Sweeping over this great continent, and over the neighboring isles from the Northern ocean to the southern seas, under the flag of the great republic, will these hundred millions of human beings assert their liberties, as we are doing to-day, or, corrupted and broken up into factions, will they present to the world a second Rome in ruins, whose decline and fall it will be the melancholy part of another Gibbon to indite? God protect and watch over us as a people, keep for us our liberties and our national honor, aid and sustain us in our amazing progress, and let a hundred years to come produce the great results indicated for them by the past, and such as were the object of the prayers of the wise and good fathers of the republic.

Let us pass in rapid review some of the evidences of the industrial progress of the United States which are displayed in its commerce, agriculture, and manufactures.

In the five years which preceded the adoption of the federal constitution, the exports and imports of the country did not exceed together fifty-five millions of dollars annually—being about one-sixth as much as the commerce of Great Britain, and one-third as much as that of France. In the last year the same commerce has reached $500,000,000—a ten-fold increase—being considerably more than that of France, and three-fifths of that of Great Britain. Eight or ten years ago the commerce of Great Britain was not larger than ours at the present time, and her trade with all the world near the close of the last century did not exceed her present trade with us.

What shall be the future of our commercial empire is more than the mind of man can now conceive. It has been gaining annually 7 or 8 per cent. on that of Great Britain, and even at this ratio, in twelve or fifteen years the two countries will share equally of the empire of the seas. But there is every reason to expect a larger ratio of increase when the great fields of the West are entirely opened and developed, when the South shall be stimulated to her utmost powers of production, when the shores of the Pacific shall be as populous as those of the Atlantic, and the commercial empire of the Indies be opened to us by a great overland railroad, and fleets of steamships—when all of our mineral and manufacturing resources shall be brought into full development—then shall open to us a com. merce which the world has never paralleled in any single nation, and which will be as considerable as that of all the combined powers of the world. Great and benignant are the results of commerce upon the families of men. Let us take the extremest limits of the ocean, the stormiest islet of the deep, struggling against the thousand billows, and what do we find?

The sailor and the trader have been there, and the return of the white wings is hailed by anxious multitudes, who bring out their richest treasures to be bartered for the veriest trifles of civilization. From the intercourse which arises, new wants are stimulated in their bosoms. They begin to think with the new objects which occasion thought; their views and ideas are naturally expanded to a wider compass, and they are insensibly moulded in the type of those who have excited their highest admiration and wonder. Mysterious, beneficent, and wise are the ways of Providence, when even the interests of men are called into requisition to work out the great problem of their existence.

The tonnage of the United States is 4,500,000 tons, as large as that of Great Britain five or six years ago, if, indeed, upon a close calculation, the two countries do not already vie with each other. At all events, the ratio of increase of our tonnage is twice as great as that of Britain. Nearly 2,000,000 tons have been built by us in the last five years, which is four times as much as in the five years preceding 1820. The North controls this tonnage, and it is calculated by Mr. Kettell realizes fifty millions a year out of the carrying trade which she is permitted to conduct for the South. The steam marine of the Union is 600,000 tons, being four times as great as in 1840.

The home or inter-State trade of the country, under the influence of perfect freedom, and without the restraint of the revenue laws, may be estimated at $1,000,000,000. The commerce which floats on western waters is estimated at $400,000,-000; and the commerce of the Great Lakes at $300,000,000.

During the war of Napoleon, the carrying trade of the world was in our hands, and produced an amount of prosperity in the country which was unexampled. In the event of another general war in Europe, were it possible for us to be kept out of the fray, an extension of our commerce would result which even figures might refuse to express.

The manufacturing progress of the United States is scarcely less marvellous than the commercial. We have invested in them $600,000,000 or $700,000,000, and our manufacturing product reaches $1,000,000,000. In 1807, we manufactured but 800 bales of cotton; in 1834, 216,000 bales; in 1852, over 600,000 bales, greatly more than is manufactured by France, and one-third as much as Great Britain, though twenty years ago we only manufactured one-fifth as much as she did. The South and the West, in the same period, have doubled the proportion which their cotton manufacture bears to that of the Union. Cotton goods constitute one-half of the whole exports of Great Britain, and seven-eighths of the whole amount consumed in Europe and America is the product of southern slave labor. In the manufacture of cotton it is computed that more than seven millions of people are immediately interested, and that $1,200,000,000 capital is invested.

I shall be brief on the subject of agriculture. In 1840 it was estimated to produce for us $600,000,000. In 1850, by a close calculation on a deficient crop, the amount swells to $1,000,000,000, and at this moment may be taken to be $1,200,000,000. We produce $150,000,000 in cotton, against $200,000 or $300,000 at the beginning of the century. Our sugar crop is already $14,000,000 or $15,000,000. There was a third more of wheat, and double as much corn, produced in 1850 than in 1840.

We have 113,000,000 acres of land in cultivation, or 300,000,000 in occupancy, or about one-sixth part of the area of the republic. These are carved out into about 1,448,000 farms, or distinct agricultural interests, with $3,500,000,000 invested in farms, implements, &c.—an average extent to each farm of 282 acres. What other country in the world can show results like these?

The physical well-being of a people has much to do with their social advancement. In the United States, fourteen-fifteenths of the free families have houses to themselves, whilst in Great Britain only six-sevenths are so favored, or about half the proportion. Comparing the different sections of the Union, it would appear that the Territories have most houses in proportion to population; the South comes next; the Southwest next; then New England; and last, the North. The number of persons to a family is smallest in the Territories, next in New England, and largest in the North.

When we come to the education of the people, we find that 2,150,000 boys, and nearly 1,900,000 girls, are at schools and colleges—being about one-fifth of the free population. The proportion in England and Wales is 1 in 8; Spain, 1 in 17; Russia, 1 in 77. The number of white persons over twenty years of age in the United States who cannot read and write is 1,053,000, about one-twelfth of the persons of that age. In England and Wales, in three years, half the persons who registered their marriages were incapable of reading and writing.

In comparing different sections of the Union with regard to education, we find that whilst in New England only 1 adult in about 375 cannot read and write; in the middle States, 2 in 100 cannot; southern States, 9 in 100 cannot; southwestern, 8; northern, 5; northwestern, 17, growing out of the great proportion of foreign-born—fourteen out of every hundred there being incapable of reading and writing, which is the same proportion of the foreign-born in New England. In the whole Union, 1 in 25 cannot read and write of the native-born, and 1 in 12 of the foreign-born.

These are gratifying results, and they should incite us to still further efforts in the cause of education. Shall a great and wealthy country pause to consider the difficulties or enumerate the cost of distributing light and instruction throughout all its extent, and of bringing home to each embryo citizen—even the veriest offspring of beggary and want—the means of becoming a nobleman in the only sense in which our institutions admit of nobility, and in which the might of intellect can make us all noble? I know of no patriot service more exalted than of that man who will come forward in our legislative halls to produce and carry out, from an enlightened appreciation of the subject in all its bearings, such educational movements as the exigencies of the country demand.

Let us diffuse knowledge throughout the length and breadth of this great country; multiply the means of information; send the schoolmaster into every hovel; dot every hill with the school-house and college; let the press, without intermission, night and day, pour forth its steady streams of light; foster science and the arts; let the civilizing and God-like influences of machinery uninterruptedly extend. Then will the future of our country open, boundless and great, beyond all example, beyond all compare, and countless ages bless its mission and acknowledge its glorious dominion.

It was our intention to have said something about pauperism and its attendant ills in our country, as compared with others, but this is unnecessary: the number is not one-thirtieth as great as in Great Britain. This is an evil, however, which advances with an advancing country. The social and agrarian doctrines of France cannot take root among us for a very long period, unless we encourage class legislation, and incite the poor to think there is something of robbery in the idea of property. The sound patriot will resist the teachings of the demagogue which lead to this. He will know the true nature of property and of its laws. He will know that it is natural—and, if natural, proper, though we may not see the reason—that poverty and want, and disease and misery, should be the next door neighbor of wealth and unbounded prosperity. The towers of the palace cast their shadows down upon the roofless hovel, as naturally as the mountains do upon the neighboring hills. Yet that nobleman has not oppressed that beggar. He may, indeed, be liberal, and generous, and just, and mourn over the misery all the wealth in the world could not relieve.

Nor is the beggar a victim of society and its laws; without that society, or those laws, he had not existed—he could not exist with the same security; his fathers before him prospered (for generations of misery in the same household is scarcely a supposable case,) and his children would have no hope. Exclaim against Nature, that she has sent you in the world half finished, maimed, diseased, imbecile, an idiot—that you were born under the frozen serpent of the North, and must struggle against tumbling icebergs, or in the death-dealing breath of torrid suns—but limit not your complaints to these. In evincing her partiality in these respects, has she proclaimed an impartiality in every other? Is it not equally an outrage upon your rights, your equality, that your neighbor is taller, or stouter, better favored, more intellectual, or that he has broader acres, greater possessions, and more comforts? All the governments in the world could not prevent these distinctions. The worst government only would attempt it, for in the effort how much injustice and wrong must be done to those who, to say the least of it, have as much right to their possessions, however earned, as you have to take them away! The remedy is within ourselves. It is for us to apply it. Be industrious, be frugal, be circumspect; if these remove not the evil, we have a claim upon the *benevolence*, not upon the *justice*, of our fellows. Sue, but not demand. If this benevolence fail, we are simply another victim of that inexplicable, yet, as we ought to believe, wise Providence, which strikes down without reason or explanation, and teaches the utter nothingness of man by her frequent indifference to his fate.

In 1828 we began the construction of railroads: in 1830 we had 41 miles; in 1840, 2,167 miles; in 1854, 15,648 miles; being twice the extent of those in Great Britain, and considerably more than in all the rest of the world together. Whilst the average cost in our country has been about $30,000 a mile, the cost in Europe has averaged about $100,000. We have put in operation in the last year about 3,000 miles, and have in course of construction a programme of 12,612 miles.

The mineral resources of the United States include almost every article of great commercial value. The coal and iron resources of some of our western States are as large as those of the whole of Britain; we have lead and copper in profusion, and the gold resources of California are almost equal to those of the fabulous reports of Ormuz and the Ind. As labor cheapens, and population centralizes, and becomes dense, the mineral resources of the Union will be developed, and it need give us little concern that they remain undeveloped now, since our capital and labor are so abundantly and profitably employed in a thousand other channels. The patrimony we shall leave to our children. The results of the gold mines of California alone, in market value, equal almost the value of the whole cotton crop of the southern States of the Union.

But, to conclude : in sketching thus rapidly the history of our country, how striking is the contrast of its early colonial periods with the present hour! It was in the sixteenth century that the leading European powers were introduced to a minute acquaintance with the continent of America. Adventurous navigation had rescued a world from savage dominion, and there were adventurous spirits enough to people that world, and identify thenceforward their destinies with it. A hundred years after, and civilization planted her abodes through all this waste. Peculiar indeed is the feeling with which these infant days of our country is regarded ; so like an illusion does it all seem—so like a dream of glowing imagery. We look back as to a classic era, and the romance of Pocahontas and of Raleigh, of Fernando de Soto, and Juan Ponce de Leon; do they thrill us less than the beatific visions of the Greek, recurring to ages long ago, when Ilion resisted the shocks of Agamemnon's heroes, and the Argo sailed away to distant Colchis? The dim antiquity seems gathered around both of them alike. But let it pass, all—the romance of our history! They imagined not, the men of that day imagined not, the stupendous results which have occurred so soon. They saw not the benign and regenerating influences of a virgin land, preserved for countless ages uncorrupted by tyranny and ignorant of oppression. Could such a soil have nurtured else than freemen? They saw it not; and do we, even we, see other than darkly yet, the grand consummation, the mighty destinies of the regions which three centuries ago were proclaimed from the masthead of a crazy ocean bark, a speck upon the distant heaven?

The developements of American character are replete with instruction, and solve one of the most remarkable problems in the history of mankind. The untried scenes of a new world, cut off by trackless oceans from contact and communion with the civilization of unnumbered generations, were sufficient to introduce, what might have been predicted of them, results new, striking, and without a precedent. The indomitable will, the stern endurance, the inflexible and hardy spirit of independence, the high daring, the lofty patriotism, the adventurous, unlimited enterprise, the genius resolute, active, intrepid, inexhaustible in resources, elastic in vigor and in freshness, buoyant ever and hoping on, and executing, amid every trying scene, every danger, and difficulty, and disaster—triumphing everywhere and in all things. Philosophy could have argued this complexion for the men whose fathers braved so much beyond the ocean, and would philosophy have won less than the fame of prophecy by her judgment?

Let us trace a few of the influences which have been at work in this country, and which more than all others have been felt in the development of its character and power.

1. With the benefit of the experience of other great powers, the United States have inherited none of the abuses which in them have been consecrated by time, and which cannot be touched by the hand of the reformer without endangering the whole frame-work of society. It is thus that the patriotism of Europe is conservative, whilst that of America may boldly approximate to radicalism. We may touch the springs of society, and rearrange its delicate machinery, without the apprehension which is felt in other governments of throwing the whole into inextricable disorder.

2. Freedom of religious faith and worship to Catholics, Protestants, and all, has been guarantied in every period of our history. The divorce of church and State is the indispensable condition of the prosperity of either. Leagued with the church, the State has ever been able to derive such sanctions for its abuses as are the most imposing upon the minds of men and the most fatal to their liberties. Degraded and corrupted by such contact, the church, in its despotism over the consciences of men, has crushed out all true religion. Better all the "isms" which our free system has brought; all the scandal of fanatic excess; far better than the tythe system, the trading in church benefits and presentations, the courts eclcesiastical, the thunders of excommunication, the princely estates of the clergy—robbing honest industry of its hard earned gains, and converting into an engine of stupendous plunder the meek and lowly religion of Christ. The religion of America is the spontaneous offering of the heart, and in elevating and enlarging it, has imparted to us no little of our power. Free to choose our form of worship, and to contribute as it may please us to its support, our people are already ministered to by 27,000 clergymen, have constructed 38,000 churches at an expense of $87,000,000, and have church-room to accommodate at one sitting 14,000,000 of people.

3. There are no priviledged classes in America—no rank, except that of honor—no nobility, except that of the intellect and the heart—no title of distinction higher than that of the gentleman, which, in its fulness of meaning in our country, involves all, and often more than all, that is claimed abroad for proudest earl or marquis, duke, or prince of the realm. The way to greatness is opened alike with us to the son of the me-

chanic and the millionaire. What a premium is here offered to the virtues—what a field for promotion to energy and talent! A splendid ancestry may, indeed, sometimes illumine the way to greatness, and furnish models for the descendants. It is more often the justification of indolence and the palliation of vice. The merit of dead men, when claimed for the living, is like stars, we are told, seen in the water, which would not be there but for their bright originals in heaven. Wealthy classes we must have and shall have—men estranged from the cares and necessities of daily business—men to be the patrons of art and of letters, and to cultivate them in elegant repose—retired scholars and gentlemen. Such are necessary to correct the strong material tendencies of our people—to teach them that there is a progress of the moral and the intellectual, as well as of the physical—that authors and artists, and poets and books, are as necessary as railroads and telegraphs—that letters are as important as land. We want these, and they are fast presenting themselves. In the forest, in contests with nature and the savage, America has been too busy in acting out her great national epic to have had time to write it. Let Europe sneer at our want of literature. We have begun at the base, and not at the apex. We are teaching the people to read books, which is more than she has ever done. The mines of thought which are being sprung throughout our reading masses will, as soon as the pressure of the physical is entirely removed, give to us Augustan and Elizabethan ages which shall not be memorable by their exception.

4. In the United States local legislation has been left where it ought to be, in the hands of local legislators, which is the greatest safeguard that could be devised against excessive and unequal legislation, the bane of all other countries. The nearer the government can be brought home to the people the more intimate will be the part they will take in it; the greater the responsibility exacted, the wiser and more intelligent the rules of action adopted. Local legislators can better understand the interests and wants of their constituency than could a central Congress legislating in detail for great communities. Under a system like ours there is no room for the tyranny of sections; but each is entirely adequate to its own security and protection. Thus is power distributed, and not concentrated. Thus may it be subjected to wise restraints, and preserved most effectually for good, and least effective for evil. We find here what may be called the compromises of the American system. Let us adhere to them. The encroachment made to-day upon the reserved rights ef the weakest and most remote of our co-sovereigns will to-morrow weave a yoke for our own necks.

If this great system is to be preserved, there must be respect paid to the rights of all of its parts. The North as well as the South, the East as well as the West, must share equally of the benefits or the burdens. Only ruin can follow the infraction of the rights and privileges of any section. Melancholy experience has taught us this, and may we profit by that experience.

5. The people of the United States have been content to take care of their own affairs, without intermeddling with those of others. The exceptions have been felt; and ought not to be called in precedent. The Father of the Republic counselled this course as suited to our exigencies, and enabling us the better to be employed in the development of our own nationality. Moral influence we may give to the struggles of brother republicans abroad—wise counsels, sound examples, without setting ourselves up as the propagandists of political principles, or entering upon a Don Quixote crusade against oppression and wrong throughout the world. Let Europe, for the present, fight out her own battles. Her old and decayed system must crumble down—her people must be born again before they can be fitted for the full blaze of the light of liberty which dazzles not our eyes. Time alone can bring about this. "Who would be free, themselves must strike the blow." The liberties of the millions now and hereafter inhabiting our country will be task enough for one nation adequately to maintain and guard. "The Greeks are at our doors." If the wise rule of our ancestors is ever to be departed from—and it is not claimed as applicable rigidly to every period of our national being—the case must be one of far greater merit than Europe has presented in the last half century. Now that the Old World is likely to be convulsed again—that the fires which have been lit by Cossack and Turk by the shores of the Bosphorus threaten general conflagration—that Poland, and Italy, and Hungary, may be found again asserting in arms their liberties and nationalities—that English bayonet and French artillery shall awaken all the dire elements of war which have slumbered so long, from the Baltic to the Mediterranean—hard indeed will it be for us to resist the pressure from our sympathies and retain our *wise neutrality.* Much will there be to gall our pride; much to tax our endurance and outrage the noblest sentiments of the heart; yet once let us yield and become involved in these great struggles, and when and where shall we be disentangled from them? The drama of our future will be one of violence and blood. Neither manhood nor religion requires from us greater love for others than for ourselves. We are doing more for republicanism through-

out the world, by furnishing it a home, and proving in it the practicability of republican institutions, when wisely framed and administered, than could be afforded by all the material aid and intervention which fleets and armies could carry. The gallantryof Ingraham, sustained by the President and by Congress, has sufficiently aroused Europe to the fact that republican America well knows how and when to extend the protection of its flag and the power of its nationality.

6. Freedom of speech and of the press are the inalienable birthright of the American citizen. With such levers, what abuse cannot be probed—what outrage redressed? We dare to speak our thoughts and to print them. This magic power of the press is at work throughout the land. Two thousand five hundred newspapers are discussing and elaborating measures of policy and cricticising the actions of public men. It is a power that is hundred-eyed and hundred-armed, and sleeps not—watchful sentinels of the liberties of the people. There is something almost divine in its action. Licentious at times though it be, prostituted to base uses, better this than the gag law and the censor, and the other restraints which despotism throws around it in Europe. The freedom of the press is the ægis of our liberty.

The density of population in the United States does not exceed seven persons to the square mile, whilst in Great Britain there are 234 to the square mile, and in Belgium 385. While the densest of our States—Massachusetts—contains 137 to the square mile, the least dense—Minnesota and Oregon—have only one inhabitant to every 30 or 40 square miles.

With the same density as Massachusetts, the United States would embrace 420 millions; with the density of Belgium, our territory is vast enough to include all the present inhabitants of the earth.

It is not in the power of man to conceive of a case more typical of the wonderful advances of our country than the growth of some of its great cities—for example, Cincinnati. About the time when the federal constitution was adopted, Mathias Denman, of New Jersey, bought for $550, eight hundred acres of the land on which the whole of all the great business streets of Cincinnati are now located. In 1800, but 750 persons had made their residences here. In 1840, there were 46,000; in 1850, 115,000—a three-fold increase in ten years. At the present moment the number cannot be less than 150,000, which will make Cincinnati the fourth or fifth city in the Union. Thus can men, in its midst, in the very activity and meridian of life, in sweeping the eye over its densely-compact streets, its marts of commerce, its richly-laden warehouses, its palaces of wealth, its splendid cathedrals of religion, its school-houses and its colleges, its quays, with their fleets of steamers, its railroads and telegraphs, approaching from every point of the compass, remember and recount scenes of the Indian wigwam and the Indian warwhoop, and when in all of its splendid and almost enchanted prospect was heard but the woodman's axe.

The State in which it is situated is another miracle of the present century. Admitted into the Union in 1802, with a population of 45,000, or two-thirds the population of Delaware, she already vies with Pennsylvania, and does not fall far short of the population of all of the New England States together. She has 820 miles of canals, built at a cost of $17,000,000, and 1,418 miles of railroads—a greater extent than any other State in the Union except New York. Her roads in progress (1853) were 1,736 miles, making a total programme of 3,154 miles. The magic lamp of Aladdin, in Eastern story, scarcely developed more rapid creations of wealth and power. The quick and infinite changes of the kaleidoscope are the only parallel for these.

The great interior valley, too, of which it is a part—the central basin of the Mississippi, and its tributaries—what enchantment at every step! The smoking cabin, the stealthy savage, the stalwart pioneer, the victim at the stake, the tomahawk and the scalp, the hunter's horn, the log house, and the picket, the interminable forests, the arrow trail! The nineteenth century opened thus upon the mighty West! It is so no more; the mansion rises, the plough speeds, the locomotive whizzes by, the paddle-wheels of the steamer dash into spray the slugged waters of every tortuous stream; fields laden with produce, wealth heaped up on every quay; the fashions of Paris, the elegance, the civilization, the intellectual culture of European courts! The spirit of the Anglo-Saxon has brooded over this waste, and chaos has broken up into life and light, and a thousand forms of attractiveness and beauty. *Westward* has been the tide of empire. It has been leaving even Ohio behind, and in its rapid footsteps making of it a very far down-east State. No longer may it be sung of her as of yore—

"Together let us rise,
Seek brighter plains and more indulgent skies,
Where fair *Ohio* rolls her amber tide,
And nature blossoms in her virgin pride."

The centre of representative population of the Union is now west of the mouth of the Ohio. Standing at this point, four great arms of an inland ocean are opened to either point of the compass. To the east the Ohio ascends 1,000 miles, penetrating in its tributaries the interior of New York, Pennsylvania, and Virginia—to the west the Missouri sweeps 3,000 miles towards the waters of the Western ocean—to the north and the south old Mississippi, father of all rivers, conveys his waters to the ocean. It has been working its way onward, that old river, further than our fancy may trace it—through all climes, and lands, and people—from where its remote source, a sleeping lake, deep set in impenetrable shades, on mountain heights, beyond all haunts of civilized life, mirrors savage and unchased beasts, it has worked itself on, father of all waters, among mountains

> "Where rolls the Oregon, and hears no sound
> Save his own dashings,"

It is not possible that the tide of emigration from abroad to our country can continue always. The improvements in the arts, and the discharge of the surplus, will render the inducements abroad to emigrate less and less. New outlets to emigration are opening in other countries, as in Australia, Canada, &c. It is against all the precedents of history that such a state of things shoul long continue. Though our territories seem to be boundless, population has not a necessary tendency to swell in the ratio of territory. But whether the increase continue or not, experience has shown, against all expectation, that this large influx of foreigners has not deteroirated the national morals, or endangered the national liberties. The danger of our country's tending towards rank and monarchy from the influx of persons brought up under such forms of government seemed to be the most pressing; but the very reverse has been the tendency, and we have run and are every day running more and more into extremes of *democracy*. The foreign element may increase this tendency, but its proportion being annually less and less to the native born, and its diffusion being very general over large sections, its effects must be neutralized. The States which have been most increased by such population have shown nothing less of the pride of republicanism, the principles of progress, and the desire for mental development, than those that have derived no such increase. It is only in the large cities that the foreign element has ever been unfavorably felt; and this is rather owing to the fact that the worst portions of such population will stop there naturally, and because in great cities vice and crime are more natural even with the natives. In many of our large northern cities there is a species of native population, known by various Billingsgates designations, who, in readiness for lawless excess, are certainly nothing behind the worst class of foreigners. A people who have derived so much from foreign increase should be the last to complain of its excesses. With one-third of our standing army of foreign birth, and with so large a foreign portion of the physical working power which has been extending our wonderful system of public improvement, and so fast filling up the wilderness, it little becomes us to express distrust. The foreigner soon assimilates to the soil, and he, and his children after him, are the ready defenders of the flag of ths country. If they are for a time more exposed than any other population to the wiles of the demagogue, we should be willing to adopt any safe and practicable checks, compatible with their rights to citizenship, within a period which shall neither be so short as to be inconsistent with a knowledge of our institutions, nor so long as to involve a condition at war with the theory of our system of a large free population, without the right of representation, and forming no part of the government.

MEMBERS OF THE CONVENTION OF 1845.

Joseph Walker,
Isaac T. Preston,
Gilbert Leonard,
John R. Grymes,
Felix Garcia,
Duncan F. Kenner,
Thomas Pugh,
C. Voorhies,
Thos. H. Lewis,
B. B. Brazeale,
Solomon W. Downs,
Piere Porche,
J. Sellers,
Thomas W. Chinn,
Wm. B. Scott,
A. G. Penn,
Thomas W. Scott,
Thomas M. Wadsworth,
A. Legendre,
C. Roselius,
W. C. C. Claiborne,
John Culbertson,
Adolph Mazereau,
Pierre Soulé,
George Eustis,
J. P. Benjamin,
Bernard Marigny,
H. B. Cenas,
Chas. M. Conrad,
O. St. Amant,
A. Boudousquie,
A. B. Roman,
B. Winchester,
H. B. Trist,
Miles Taylor,
I. Garrett,
Jacob Humble,
M. Bourg,
J. C. Beatty,
Justin Aubert,
George S. Guion,
V. P. Winder,
Z. Labauve,
Amasa Read,
A. Waddill,
Jas. McCalop,
Cyrus Ratliff,
J. B. Wederstrand,
A. M. Dunn,
Lafayette Saunders,
W. Burton,
A. H. McKay,
W. Brumfield,
Terrence Carriere,
A. R. Splane,
Phanor Prudhome,
Zenon Ledoux, Jr.,
R. J. Chambliss,
Paul Briant,
J. B. Derbes,
D. O. Brian,
W. M. Prescott,
S. M. Wikoff,
Green Hudspeth,
G. R. King,
R. Taylor,
Pierre Couvillion,
W. B. Prescott,
R. C. Hinson,
James F. Brent,
D. Stephens,
Thomas C. Porter,
George Mayo,
G. W. Peets.

ERRATA.

Page 88, under the head of "Members of the House of Representatives," Parish of Ascension, *insert* J. A. Richard, Representative.

Page 96, *read* Thomas Askew, Tax Collector, *instead* of Asken.

Page 111, *read* B. F. Cauthon, Clerk of Court, Parish of Washita, *instead* of Cuuthom.

Page 104, *read* John A. McHugh, Justice of the Peace, Baton Rouge, *instead* of John A. Messeugh.

Page 93, *read* Joint Committee for Revision of the Statutes of the State, *instead* Joint Committee.

Page 134, *read* United States Land Offices and Officers, *instead* United States and Officers.

TABLE OF CONTENTS.

ADVERTISEMENTS.

Baton Rouge Literary Depot.

J. M'CORMICK & CO.,

Corner of Third and Laurel Streets,

BATON ROUGE, LA.,

Have constantly on hand a large and well selected assortment of

SCHOOL BOOKS,

consisting of the Latest and most approved editions published. A large large assortment of

STATIONERY,

Consisting of Papers of American and English Manufacture—a beautiful variety of NOTE PAPER, LETTER PAPER, FOOLSCAP, SILK PAPER, etc., etc. Also, STEEL PENS, INK, WAFERS, WRAPPING PAPER, PORT-FOLIOS, HERBERIUMS, SCRAP BOOKS, DRAWING CARDS, SLATES, PENCILS, TWINE, REELS, QUILLS, INKSTANDS, &c, ENVELOPES—Wedding, a beautiful article; Official, white and colored; Plain and Fancy Note Envelopes.

BLANK BOOKS,

Day Books, Ledger, Bill Books, Receipt Books, Pass Books, Memorandum Books, fancy and plain.

Standard Literary & Scientific Works,

Always on hand, and furnished to order. New works received from the Publishers every month.

ALBUMS AND GIFT BOOKS—a large and beautiful assortment always on hand.

MAGAZINES—Graham's Magazine, Godey's Lady's Book, Harper's Magazine, Southern Quarterly Review, &c., &c., received regularly, and sent to any address at Publisher's prices.

LAW BOOKS—On hand, or ordered at the shortest notice.

VALENTINES—A great variety.

General Agents.

Subscriptions to Newspapers and Magazines received. ☞ BUSINESS AT THE CAPITOL transacted for persons abroad with promptness ond fidelity.

Baton Rouge, 1854.

NOTICE TO BUILDERS.

J. W. BROWN,

Architect and Builder,

BATON ROUGE,

IS PREPARED TO MANUFACTURE BY

STEAM POWER,

At the shortest notice, all kinds of

SASH, BLINDS,

WINDOWS, DOORS, &c.

☞ Letters addressed to him at the Post Office, Baton Rouge will meet with immediate attention.

Baton Rouge, December, 1854.

JOHN TILANO,

WORKER IN

Copper, Tin, and Sheet-Iron,

CHURCH STREET,

Near the Catholic Church,

BATON ROUGE, La.

JOHN TILANO, would respectfully inform the public that he is ready, at all times, to make or repair STEAM, SUPPLY, COLD WATER, ESCAPE, and STOVE PIPES.

TIN ROOFING, TIN or COPPER GUTTERS, and SPOUTS, put up at short notice.

ALWAYS ON HAND A COMPLETE ASSORTMENT OF

TIN WARE, SUGAR-HOUSE LAMPS,

LANTERNS, OIL CANS, &C.

☞ All orders from the country promptly and carefully attended to.

Carriage & Harness Ware-rooms,

AND PLANTERS' EMPORIUM,

CORNER OF CHURCH AND MAIN STREETS,
BATON ROUGE, LA.

W. F. TUNNARD & CO.,

Keep constantly on hand at their Establishment Carriages and Harness of every variety, from the best Northern Manufactories. Also, Build to order, and repair all kinds of Carriages in the best manner.

WAGONS, CARTS, WHEEL and DIRT-BARROWS, with every variety of Plantation Work and Plantation Harness manufactured and supplied to order—of the best workmanship and material.

IRON, of all sizes constantly on hand. All kinds of Smith-work, including Balcony, Verandah and Cemetery Railings, made and put up of the latest styles.

Also, LIGHTNING RODS on the most approved Scientific principles, and of the latest improvements, erected, or sent to order.

BARKER'S FORCE PUMP.

They have also purchased the Patent-right of the celebrated Barker's Force Pump, for the Parishes of East and West Baton Rouge, East and West Feliciana, and Iberville, and have a full assortment of different sizes, to which the attention of the public is called. They are admirably adapted for Pumping Molasses from Cisterns, and can be used as a Force and Lifting Pump, and are guaranteed as the best pump in use.

J. L. VIALET,

Apothecary and Druggist,

THIRD ST., BATON ROUGE, La.,

Takes the liberty of calling the attention of Country Dealers and Planters to his large and extensive assortment of

Drugs, Medicines, Chemicals, Patent Medicines, &c.,

embracing all articles usually found in Drug Stores, and which he offers on the most favorable terms.

Taking great pains in the selection of his goods, he thinks he can suit all who may wish for Drugs of reliable quality, and feels no hesitation in warranting that he can give *entire satisfaction* in this respect to those who may be inclined to send their orders.

Orders respectfully solicited.

Baton Rouge, La., Dec. 1, 1854.

THEODORE GOLDMAN,

Watchmaker and Jeweller,

HARNEY HOUSE ROW, BATON ROUGE.

DANIEL BUCKLEY,

Blacksmithing & Wagon Making,

CHURCH STREET, BATON ROUGE.

CANE WAGONS MANUFACTURED.

M. CONNOR,

TAILOR,

THIRD ST., BATON ROUGE, LA

S. M. HART & Co.,

Commission & Forwarding Merchants,

And Wholesale Dealers in

GROCERIES, WESTERN PRODUCE,

And Plantation Supplies Generally.

BATON ROUGE, LA.

A. MONTAN & Bro.,

WHOLESALE & RETAIL

GROCERS,

Corner of Church and Third Streets,

BATON ROUGE, LA.

Bogan & Legendre,

Workers in Tin Copper & Sheet-iron,

Third Street, opposite Beal's Stable,

BATON ROUGE, LA.

A. HAGER,

KETTLE SETTER,

BATON ROUGE, LA.

TRUDEAU, HUTCHISON & Co.,

STEAM BRICK YARD,

BATON ROUGE, LA.

Jos. Kressebuch,

MERCHANT TAILOR,

LAFAYETTE STREET,

BATON ROUGE, LA.

J. W. BURGESS. J. C. LANOUE.

Clothing! Clothing!!

GENTLEMEN'S FURNISHING STORE.

Third Street, next door to the Post Office.

HAS ON HAND A LARGE AND SPLENDID STOCK OF

Gentlemen's Clothing,

HATS, &c.

We invite our friends and the public generally, to call and examine our stock before purchasing elsewhere. Our motto is "QUICK SALES AND SMALL PROFITS." TERMS—*CASH.*

BURGESS & LANOUE.

AGENCY.

GEORGE P. BRIANT,

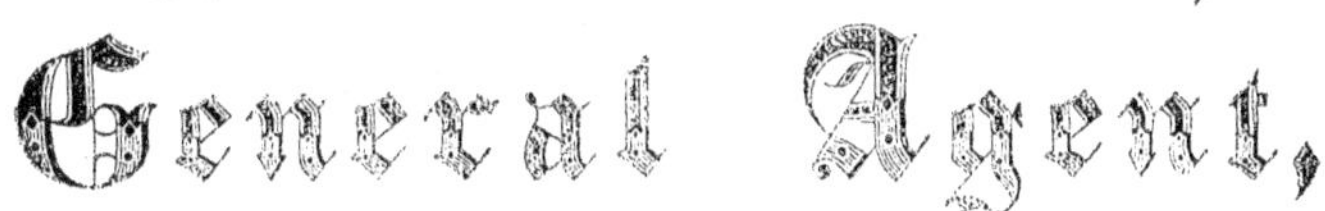

BATON ROUGE, LOUISIANA,

Will attend to the COLLECTION OF CLAIMS, PURCHASES AND ENTREES OF LAND, &c. To be found in STATE TREASURER'S OFFICE, where he is employed as Clerk. For information, refer to State and Parish Officers.

ROBERT BEAL'S

LIVERY STABLE,

THIRD STREET,

BETWEEN CHURCH & LAUREL.

Carriages, Buggies and Horses,

Always on hand, for Hire on reasonable terms for CASH.

Baton Rouge, December, 1854.

HUTCHINSON & CLINE'S

LIVERY STABLE.

Carriages, Buggies,

AND SADDLE HORSES,

Always on hand for Hire,

HORSES BOUGHT;

HORSES FOR SALE.

BATON ROUGE, Dec. 1854.

JAMES McVEY,

BUILDER.

BATON ROUGE, LA.

A. W. CAMERON,

BATON ROUGE, LA.

GOLDMAN & WEILMAN,

DEALERS IN

Dry Goods and Clothing,

Corner of Lafayette and Laurel Streets,

BATON ROUGE, La.

DR. J. A. TROUSDALE,

SURGEON DENTIST,

Baton Rouge, La.

☞ *Office in the rooms lately occupied by Dr. Mann, on Lafayette Street, over Quiggins' Shoe Store.*

LARGUIER & LANOUE,

DEALERS IN

Hardware, Cutlery, &c.

COR. LAFAYETTE AND FLORIDA STREETS,

BATON ROUGE, LA.

R. B. GREEN,

Wheel Wright

AND

MACHINIST,

COVINGTON, La.,

Is prepared to receive orders for putting up all kinds of LUMBER MILLS, SUGAR MILLS, COTTON GINS, STEAM ENGINES, &c., including any Machinery used on plantations.

Hardware! Hardware!! Hardware!!!

D. C. MONTAN,

CHURCH STREET,

BETWEEN LAFAYETTE AND THIRD STREETS, BATON ROUGE, LA.,

Has on hand a large and superior stock of

HARDWARE

And PLANTERS, MECHANICS and others, would do well to call and examine his stock and PRICES, before purchasing elsewhere.

BATON ROUGE FOUNDRY.

HILL & Co.,

MANUFACTURERS OF MACHINERY,

IRON & BRASS CASTINGS,

Of the Heaviest Dimensions.

BATON ROUGE.

I. N. LEMON,

DEALER IN

Drugs, Medicines & Paints

CLINTON, LA.

Geo. M. Heroman,

BOOKSELLER & STATIONER,

AND DEALER IN

Medicines, Jewelry, Hollow-ware &c.,

BATON ROUGE, La.

A. BRADFORD. R. MONTEITH.

A. BRADFORD & CO.,

Manufacturers and Dealers in

Saddlery, Harness, Trunks,

WHIPS, &c., AND SADDLERS' MATERIALS,

BATON ROUGE, LA.

R. G. BEALE,

Attorney and Counsellor at Law,

BATON ROUGE, La.

A. S. HERRON,

ATTORNEY AND COUNSELLOR AT LAW.

BATON ROUGE, LA.

U. B. PHILLIPS,

Attorney & Counsellor at Law,

BATON ROUGE, La.

JAS. GORLINSKI,

Surveyor & Civil Engineer,

BATON ROUGE, LA.

GEORGE S. LACEY,

Attorney and Counsellor at Law,

No. 23 COMMERCIAL PLACE,

NEW ORLEANS, La.

JOHN JAY LANE,
New Orleans.

W. J. LACEY.
Baton Rouge.

LANE & LACEY,

ATTORNEYS AT LAW,

NEW ORLEANS & BATON ROUGE.

JOHN M'VEA.

CHARLES M'VEA

John & Charles McVea,

Attorneys at Law,

Clinton and Jackson, La.

W. J. KERNAN,

ATTORNEY AT LAW,

Practices in East and West Feliciana.

CLINTON, LA.

J. J. BURK,

Attorney and Counsellor at Law,

BATON ROUGE, La.

G. C. McWHORTER,

ATTORNEY AND COUNSELLOR AT LAW,

BATON ROUGE, LA

J. W. SEYMOUR,

Attorney and Counseller at Law,

OFFICE, ON LAUREL STREET.

BATON ROUGE, LA.

S. P. GREVES,

ATTORNEY AT LAW,

Baton Rouge, La.

Office, on Lafayette street.

HARNEY HOUSE.

BATON ROUGE, La.

Wm. MARKHAM, Proprietor.

This well known establishment has been thoroughly renovated, and is now open for the accommodation of Travellers and Boarders.

Baton Rouge, Dec. 1854.

BATON ROUGE ACADEMY.

RUFUS WILSON, PRINCIPAL.

SPRING SESSION COMMENCES MARCH 1st.
FALL SESSION COMMENCES SEPT. 15th.

Baton Rouge Female Seminary.

Mrs. M. W. READ, Principal.

Miss E. A. DODSON, Teacher of Music.

CICERO HUTCHINS,
Miss BOYCE, } **Teachers.**

3

BOOKS AND STATIONERY.

New Orleans Stationers' Warehouse,

NO. 60 CAMP STREET.

SCHOOL BOOKS AND STATIONERY.

To School Teachers, Country Merchants and Parents:

The attention of those purchasing School Books and Stationery, either for their own use or to sell, is respectfully invited to the assortment of the subscriber, who offers all kinds of

School Books and Stationery,

as low as any other establishment in this city, and has constantly on hand all works in the various departments of Education in general use.

Also, an extensive assortment of—

AND MISCELLANEOUS WORKS,

in every department of Literature, Science and Art, together with every article of Stationery.

J. B. STEEL,
BOOK-SELLER & STATIONER,
No. 60 Camp street.

New Orleans, December, 1854.

E. Johnson & Co.

STATIONERS,

No. 68 Camp Street,

NEW ORLEANS.

Printing & Book Binding

Executed with Neatness and Despatch.

NORMAN'S

No. 14 CAMP STREET,

NEW ORLEANS.

Books of Standard Literature,

ELEGANTLY ILLUSTRATED WORKS,

CHEAP PUBLICATIONS,

MAGAZINES, &C.

SCHOOL BOOKS AT PUBLISHERS' PRICES.

G. N. MORISON,

IMPORTER AND

Wholesale Druggist,

No. 12 MAGAZINE STREET,

NEW ORLEANS.

W. J. A. ROBERTS,

ATTORNEY AT LAW,

95 COMMON STREET,

NEW ORLEANS.

N. C. FOLGER,

WHOLESALE AND RETAIL

CLOTHING STORE,

Nos. 17 and 19 OLD LEVEE,

Corner of Customhouse Street,

NEW ORLEANS.

My General Depot of Plantation Clothing

COMPRISES THE FOLLOWING:

For Winter Wear.—5000 Heavy Kersey Monkey Jackets, 5000 ditto Pantaloons, 10,000 red twilled Flannel Shirts, 10,000 Hickory Shirts, 500 dozen heavy Kentucky knit Wool Socks, 1000 Blanket Capots, Woolen Caps, white and black Wool Hats, Glazed Hats, Oil Hats, &c., &c.

For Summer Wear.—3000 Cottonade Pantaloons, 3000 Planters' Linen, 2000 Cottonade Harney Jackets, 2000 Planters' Linen ditto, 10,000 Hickory and Check Shirts, Straw Hats, Musquito Bars, &c., &c.

For Women.—2000 Women's Linsey Frocks, 2000 Cottonade ditto, 2000 Kersey Joseys, (used instead of Jackets,) 2000 brown Cottonade Chemises. &c., &c.

Oil Clothing.—2000 Oil Jackets, 1500 Oil Pants; 2000 Oil Aprons and 2000 Oil Caps with Hoods for the head—invented by the Subscriber, and patent right secured.

This Oil Cloth Clothing has been made up expressly for field hands, to protect them from the injurious effects of the heavy dew in the early morning, it being well known to Planters that the negroes have their clothing completely saturated with the dew from the leaves of the plants when at work in the early hours of the day.

Forest Cloth Pants and Monkey Jackets, grey and white Blankets, &c., &c.

For Fine Clothing see next page.

IN MY STOCK OF

FINE CLOTHING

Will be found the following articles, besides many more which cannot be enumerated here.

DRESS and FROCK COATS,

Black, Blue, Olive, Dahlia, Maroon, &c., Cloth Dress and Frock Coats.

PALETOTS and SACS.

Black, Brown, Maroon, Blue, Olive-green, &c., cloth Paletots and Sacs; Black and Colored Tweeds and Cassimere Paletots and Sacs; Blanket Sacs and Paletots.

OVERCOATS.

Heavy Devonshire Pilot and Beaver Cloth Over Coats, Paletots and Sacs.

PANTALOONS.

Black Cassimere and Doeskin Pants, a general assortment of colored Cassimere, Tweeds and Satinet Pants.

VESTS.

Black Cassimere, Black Satin, Colored Cashmere and Fancy Silk Vests, single and double breasted.

BOY'S AND YOUTH'S CLOTHING.

A complete assortment of Frock Coats, Sacs, Paletots, Harney Jackets, Pantaloons, Vests, Shirts, &c., for Youths, Boys and Children.

NEGRO TRADER'S CLOTHING.

Blue Satinet Harney Jackets and Pantaloons, Cassimere Vests, white Cotton Shirts, Hats, Drawers, Under Shirts, &c.

ALSO, a large assortment of Shirts, of all sizes, from small Boy's to the largest Men's; Drawers, Under Shirts, Cravats, Suspenders, Half-hose, Gloves, India Rubber Coats, Leggins, Cloaks, Life Preservers; Carpet Bags, Valises and Trunks, of the very best make.

☞N. B.—In my assortment of Plantation Clothing, will be found Youths' and Boys' sizes.

N. C. FOLGER,
Nos. 17 *and* 19 *Old Levee.*

New Orleans, December, 1854.

BATON ROUGE
Collegiate Institute
FOR YOUNG LADIES.

The second session of this Institution will commence on the FIRST MONDAY IN OCTOBER, and continue nine months without a vacation, except the Holidays. The course of studies will embrace the approved and standard Class Books in the departments of English Literature, Ancient and Modern Languages, Natural Sciences and Mathematics adopted at the best and most popular Seminaries.

Application will be made at the ensuing Legislature for a charter with full power to grant a Diploma to such students as shall have completed the entire Collegiate Course. The Principal will be assisted by a Board of competent and experienced Teachers, adequate to the wants and objects of the Institute. Arrangements have been made to afford superior accommodations to pupils, who will be under the constant supervision of the Principal and Teachers; and the utmost attention will be given to the formation of correct manners and deportment, and to whatever may contribute to their health, comfort and happiness.

As the Institute is free from all partisan and denominational influence, pupils will be allowed to attend whatever place of worship their parents and guardians may prefer. Students will be admitted at any time during the session, and charged only for the period of attendance; but no deduction for absence, except in cases of protracted illness.

Day scholars will be charged monthly for Tuition at the rate of three, four and five dollars per month; Music and Ornamental branches extra. Boarders will be charged one-half in advance, the remainder at the close of the session, except by special agreement.

Vocal Music will be taught in the school without charge.

TERMS:

For Board, Washing, Fuel, Lights and Tuition, per session of nine months—

In the Primary Department, - - - - - - $200

In the Collegiate Department, including Music and the Ornamental branches, from - - $250 to $300.

☞ NO EXTRAS.

M. H. SLOSSON, Principal.

Baton Rouge, La., Dec. 1, 1854.

NEW ORLEANS

Female Collegiate Institution,

CONDUCTED BY

MRS. MACAULAY,

NO. 252 CAMP STREET.

This Institution has been in successful operation for a series of years. The best teachers are employed in giving instruction in the English, French, Spanish, Italian and Latin Languages.

The Music Teachers who give lessons on the Piano, Harp and Guitar, together with Vocal Music, possess the highest order of attainments, combined with long experience and success.

Young ladies residing in the Institution have every facility afforded them to acquire a practical knowledge of the French language, to perfect their Musical studies and pursue the elegant accomplishments of drawing and painting.

The premises, since the recent improvements, are perhaps the best in this city, and boarders have every attention paid to their health, comfort and improvement.

The institution is furnished with a well selected library, to the use of which the scholars are entitled free of expense.

For particulars apply in person, or by letter, at the Institution.

FELICIANA HIGH SCHOOL,

JACKSON, LOUISIANA.

W. H. N. MAGRUDER, A. M., } *Associate Principals.*
W. H. POTTER, A. M., }

JAMES McKEIGNEY, A. M., *Assistant.*

W. H. POTTER,

Teacher of Mathematics and Natural Sciences.

W. H. N. MAGRUDER,

Teacher of the Latin and Greek Languages and English Literature.

JAMES McKEIGNEY,

Assistant Teacher of English, Latin and Greek and Professor of French and the Commercial Department.

The Principals have secured the services of Prof. McKeigney for the purpose of extending the course of instructions hitherto adopted in this Institution so as to embrace the

FRENCH LANGUAGE,

to the teaching of which particular attention will be paid, and a thorough

COMMERCIAL COURSE,

including Book-Keeping and Commercial Calculations in their various applications to mercantile pursuits, as taught in the best Commercial Colleges in the United States.

This arrangement is intended to supply a deficiency too common in most Institutions, by affording young gentlemen who may not desire to pursue a full Collegiate course of studies an opportunity of thoroughly preparing themselves for the active duties of the counting room.

Jackson, La., Dec. 1, 1854.

www.ingramcontent.com/pod-product-compliance
Lightning Source LLC
LaVergne TN
LVHW011220110826
845150LV00006B/1490

* 9 7 8 1 4 2 5 5 1 6 2 9 1 *